W9-CBX-633

ROCKS, MINERALS, GEMS, CRYSTALS, FOSSILS

ROCKS, MINERALS, GEMS, CRYSTALS, FOSSILS

THE COMPLETE COLLECTOR'S COMPANION

Edited by Harriet Stewart-Jones

CHARTWELL BOOKS, INC.

A QUINTET BOOK

Published by Chartwell Books
A Division of Book Sales, Inc.
PO Box 7100
Edison, New Jersey 08818-7100

This edition produced for sale in the U.S.A., its territories and dependencies only.

ISBN 0-7858-0242-8

This book was designed and produced by
Quintet Publishing Limited
6 Blundell Street
London N7 9BH

Creative Director: Richard Dewing
Designer: Ian Hunt
Project Editor: Diana Steedman

The material used in this publication previously appeared in *Identifying Rocks and Minerals* by Basil Booth, *Identifying Gems & Precious Stones* by Cally Hall, *Identifying Shells* by Fred Woodward, *Fossil Identifier* by Scott Weidensaul.

Typeset in Great Britain by
Central Southern Typesetters, Eastbourne
Manufactured in Singapore by Eray Scan Pte Ltd.
Printed in Singapore by
Star Standard Industries (Pte) Ltd.

Contents

Part I Minerals & Gems

Part II Rocks

Part III Shells

Part IV Fossils

INTRODUCTION

The durability, beauty, variety and widespread availability of minerals, rocks, shells and fossils make them ideal subjects for the amateur collector. Anyone who has spent many a happy hour collecting pebbles and shells on the beach as a child, marveling at the different shapes and colors to be found, can appreciate the enjoyment to be had from finding, studying and identifying these fascinating products of our natural environment.

Of course, gems, rocks, shells and fossils are all, generally speaking, made of minerals. But they are put together in different forms and by different means, either as a result of inorganic processes, as in a piece of granite, or by the action of some organism, as in shells, or a combination of both, as in fossils.

In this book we have put together four sections on minerals and gems, rocks, shells, and fossils and carefully selected the entries to give a wide range of samples from around the world. Detailed information on the form, color and occurrence of each sample is given along with a clear color photograph.

Each section has its own introduction giving background information on how the rocks, shells or fossils formed, and how to identify them and recognize their various properties.

Part I MINERALS & GEMS

Minerals are fundamental components of the earth beneath our feet. There are something like 3000 different minerals, with forms ranging from well-formed crystals of shiny, transparent quartz to amorphous, crumbly yellow limonite. So what do we mean by the term mineral? A mineral is defined as a naturally formed, solid, inorganic substance with a composition that is either fixed or that varies within a defined range, and a characteristic atomic structure.

Some minerals have been valued throughout history for their beauty, durability and rarity. These are the gemstones, fashioned to be worn as jewelry, used to decorate objects, exquisitely carved to be admired, or collected to impress.

PROPERTIES

The characteristic composition and atomic structure of a mineral are expressed in its physical properties, such as its crystalline form, its color and its hardness, and it is these physical properties that are used in identification. In order to appreciate how these physical properties are produced and to understand some of the technical terms used in this book, it is important to look at the way in which crystals are formed and defined.

CRYSTAL SYSTEMS

Many minerals have a crystalline structure, and although it is unusual for perfect crystals to form under natural conditions, the shape of the crystals in a sample of mineral will give the collector a valuable clue to its identity. If a mineral is made up of a mass of small, poorly formed crystals such that the faces cannot be distinguished, it is termed massive.

The **habit** of a crystal is the usual shape it takes. The habit can be described as one or more of the crystal **forms** defined by sets of parallel faces and their angles. Emerald, for example, is found as hexagonal prisms (see diagram) made up of two forms. A form consists of a number of identical faces and is termed a "closed form" if it can enclose space, or "open" if it cannot.

If you rotate a sugar cube about an axis running straight through the middle of two opposite faces, you see four identical square sides, one after another. A cube is therefore said to have four-fold **symmetry**. Further examination would show that there are three such **axes** of four-fold symmetry. These axes form the basis of the classification of crystal systems.

There are seven **crystal systems:** cubic (or isometric), tetragonal, orthorhombic, monoclinic, triclinic, hexagonal and trigonal, as described in the box on page 8.

A crystal has a number of **faces**, each of which is given a number according to the axes intersecting it. This number is called the **Millar index**.

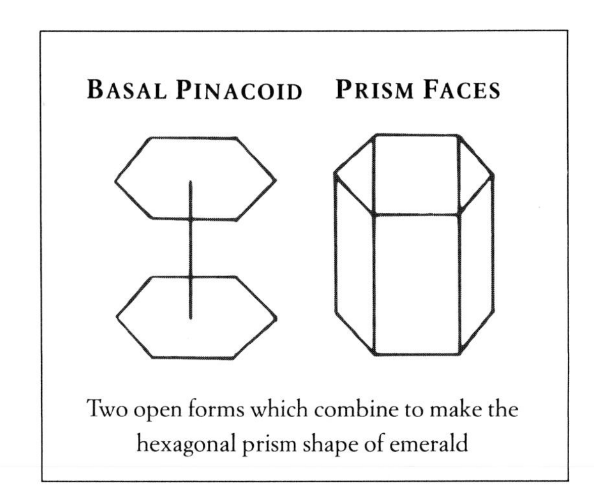

Two open forms which combine to make the hexagonal prism shape of emerald

COLOR

Some colors are striking and serve a diagnostic purpose, while others are of lesser value. Minerals with a characteristic color include malachite (green) and pyrites (brassy yellow); minerals of variable color include fluorspar , barytes and quartz.

ABOVE *Malachite is a distinctive green color. Both the color and the streak are the same.*

CRYSTAL SYSTEMS			
CLASSIFICATION	FACE SHAPE AND AXIS ORIENTATION	FORM	EXAMPLES
ISOMETRIC (or cubic)	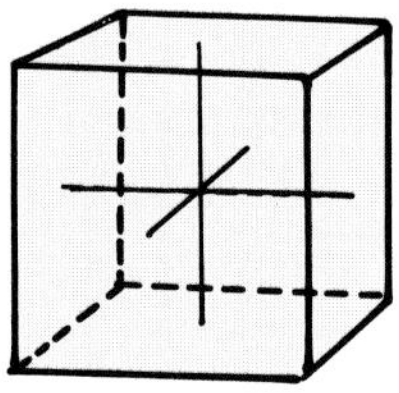	All three axes are the same length and are at right angles to each other.	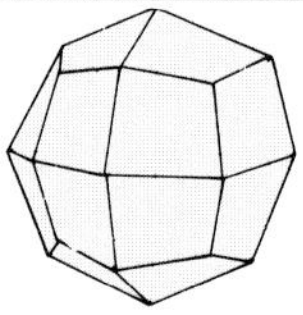 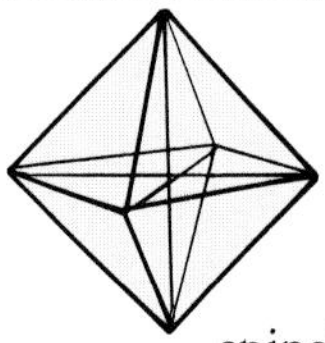 garnet (icositetrahedron) spinel (octahedron)
TETRAGONAL	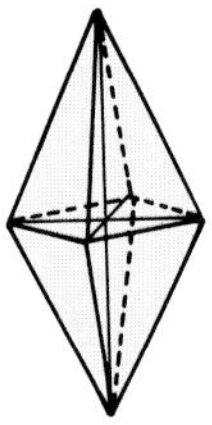	Three axes which are at right angles to each other. The two on the same plane are equal in length while the third is perpendicular to this plane and of different length.	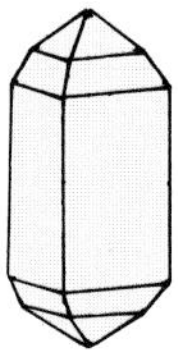 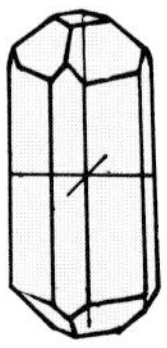 zircon scapolite
HEXAGONAL	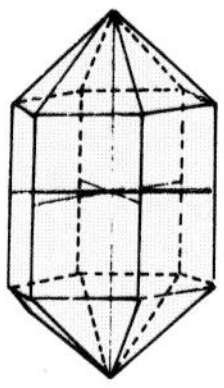	Three of the four axes are in one plane and intersect at 60°. The fourth axis is perpendicular and unequal in length to the other. There are six planes of symmetry.	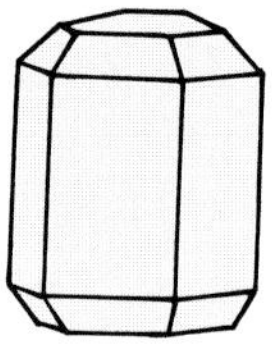 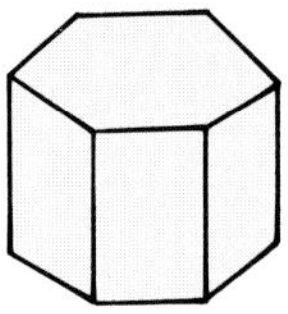 apatite beryl
TRIGONAL	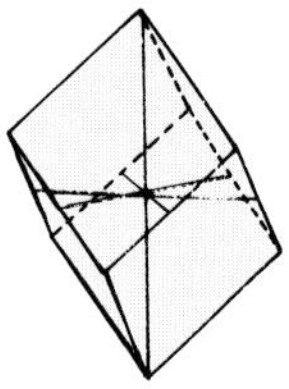	Similar to the hexagonal system. There are three axes at 60° to each other in the same plane. The fourth axis is perpendicular. There are three planes of symmetry.	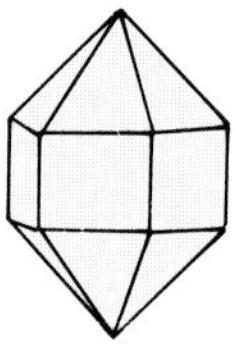 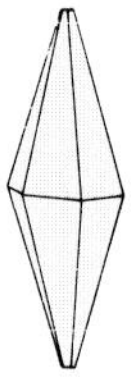 quartz sapphire
ORTHORHOMBIC	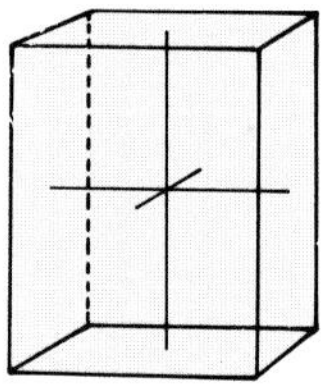	Three axes of unequal length. Two are at right angles to one another and the third is perpendicular.	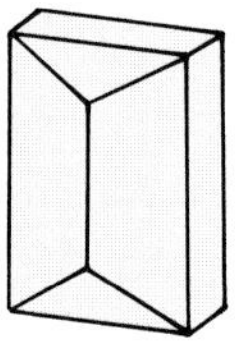 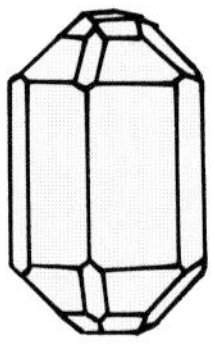 peridot topaz
MONOCLINIC	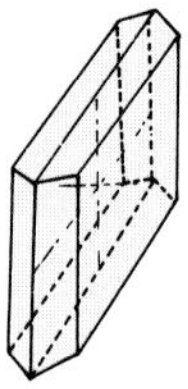	There are three axes of unequal length. Two intersect at an oblique angle in one plane and the third is perpendicular.	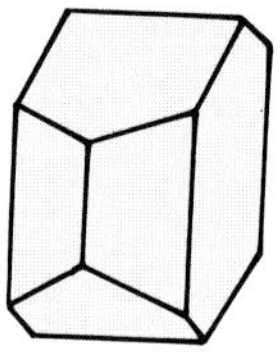 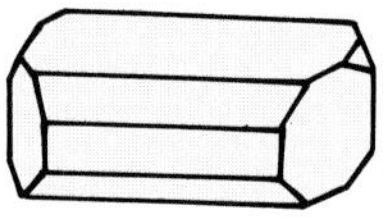 orthoclase feldspar epidote
TRICLINIC	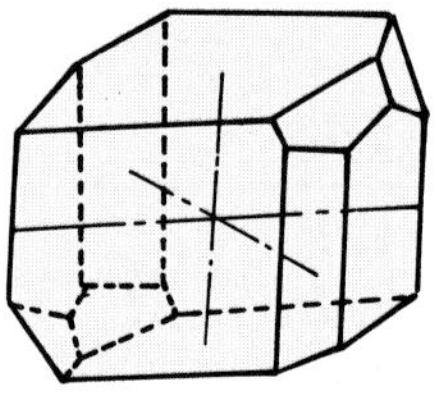	Three axes of unequal length all inclined to one another at different angles.	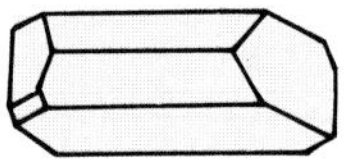 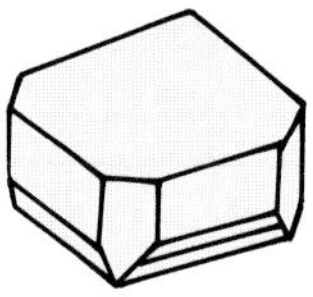 alkali feldspar (amazonite) rhodonite

When white light, made up of all the spectral colors, travels through a transparent or translucent mineral, some of the colors may be absorbed within the crystal structure. The colors that emerge combine to give the color of the mineral. If no part of the spectrum is absorbed the crystal will appear colorless. The **"absorption spectrum"** produced when white light passes through a gemstone can be viewed using an instrument called a spectroscope. Dark lines are seen in the part of the spectrum that has been absorbed by the stone. The spectroscope may be used to distinguish between stones of similar color.

A gemstone viewed in white light may appear to be one color but viewing it through a colored filter may reveal underlying colors which can help to identify the stone. A **Chelsea color filter**, for example, cuts out all of the spectrum except red and green light and through the filter a true emerald appears red while imitation emeralds appear green. The appearance under ultraviolet light and X-rays can also aid identification.

The ability of a gemstone to split white light into the colors of the spectrum is called **dispersion**. It is usually measured by finding the difference in refractive index of the stone for a red ray, which is refracted least, and a blue ray which is refracted most.

Refraction and Reflection of Light

The behavior of light entering a crystal is dependent upon the internal atomic structure of the mineral and can be used as a means of identification.

Isometric (cubic) minerals and non-crystalline minerals are isotropic (have the same optical properties in all directions). When light enters them it is slowed down and its course is changed (the light ray is bent or refracted). Each ray of light is slowed down and refracted by the same amount and the mineral is said to be **singly refractive**. Light entering minerals crystallizing in any of the other six crystal systems is split into two rays and each ray is refracted by a different amount. These crystals are said to be **doubly refractive**.

Doubly refractive gemstones may appear to be different colors and different shades of the body color when viewed from different directions. They are said to be **pleochroic**. Gemstones that show two colors are dichroic and belong to the tetragonal, trigonal or hexagonal crystal symmetry classes. Gemstones that show three colors are trichroic and belong to the orthorhombic, monoclinic or triclinic crystal symmetry classes.

The **refractive index (RI)** indicates the amount that the light rays are bent by a mineral and it is measured by a refractometer. A singly refractive mineral has one refractive index but a doubly refractive mineral has a range of refractive indices. The difference between the minimum and maximum refractive indices in such a crystal is called its **birefringence**. When the birefringence is high the light rays can be seen to reflect off different parts of the back of the stone causing an apparent doubling of the back facets when viewed through the front facet.

Light that is reflected from fibres or fibrous cavities within the mineral may appear as a cat's-eye **(chatoyancy)** or a star **(asterism)** when cut with a domed top *(en cabochon)*. Cat's-eyes can be seen when the light is reflected from parallel arrangements of inclusions as in chrysoberyl cat's-eyes. Star-stones are seen when several sets of parallel fibres reflect light.

Other Characteristics

Luster The luster describes the way in which light is reflected off the surface of a mineral or gemstone. The terms used are **metallic** (like polished metal), **adamantine** (brilliant, like diamonds), **vitreous** (like broken glass), **resinous** (like resin or wax), **pearly, silky, splendent** (brilliant reflectivity), **shining** (reflects an image but not

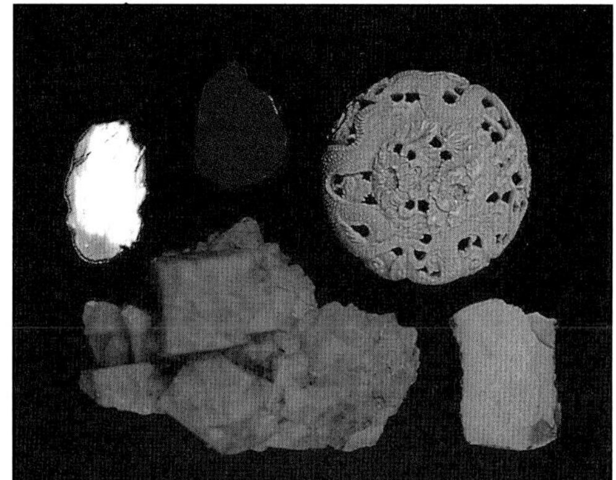

Left *Pyrites (iron sulphide) displays a brilliant metallic luster.*

clearly), **glistening** (reflects light but not an image) and **glimmering** (imperfect reflections from points on specimen).

Streak The streak is the color produced when a mineral is powdered, either by crushing or by drawing across a piece of unglazed porcelain – a streak plate. It is frequently quite different from the apparent color of the mineral surface.

Transparency Minerals can be either **transparent** – the outline of objects can be seen clearly through the specimen, **semitransparent** – objects can be seen but are indistinct, **translucent** – light passes through the specimen but objects cannot be seen, or **opaque** – no light passes through the specimen.

Cleavage Some minerals tend to break smoothly and evenly along well-defined planes of weakness called cleavage planes. These are related to the crystal structure of the mineral. Cleavage is either **perfect, distinct, indistinct** or **none** and the cleavage planes are numbered using Millar indices.

Fracture Some minerals give a distinctive type of break or fracture when hit with a hammer. Fracture may be described as **conchoidal** (shell-like), **subconchoidal** (indistinct conchoidal), **even** (surface flat but slightly rough), **uneven** (surface rough and irregular), **hackly** (with sharp points) or **earthy** (surface dull and crumbly).

Hardness The German mineralogist Friedrich Mohs developed a scale to quantify the hardness of minerals. He took ten minerals and placed them in order so that each was scratched by those above it on the scale but was in turn scratched by those beneath it on the scale.

SCALE	COMPARISON	MINERAL TEST
1	TALC	Powdered by finger nail
2	GYPSUM	Scratched by finger nail
3	CALCITE	Scratched by copper coin
4	FLUORSPAR	Easily scratched by pocket knife
5	APATITE	Just scratched by pocket knife
6	ORTHOCLASE	Scratched by steel file
7	QUARTZ	Scratches glass window
8	TOPAZ	Easily scratches quartz
9	CORUNDUM	Easily scratches topaz
10	DIAMOND	Hardest known substance, cannot be scratched

Tenacity Another related test is for tenacity. Minerals are termed **sectile** if they are easily cut by a knife, **brittle** if they crumble when hit by a hammer, **malleable** if cut slices can be flattened by hitting with a hammer, or **flexible** if they will bend without breaking.

Twinning Sometimes a crystal will grow in two different directions from one face. This is known as twinning and is especially common in the isometric system. Twinned crystals can be recognized by the presence of re-entrant angles.

Specific gravity The specific gravity of a mineral is its weight compared with the weight of an equal volume of water. A specimen of fluorite, therefore, with a specific gravity of over 3, would be much lighter than a similar sized piece of, say, galena, which has a specific gravity of 7.6.

Magnetism Some minerals are magnetic and this property can be used to identify stones of similar color. Pyrope garnet is moderately magnetic and can be separated from non-magnetic red spinel. Sinhalite is only weakly magnetic and so can be differentiated from brown peridot, which is moderately magnetic.

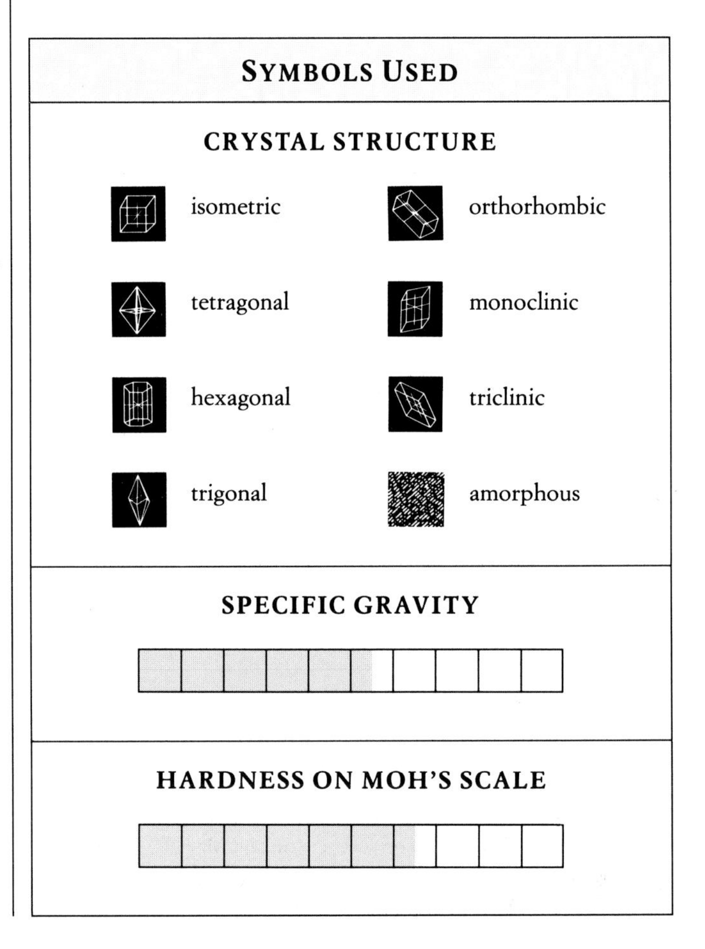

NATIVE ELEMENTS AND ALLOYS

COPPER

PROPERTIES **Distinctive features:** Color, malleability, ductility, association with malachite and other copper ores. Dissolves in nitric acid, producing red nitrous fumes (care is needed for this test). **Colour:** Copper-red. **Luster:** Metallic. **Streak:** Metallic, coppery, shining. **Transparency:** Opaque. **Cleavage:** None. **Fracture:** Hackly. **Tenacity:** Ductile, malleable. **Forms:** Twisted, wirelike, platy, crystals uncommon. **Twinning:** On 111. **Varieties:** Veins, strings, sheets, crystal masses.
OCCURRENCE Native copper is usually of secondary origin in copper ore veins, sandstone, limestone, slate and near igneous rocks. Russia, south-west UK, Australia (New South Wales), Bolivia, Mexico and the USA.
USES Electrical conductor in wires, electronics, alloyed with tin (to produce bronze) and zinc (to produce brass).

SPECIFIC GRAVITY 8.8–8.9 **HARDNESS** 2.5–3.00 **CRYSTAL SYSTEM** ISOMETRIC

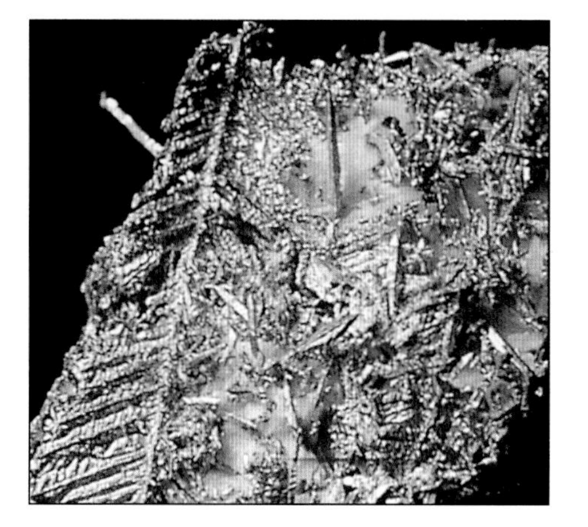

SILVER

PROPERTIES **Distinctive features:** Malleability, color and specific gravity. **Color:** Silvery white. **Luster:** Metallic. **Streak:** Silvery white. **Transparency:** Opaque. **Cleavage:** None. **Fracture:** Hackly. **Tenacity:** Ductile, malleable. **Forms:** Distorted crystals, reticulated and arborescent. **Twinning:** None. **Varieties:** Usually alloyed with gold or copper.
OCCURRENCE Native silver is rare and is often associated with silver minerals. Norway, Central Europe, Australia (New South Wales), Chile, Mexico, the USA and Canada.
USES Coinage, jewelry, ornaments, electronics.

SPECIFIC GRAVITY 10.10–10.50 **HARDNESS** 2.5–3 **CRYSTAL SYSTEM** ISOMETRIC

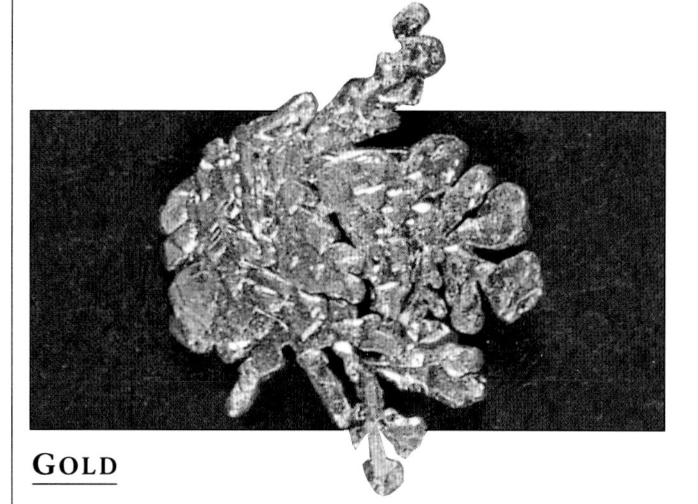

GOLD

PROPERTIES **Distinctive features:** Malleability, color, association with pyrites, galena and chalcopyrite. **Color:** Deep gold-yellow to pale yellow. **Luster:** Metallic. **Streak:** Golden-yellow to reddish. **Transparency:** Opaque. **Cleavage:** None. **Fracture:** Hackly. **Tenacity:** Ductile, malleable. **Forms:** Flat plates, arborescent, crystals rare. **Twinning:** On 111. **Varieties:** Usually alloyed with silver; ordinary gold is 10 per cent silver, electrum is 38 per cent silver and is, therefore, a pale yellow to silvery color, while other varieties contain up to 20 per cent copper and palladium.
OCCURRENCE Worldwide, mostly in quartz veins and placer deposits, although it does occur in igneous, metamorphic and sedimentary rocks, but particularly Ural Mountains, Siberia, Alps, India, China, New Zealand, Queensland, South Africa (Transvaal), Colombia, Mexico, Yukon and the USA.
USES Monetary standard, jewelry, electronics, aircraft window screening.

SPECIFIC GRAVITY 15.6–19.33 **HARDNESS** 2.5–3 **CRYSTAL SYSTEM** ISOMETRIC

DIAMOND

PROPERTIES Most diamonds are colorless, but white or, rarely, yellow, orange, brown, blue or green stones are found. Diamond crystals form as cubes, octahedra and dodecahedra. It has an adamantine luster and very good "fire" (dispersion), which makes it the most popular gemstone. The bluish-white fluorescence under ultraviolet light is used in identification. It is extremely hard.
OCCURRENCE The ancient diamond mines of southern India have been the source of some of the world's most famous diamonds, such as the Koh-i-nor and Jehangir. Industrial and gem-quality stones are widespread in Brazil and South Africa, and alluvial diamonds have been found in almost every state of the USA. Other localities include Australia, Borneo, Botswana, China, Ghana, Guyana, Russia, Tanzania, Venezuela, Zaire and Zimbabwe.
USES Gemstones, abrasives, in cutting tools and drill bits, for polishing gemstones. Diamonds are usually cut in the brilliant style. They have been imitated by many colorless minerals and by glass, but the fire is distinctive.

SPECIFIC GRAVITY 3.52 **HARDNESS** 10 **CRYSTAL SYSTEM** ISOMETRIC

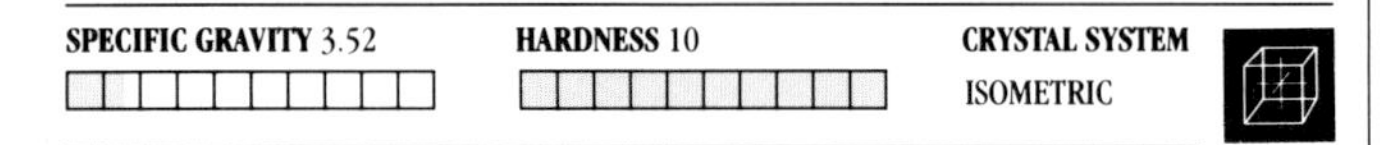

GRAPHITE

PROPERTIES **Distinctive features:** Silvery black color with pencil black streak. Very soft with greasy feel. Extremely dirty to handle. **Color:** Steel black to gray. **Luster:** Metallic, dull, earthy. **Streak:** Black. **Transparency:** Opaque. **Cleavage:** Perfect basal. **Fracture:** Rough when not on cleavage. **Forms:** Tabular crystals – six-sided, foliated masses, granular to compact masses.

OCCURRENCE In gneiss, schists, limestones and quartzites. Siberian gneisses, Sri Lankan granulites, Finnish limestones, Mexico and the USA.
USES "Lead" in pencils, graphite lubricants, paints, high temperature crucibles, electrodes.

SPECIFIC GRAVITY 2.09–2.23 **HARDNESS** 1.0–2.0 **CRYSTAL SYSTEM** TRIGONAL

SULPHUR

PROPERTIES **Distinctive features:** Yellow color, melts and burns readily with blue flame, giving off choking sulphur dioxide fumes. Often contaminated with clay or bitumen. **Color:** Bright yellow to red or yellow-gray. **Luster:** Resinous. **Streak:** White. **Transparency:** Transparent to translucent. **Cleavage:** On 001, 110, 111. **Fracture:** Conchoidal to sectile. **Tenacity:** Ductile when heated. **Forms:** Pyramidal to tabular. **Twinning:** Rare.
OCCURRENCE Mostly in young sedimentary rocks, often clays, associated with bitumen. Frequently as small crystals around fumaroles on volcanoes. Sicily (large crystals, associated with selenite and calcite) and the USA (mainly in Louisiana and Texas, but also found around fumaroles in Yellowstone Park, Sulphur Bank mercury mine in California and in many other states).
USES Making sulphuric acid, gunpowder, fireworks, insecticides and fungicides, vulcanizing rubber, medicines.

SPECIFIC GRAVITY 2.05–2.09 **HARDNESS** 1.5–2.5 **CRYSTAL SYSTEM** ORTHORHOMBIC

SULPHIDES

SPHALERITE

PROPERTIES **Distinctive features:** Resinous luster and color and often associated with galena, pyrite, quartz, calcite, barytes and fluorite. **Color:** Dull yellow-brown to black, also greenish to white, but nearly colorless when pure. **Luster:** Resinous and adamantine. **Streak:** Pale brown to light yellow. **Transparency:** Transparent to translucent. **Cleavage:** Perfect on 110. **Fracture:** Conchoidal. **Forms:** Dodecahedra, massive to granular, sometimes amorphous. **Twinning:** Common on 111.
OCCURRENCE Can occur in veins in most rocks, where it is associated with galena, pyrite, quartz and calcite. Romania, Italy (Tuscany), Switzerland, Spain, UK, Sweden, Mexico, Canada and the USA.
USES Principal ore of zinc.

SPECIFIC GRAVITY 3.9–4.1	HARDNESS 3.5–4.0	CRYSTAL SYSTEM ISOMETRIC

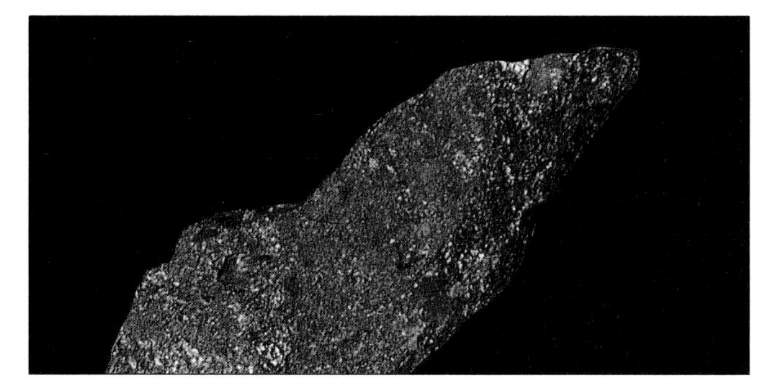

CHALCOPYRITE

PROPERTIES **Distinctive features:** Similar to pyrite but deeper in color and often iridescent. Usually massive, brittle and soluble in nitric acid. **Color:** Tarnished brassy gold, often iridescent. **Luster:** Metallic. **Streak:** Green-black. **Transparency:** Opaque. **Cleavage:** Variable on 201. **Fracture:** Uneven. **Forms:** Usually massive, sometimes rounded. Crystals less common than for pyrites. **Twinning:** On 111 or 101.
OCCURRENCE Metalliferous veins in granites, gneisses and schists. Often associated with bornite, malachite, azurite and quartz. Germany, Italy, France, UK, Spain, Sweden, South America, Australasia, Namibia and the USA.
USES Principal ore of copper.

SPECIFIC GRAVITY 4.1–4.3	HARDNESS 3.5–4.0	CRYSTAL SYSTEM ISOMETRIC

CINNABAR

PROPERTIES **Distinctive features:** Color and streak, high specific gravity and its softness. When heated in a tube it yields globules of mercury metal which settle on the sides of the tube. **Color:** Cochineal red to brownish-red. **Luster:** Adamantine to dull. **Streak:** Scarlet. **Transparency:** Transparent to opaque. **Cleavage:** Perfect on 1010. **Fracture:** Uneven to subconchoidal. **Forms:** Rhombohedral to tabular in habit. Also granular and massive. **Twinning:** Interpenetrant.
OCCURRENCE Russia, Serbia, Czech Republic, Slovakia, Bavaria (good crystals), Italy, Spain, Peru, China and the USA.
USES Only common, and therefore principal, ore of mercury.

SPECIFIC GRAVITY 8.0–8.2	HARDNESS 2.0–2.5	CRYSTAL SYSTEM HEXAGONAL

GALENA

PROPERTIES **Distinctive features:** Cubic, cleavage, color, high specific gravity. **Color:** Lead grey, often silvery. **Luster:** Metallic, shining. **Streak:** Lead gray. **Transparency:** Opaque. **Cleavage:** Perfect on 100, 010 and 001. **Fracture:** Flat on cubic form to even. **Forms:** Mainly cubes, tabular, sometimes skeletal crystals. **Twinning:** On 111, interpenetrant and contact twins common.

OCCURRENCE Widespread in beds and veins due to hydrothermal action of mineralizing fluids. Found in limestones, dolomites, granites and other crystalline rocks and is often associated with sphalerite, pyrite, calcite and quartz. France, Austria, UK, Australia, Chile, Peru and the USA (extensive deposits in Missouri, Illinois and Iowa).

USES Chief ore of lead and important source of silver.

SPECIFIC GRAVITY 7.4–7.6	HARDNESS 2.5–2.75	CRYSTAL SYSTEM ISOMETRIC

ORPIMENT

PROPERTIES **Distinctive features:** Lemon yellow, often tinged with fine streaks of orange, its lustre and flexibility in thin plates. When heated in a closed tube, it yields a dark red liquid that becomes yellow when cold. *Note:* Arsenic trisulphide is poisonous. **Color:** Lemon yellow to medium yellow. **Luster:** Pearly to resinous. **Streak:** Slightly paler than color. **Transparency:** Subtransparent to translucent. **Cleavage:** Perfect on 010 and striated. **Fracture:** Rough. **Tenacity:** Sectile. **Forms:** Massive and foliated, but the tiny crystals are difficult to see.

OCCURRENCE Often associated with the equally poisonous orange-red realgar, arsenic sulphide. Eastern Europe, Japan and the USA.

USES Pigment and for removing hair from animal skins.

SPECIFIC GRAVITY 3.4–3.5	HARDNESS 1.5–2	CRYSTAL SYSTEM MONOCLINIC

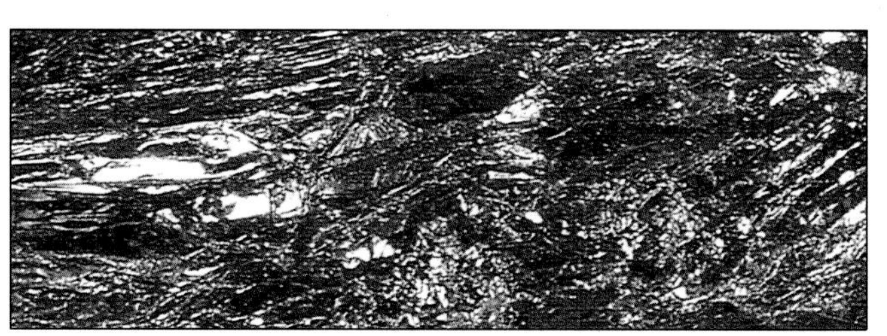

MOLYBDENITE

PROPERTIES **Distinctive features:** Soft, flexible, silvery, foliated scales and has a greasy feel. When heated in a tube, it yields sulphurous fumes and a pale yellow sublimate. **Color:** Silvery lead gray. **Luster:** Metallic. **Streak:** Gray to greenish-gray. **Transparency:** Opaque. **Cleavage:** Perfect basal on 0001. **Fracture:** Not applicable. **Tenacity:** Flexible, but not elastic. **Forms:** Tabular prisms, often short and tapering and often foliated or massive.

OCCURRENCE In granite pegmatites and quartz veins, also in syenites and gneisses. Norway, UK, Australia (Queensland), Namibia and the USA.

USES Principal ore of molybdenum.

SPECIFIC GRAVITY 4.7–4.8	HARDNESS 1.0–1.5	CRYSTAL SYSTEM HEXAGONAL

STIBNITE

PROPERTIES **Distinctive features:** Color, softness, cleavage. Also, when heated in a tube, it yields sulphur dioxide and fumes of antimony oxide, the latter condensing to form a white powder. **Color:** Steel grey to dull grey, often with a black, iridescent tarnish. **Luster:** Metallic; splendent on fresh crystal surfaces. **Streak:** Same as color. **Transparency:** Opaque. **Cleavage:** Perfect on 010, less so on 001. **Fracture:** Small-scale

subconchoidal. **Tenacity:** Somewhat sectile. **Forms:** Masses of radiating elongated crystals. Also massive and granular. **Twinning:** None. **Varieties:** Metastibnite, which is an earthy, reddish deposit found at Steamboat Springs, Nevada in USA.
OCCURRENCE Mostly in quartz veins in granites, but also in schists and limestones. China, Algeria, Mexico, Germany, Romania, Italy, Borneo, Peru and the USA.
USES Principal source of antimony.

SPECIFIC GRAVITY 4.56–4.62	HARDNESS 2.0	CRYSTAL SYSTEM ORTHORHOMBIC

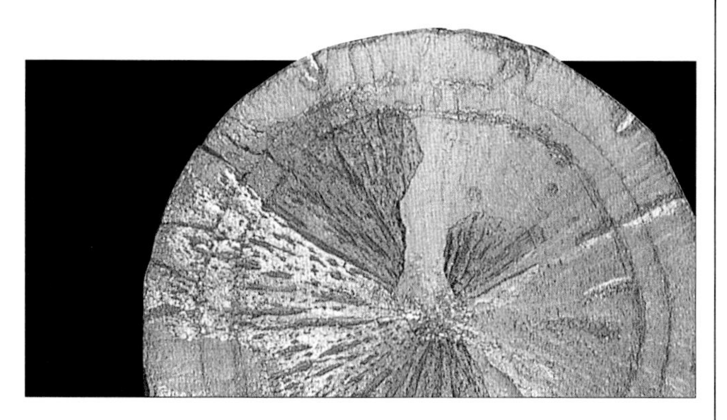

PYRITE

PROPERTIES **Distinctive features:** Glistening to metallic brassy gold cubic and pyritohedron crystals and produces a greenish-black streak. **Color:** Pale brassy gold. **Luster:** Metallic to glistening. **Streak:** Greenish-black to brown-black. **Transparency:** Opaque. **Cleavage:** Poor on 100 and 111. **Fracture:** Usually uneven, sometimes conchoidal. **Forms:** Cubes, pyritohedrons. Often intergrown, massive, radiated, granular, globular and stalactitic. **Twinning:** Interpenetrant twins common on 110.
OCCURRENCE Universal – the most common sulphide. Eastern Europe, Switzerland, Italy (large crystals up to 16cm (6in)), Spain, UK and the USA.
USES As source of gold and copper, which it contains in small amounts. Also to produce sulphur, sulphuric acid and iron sulphate.

SPECIFIC GRAVITY 4.95–4.97	HARDNESS 6.0–6.5	CRYSTAL SYSTEM ISOMETRIC

ARSENOPYRITE

PROPERTIES **Distinctive features:** Color, streak. Also, when heated in an open tube, it gives off sulphurous fumes and produces a white sublimate of arsenic trioxide. **Color:** Silvery tin white to iron gray. **Luster:** Metallic. **Streak:** Black to dark gray. **Transparency:** Opaque. **Cleavage:** Good on 110. **Fracture:**

Uneven. **Tenacity:** Brittle. **Forms:** Prismatic crystals, often flattened. Granular. **Twinning:** On 110, occasionally on 101.
OCCURRENCE Associated with cassiterite, wolframite, sphalerite and galena mineralized veins in granite and associated rocks. Also in limestones and dolomites and frequently associated with gold. Austria, Germany, Switzerland, Sweden, UK, Bolivia, Canada and the USA.
USES Principal ore of arsenic.

SPECIFIC GRAVITY 5.9–6.2	HARDNESS 5.5–6.0	CRYSTAL SYSTEM ORTHORHOMBIC

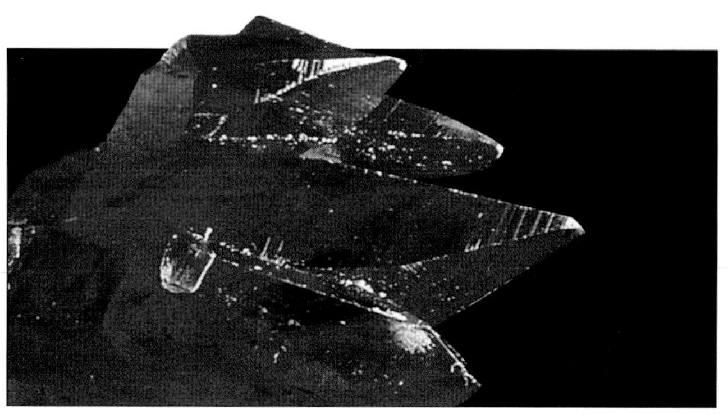

PROUSTITE

PROPERTIES **Distinctive features:** Color, streak and, when heated in a closed tube, it fuses, emits sulphurous fumes and leaves a white sublimate of arsenic trioxide. **Colour:** Dark red to vermilion. **Luster:** Adamantine. **Streak:** Same as colour. **Transparency:** Transparent to translucent. **Cleavage:** Good on 1011. **Fracture:** Uneven to occasionally conchoidal. **Tenacity:** Brittle. **Twinning:** On 1014 and 1011.
OCCURRENCE In hydrothermal silver veins and associated with galena and sphalerite. Slovakia, Czech Republic, Germany, France, Chile and Mexico.
USES Mineral collections.

SPECIFIC GRAVITY 5.57–5.64	HARDNESS 2.0–2.5	CRYSTAL SYSTEM HEXAGONAL

CHRYSOBERYL

PROPERTIES Chrysoberyls are green, greenish-yellow or brown in color. There are two varieties: alexandrite and cat's-eye chrysoberyl. The alexandrites are distinctive in that in daylight they are green, but when viewed under artificial light they appear red. Some replacement of aluminum by chromium gives the green color.

Chrysoberyl is found as prismatic crystals which are usually flattened parallel to one pair of the faces. Alexandrite may be found as three intergrown crystals which give the appearance of having hexagonal symmetry; these are called "trillings". There are three directions of cleavage which are weak, and fracture is conchoidal.

OCCURRENCE The best alexandrites are found in the Ural Mountains. Russian chrysoberyl has two-phase inclusions and feathers. Large crystals of chrysoberyl are found as water-worn pebbles in Sri Lanka. Other localities include the Mogok area of Burma, Brazil, Zimbabwe, Madagascar, Zambia and Tanzania.

USES Gemstones. The mixed cut (brilliant-cut crown and step-cut pavilion) is usually used for chrysoberyl. To show the cat's-eye the stone must be cut *en cabachon*. Synthetic chrysoberyl, synthetic corundum and synthetic spinel are made to imitate alexandrite and its color change.

SPECIFIC GRAVITY 3.68–3.78 **HARDNESS** 8.5 **CRYSTAL SYSTEM** ORTHORHOMBIC

SPINEL

PROPERTIES Spinels are found in a number of colors including shades of red, blue, violet, purple and mauve. Dark green and brown iron-rich spinels are usually too dark to be used in jewelry. Star-stones are also found occasionally.

Spinel is found as octahedral crystals which may be twinned, and as perfect crystals. It is also found as pebbles in gem gravels. Luster is vitreous. Red spinels show a characteristic absorption spectrum, with a group of fine lines in the red. A weak red glow is seen when a red spinel is placed under short-wave ultraviolet light, while a much stronger and brighter glow is seen under long-wave ultraviolet light. It is singly refractive.

OCCURRENCE Spinel is generally found in association with corundum, usually in alluvial deposits such as those of Burma and Sri Lanka. Other localities include Afghanistan, Thailand, Australia, Sweden, Brazil and the USA.

USES Gemstones. Spinels are fashioned in the mixed-cut or step-cut styles. The star-stones when cut *en cabochon* show a four-rayed star. Spinel can be made synthetically and colored to imitate other gemstones such as aquamarine and zircon.

SPECIFIC GRAVITY 3.60–3.70 **HARDNESS** 8.0 **CRYSTAL SYSTEM** ISOMETRIC

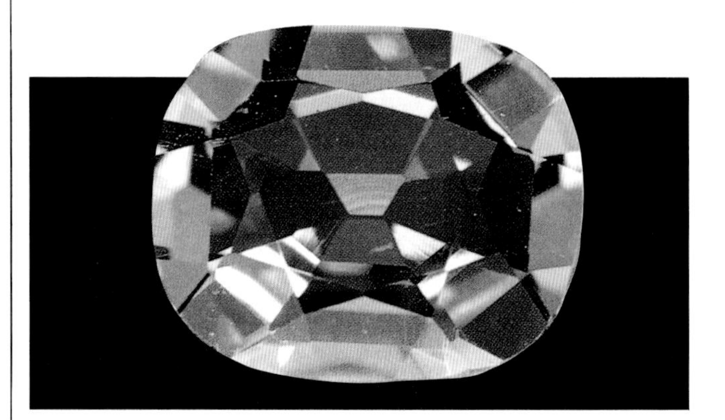

TAAFFEITE

PROPERTIES Taaffeite is an extremely rare mineral which is of interest as it is the first mineral to have been identified when already cut as a gemstone. The first specimen was found in 1945 by Count Taaffe of Dublin amongst a jeweler's box of mixed stones. The pale mauve stone weighing 1.419 carats resembled spinel but was doubly refractive whereas spinel is singly refractive. A second taaffeite specimen (0.86 carats) was found in 1949 and a third in 1957; since then only a few more have been found, including a ruby-red specimen and a sapphire-blue.

OCCURRENCE Taaffeite specimens have been found in Sri Lanka, China and Russia.

USES Gemstones. Taaffeites are usually faceted as round brilliants. It is not imitated or synthesized.

SPECIFIC GRAVITY 3.62 **HARDNESS** 8.0 **CRYSTAL SYSTEM** HEXAGONAL

Ruby

CORUNDUM VARIETY

Properties Pure corundum is colorless and the gem color is caused by small amounts of impurities. The rich red color of ruby is caused by chromium. The crystal habit varies with locality. Fracture is uneven or conchoidal. There is no true cleavage but a line of weakness may be present. Luster is vitreous.

The absorption spectrum is characterized by fine lines in the red and when rubies are viewed through crossed filters the chromium causes a luminescence that can be seen as a red glow. It is doubly refractive.

Occurrence The highest quality rubies come from the Mogok area of Burma. Thailand provides most of the world's rubies but they are brownish-red and darker than the Burmese ones. Tanzanian rubies are distinctive short prismatic crystals in a bright green rock. Other localities include Afghanistan, Australia, Brazil, Cambodia, India, Malawi, Pakistan and the USA.

Uses Rubies are faceted or cut *en cabochon*. They may have rutile inclusions which appear as a sheen known as "silk" or show a six-pointed star when cut *en cabochon*.

Rubies were first made synthetically towards the end of the nineteenth century and soon became the first gems to be made in commercial quantities. Synthetic rubies are now used instead of real gems as bearings in watches and precision instruments.

SPECIFIC GRAVITY 4.0 | **HARDNESS** 9.0 | **CRYSTAL SYSTEM** TRIGONAL

Sapphire

CORUNDUM VARIETY

Properties The name sapphire is given to any color of corundum other than red. They can be black, purple, violet, blue, green, yellow or orange. The blue colors are caused by traces of titanium and iron.

The form the crystals take depends on the variety and locality. Fracture is uneven or conchoidal with no real cleavage. Luster is vitreous. Sapphire is doubly refractive.

Occurrence Good-quality sapphires come from Burma. They often have black, feather-like inclusions. Cornflower blue sapphires are found in pegmatite rocks and as water-worn pebbles in Kashmir. Sri Lankan sapphires are pale blue, violet, yellow, white, green, pink and a rare orange-pink. Other localities include Queensland and New South Wales, Australia, Brazil, Cambodia, Kenya, Malawi, Tanzania, Thailand and Zimbabwe.

Uses Gemstones, abrasives and grinding powders. For parti-colored gemstones, the cutter places the clear part at the front of the gem so that it appears blue from the front. Stones are usually faceted as mixed-cut gems. Star-stones are cut *en cabochon*.

Corundums are imitated by spinel, garnet and glass. Most of the blue glasses show strong red through the Chelsea color filter, unlike sapphires.

SPECIFIC GRAVITY 4.0 | **HARDNESS** 9.0 | **CRYSTAL SYSTEM** TRIGONAL

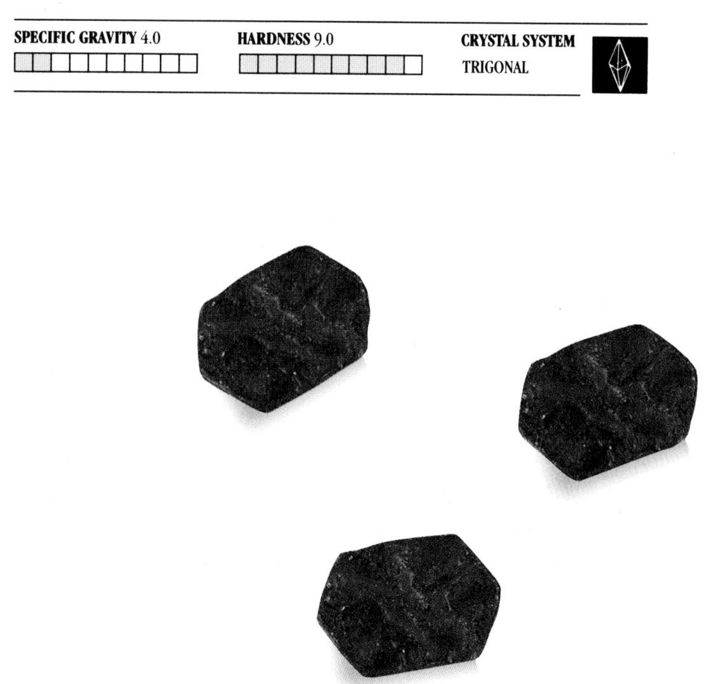

ROCK CRYSTAL

QUARTZ VARIETY

PROPERTIES Rock crystal is found as hexagonal prisms which are characterized by horizontal striations on the prism faces and it has a vitreous luster. Twinning is common and some crystals are doubly terminated. There is no distinct cleavage and fracture is conchoidal. It is doubly refractive. Rock crystal is often clear, but if there are inclusions they are usually two-phase. Tourmalinated quartz has inclusions of black tourmaline crystals. "Rainbow quartz" or "iris quartz" is rock crystal that has cracks which produce rainbow colors due to interference of light at the thin films of air in the cracks. Rock crystal is transparent to ultraviolet rays, as is all quartz.

OCCURRENCE Rock crystal is found all over the world, and is one of the most common minerals in the Earth's crust. Good crystals are found in the Swiss and French Alps, but the most important locality is Brazil.

USES Manufacture of glass and porcelain, ornamental, jewelry, abrasives. Rock crystal has been used as faceted stones and beads and in composite stones, to imitate other gemstones. Flat rock crystal beads (rondels) are often used to separate colored stones.

Rock crystal may be imitated by glass, but can be distinguished from glass by its birefringence and by the fact that it does not contain air bubbles.

SPECIFIC GRAVITY 2.65 | **HARDNESS** 7.0 | **CRYSTAL SYSTEM** TRIGONAL

AMETHYST

QUARTZ VARIETY

PROPERTIES Amethyst varies in color from pale violet to dark purple and may be parti-colored with clear or yellow quartz. The tips of the crystals are often darkest and may grade to colorless quartz.

Amethyst changes color with heat and stones from different localities show different color changes to brown, yellow and sometimes green. However, these changes are unpredictable and the color may fade. Amethyst has distinct dichroism, showing a bluish-purple and a reddish-purple. This distinguishes it from heat-treated stones which do not show any dichroism. Amethyst

does not have a characteristic absorption spectrum. Inclusions are usually feather-like, or may resemble a thumb print or tiger stripes.

OCCURRENCE The Ural Mountains of Russia have been the main source of a reddish-colored amethyst. Other good sources include Germany, Namibia, Western Australia, Sri Lanka, USA and Zambia. Brazilian and Uruguayan amethyst is found in cavities in igneous rocks. Violet-colored amethyst is found in Canada and many geodes containing amethyst are found in the Deccan trap area of India.

USES Crystals of amethyst are cut in the mixed-cut style or the step-cut style and are often fashioned into beads. Synthetic corundum and glass can be made in a color to imitate amethyst.

SPECIFIC GRAVITY 2.65 | **HARDNESS** 7.0 | **CRYSTAL SYSTEM** TRIGONAL

CITRINE

QUARTZ VARIETY

PROPERTIES The distinctive colour of citrine is due to the presence of iron and varies from pure yellow, dull yellow, honey or brownish yellow. Citrine is dichroic but has no characteristic absorption spectrum or fluorescence. The crystals will turn white if heated and dark brown if exposed to X-rays. They are often parti-colored. Cut crystals have a good luster. Larger citrine crystals take the form of prisms with pyramid ends.

OCCURRENCE Citrine is rare, but does occur in Brazil, France, Madagascar and the USA (Colorado).
USES Faceted cuts are used for fine transparent gemstones, while the remaining varieties are cut as cabochons.

Natural yellow citrine is rare and most commercial stones are actually heat-treated amethysts. Some heat-treated stones have a red tint and show no pleochroism. Citrine is used to imitate the more expensive gemstone, topaz.

SPECIFIC GRAVITY 2.65 | **HARDNESS** 7.0 | **CRYSTAL SYSTEM** TRIGONAL

BROWN QUARTZ

QUARTZ VARIETY

PROPERTIES Brown quartz varies in color from yellow-brown cairngorm and gray smoky quartz to the almost black quartz sometimes called morion. Morion can be heat-treated to lighten its color and make a more attractive stone. The smoky variety is thought to be rock crystal which has been irradiated.

Brown quartz is found as hexagonal prisms. It is doubly refractive but has no characteristic absorption spectrum or luminescence under ultraviolet light or X-rays. It often has rutile inclusions, which may add to the beauty and interest of the stone.
OCCURRENCE The main localities for brown quartz are in the Swiss Alps. Good crystals of smoky quartz are found in Pike's Peak, Colorado (USA). Other localities include Australia, Japan and Spain.
USES Brown quartz is often faceted for gemstones or carved for *objets d'art*. Most of the cairngorm variety of brown quartz is Brazilian amethyst that has been heat-treated to give the brown color.

SPECIFIC GRAVITY 2.65 | **HARDNESS** 7.0 | **CRYSTAL SYSTEM** TRIGONAL

ROSE QUARTZ

QUARTZ VARIETY

PROPERTIES Rose quartz varies in color from pale whitish-pink to dark rose pink. Magnesium and titanium have both been suggested as the impurity which causes the color. Transparent rose quartz is very rare and the stones are usually rather cloudy.

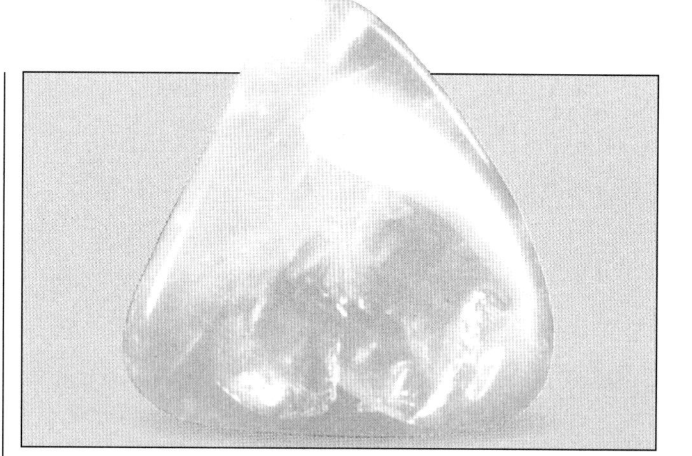

The crystals are brittle and often cracked. The stones tend to lose their color when heated and turn black when exposed to radiation. Dichroism is apparent in the darker colored stones.
OCCURRENCE Quality rose quartz is found in Brazil, Madagascar and the USA (California and Maine).
USES Some rose quartz contains tiny rutile needles which cause a star effect. This is best seen when the stone is cut *en cabochon* and light is directed up through the stone. Rose quartz may be faceted although it is more usually fashioned as cabochons, beads or carved for ornaments.

SPECIFIC GRAVITY 2.65 | **HARDNESS** 7.0 | **CRYSTAL SYSTEM** TRIGONAL

MILKY QUARTZ

QUARTZ VARIETY

PROPERTIES Milky quartz is of variable opacity, white and may be layered or striped with milky bands. The distinctive coloration is due to inclusions of numerous bubbles of gas and liquid in the crystal.
OCCURRENCE Milky quartz is found in pegmatites and hydrothermal veins and is one of the most common materials found in the Earth's surface. Massive crystals have been found in Siberia. Other localities include Central Europe, Brazil, Madagascar, Namibia and the USA.

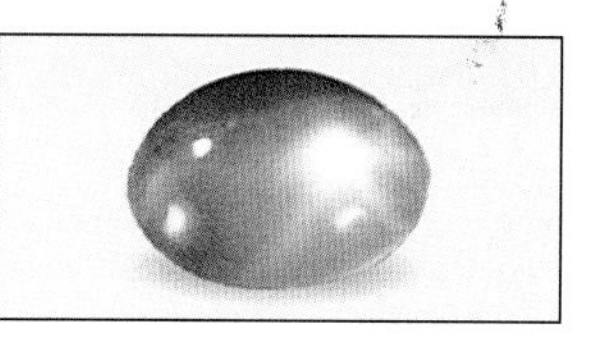

USES Milky quartz is rarely cut as a gemstone but is often cut into beads or ornaments. It may contain grains of gold and is usually cut *en cabochon* to show these.

SPECIFIC GRAVITY 2.65 | **HARDNESS** 7.0 | **CRYSTAL SYSTEM** TRIGONAL

QUARTZ CAT'S-EYE

QUARTZ VARIETY

PROPERTIES Quartz cat's-eye is one of a group formed from fibrous quartz aggregates. It is semi-transparent and the fibres are clearly seen. Another variety, tiger's-eye, varies in color from gold-yellow to gold-brown stripes against a blackish background. Hawk's-eye is blue. Quartz cat's-eye contains parallel lines of asbestos fibers. It becomes greenish gray or green when ground. Tiger's-eyes and hawk's-eyes form when blue crocidolite asbestos is replaced by quartz. The asbestos breaks down leaving a residue of brown iron oxides, which gives the golden brown colors in tiger's-eye. Hawk's-eye retains the original blue color of asbestos.
OCCURRENCE Quartz cat's-eye is found in Burma, India, Sri Lanka and Germany. Tiger's-eye and hawk's-eye are mainly found in South Africa, but other localities include Australia, Burma, India and the USA.
USES Tiger's-eye is often used for carving boxes and other ornamental items. It can also be cut to show the chatoyant effect. Quartz cat's-eye is usually cut into round polished pieces for jewelry. It may be distinguished from chrysoberyl cat's-eye by its lower refractive index.

SPECIFIC GRAVITY 2.65 | **HARDNESS** 7.0 | **CRYSTAL SYSTEM** TRIGONAL

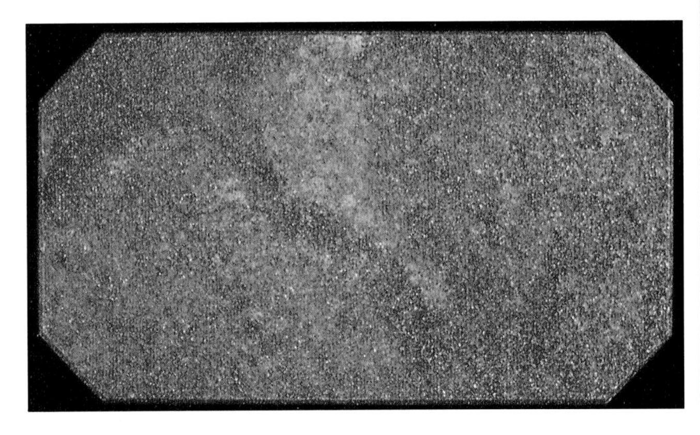

AVENTURINE QUARTZ

QUARTZ VARIETY

PROPERTIES Aventurine quartz contains mica plates which give it a sheen, with spangles of different colors. Green aventurine quartz contains green mica. Other aventurine quartzes include the brownish-red stones, which contain cubes of the mineral pyrite. Other varieties of aventurine include bluish-white and bluish-green material.
OCCURRENCE The main localities for good-quality aventurine include Brazil, India, Siberia and Tanzania.
USES Aventurine is used for ornamental objects and may also be cut *en cabochon*.

SPECIFIC GRAVITY 2.65 | **HARDNESS** 7.0 | **CRYSTAL SYSTEM** TRIGONAL

CHALCEDONY

QUARTZ VARIETY

PROPERTIES Chalcedony is a variety of quartz with a crystalline structure that is so small it can only be seen with the use of a microscope (microcrystalline). The word chalcedony covers a group of quartzes, including all agates, carnelian and chrysoprase, which form from thin layers of tiny quartz fibres. Pure chalcedony, however, has its own distinct properties. It is translucent and has a white or bluish color, but it may be colored green by chromium. The banding of chalcedony cannot be seen without a microscope. Under ultraviolet light the luminescence varies from bluish-white to yellowish-green. It is doubly refractive.
OCCURRENCE Good-quality chalcedony is found in Brazil, India, Madagascar and Uruguay.
USES The fibrous structure gives chalcedony its toughness and makes it ideal for carving, particularly popular in Germany. Chalcedony is porous and may be dyed with a variety of metallic salts.

SPECIFIC GRAVITY 2.60 | **HARDNESS** 7.0 | **CRYSTAL SYSTEM** TRIGONAL

JASPER

QUARTZ VARIETY

PROPERTIES Jasper is an impure variety of microcrystalline quartz. It consists of a network of interlocking quartz crystals. Jasper is opaque and may contain a mixture of reds and browns or greyish-blues and greens, caused by impurities. Riband (ribbon) jasper is striped and takes a good polish but may break along lines where the colors meet. Orbicular jasper has white or grey "eyes" surrounded by red. Bloodstone or heliotrope is dark green with scattered red spots. Plasma is usually green with white

or yellow spots. Hornstone is a grey form which is sometimes stained blue to imitate lapis lazuli. Prase is a dull green rock sometimes coloured by actinolite fibres.
OCCURRENCE Worldwide. A red jasper is found in India and Venezuela, but the most varied types are found in the USA, in particular in Santa Clara, California, where orbicular jasper is found.
USES Jasper is often cut in slabs for fireplace surrounds, tables and facing materials. It is also used for carvings and in mosaics and inlays. Jasper may form within fossil wood and when polished this petrified wood is attractive in brooches or cut *en cabachon*.

SPECIFIC GRAVITY 2.60	HARDNESS 7.0	CRYSTAL SYSTEM TRIGONAL

AGATES

QUARTZ VARIETY

PROPERTIES Agates are banded forms of chalcedony. The bands may be multicoloured or different shades of the same color. Coloration is due to trace elements and the banding is due to the progressive solidification of the material. When agate contains dendritic (tree-like) inclusions it is called moss agate or mocha stone. The inclusions may be black (manganese dioxide), green (chlorite), red (iron) or a mixture. Fire agate has iridescent colors which are produced by the interference of light at the layers of iron oxide within the chalcedony.
OCCURRENCE Agate localities include Brazil, Egypt, Scotland and Uruguay. The best green moss agate comes from India.
USES Agate is usually cut and polished and may be stained many different colors. It may chip and splinter when struck.

SPECIFIC GRAVITY 2.60	HARDNESS 7.0	CRYSTAL SYSTEM TRIGONAL

SARD, SARDONYX AND ONYX

QUARTZ VARIETY

PROPERTIES Sard is the brownish-red variety of chalcedony. Sardonyx has straight bands of white together with bands of brownish-red sard. Onyx is made up of black and white bands. It is similar to agate except that the bands are straight.
OCCURRENCE Localities include Brazil and Uruguay.
USES Sard, sardonyx and onyx are carved and polished for use as beads and cameos. Black onyx has almost always been stained. Natural black onyx is rare and so it is produced by chemically treating agate.

SPECIFIC GRAVITY 2.60	HARDNESS 7.0	CRYSTAL SYSTEM TRIGONAL

CHRYSOPRASE

QUARTZ VARIETY

PROPERTIES Chrysoprase is a form of chalcedony. It is translucent and apple green.
OCCURRENCE Most early chrysoprase came from Bohemia. A more recent source is Marlborough in Queensland, Australia.
USES It is usually cut *en cabochon*, as beads, which are thought to date from Greek and Roman times. Like other rare gemstones, chrysoprase is imitated. These imitations include glass and stained agate.

SPECIFIC GRAVITY 2.60	HARDNESS 7.0	CRYSTAL SYSTEM TRIGONAL

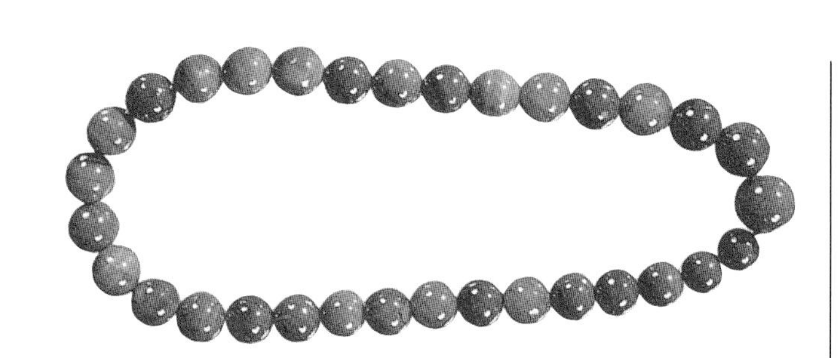

CARNELIAN

QUARTZ VARIETY

PROPERTIES Carnelian, also known as cornelian, is the translucent red variety of chalcedony. The red color comes from the presence of iron oxides.
OCCURRENCE Carnelian is found as rolled pebbles in Brazil, China, Egypt and India. Other localities include Colombia, Germany, Japan, Scotland and the USA.
USES Carnelian is carved or cut and polished *en cabochon*. Most commercial carnelian is stained chalcedony.

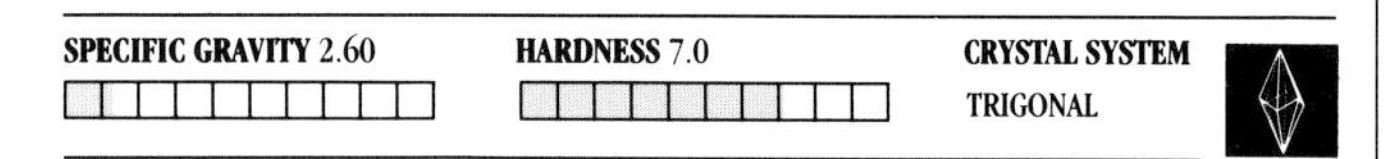

SPECIFIC GRAVITY 2.60 **HARDNESS** 7.0 **CRYSTAL SYSTEM** TRIGONAL

BAUXITE

PROPERTIES **Distinctive features:** Massive, red to reddish-yellow, earthy and amorphous. **Color:** Shades of red to yellow, occasionally white. **Luster:** Earthy. **Streak:** Reddish. **Transparency:** Opaque. **Cleavage:** None. **Fracture:** Earthy. **Forms:** Mostly in reddish, earthy-like masses, but sometimes occurs as fine grains. **Twinning:** None. **Varieties:** Concretions of grains, clay or earthy-like masses.
OCCURRENCE Formed by weathering of aluminum rocks under tropical conditions and deposited as a colloid. France, Germany, Romania, Italy, Venezuela and the USA.
USES Principal ore of aluminium; also used in ceramics.

SPECIFIC GRAVITY 2.5 **HARDNESS** Not applicable **CRYSTAL SYSTEM** COLLOIDAL

CROCIDOLITE

QUARTZ VARIETY

PROPERTIES **Distinctive features:** Glistening fibrous to hair-like blue to green crystals. **Color:** Medium to pale blue to medium green. **Luster:** Silky. **Streak:** Bluish. **Transparency:** Transparent. **Cleavage:** Perfect on 110. **Fracture:** Uneven. **Tenacity:** Brittle to flexible. **Forms:** Fibrous masses of thin, prismatic crystals. **Twinning:** None. **Varieties:** Synonymous is blue asbestos and when it is replaced by quartz it forms the mineral tiger's eye.
OCCURRENCE In veins and pegmatites in granites and syenites. South Africa, Austria, France, Bolivia, UK and the USA.
USES Mineral collections.

SPECIFIC GRAVITY 3.0 **HARDNESS** 6.0 **CRYSTAL SYSTEM** MONOCLINIC

LIMONITE

PROPERTIES **Distinctive features:** Ochreous yellow, earthy, amorphous. **Color:** Deep ochreous yellow to brown and black. **Luster:** Earthy, dull. **Streak:** Ochreous yellow. **Transparency:** Opaque. **Cleavage:** None. **Fracture:** Earthy. **Forms:** Compact to stalactitic and botryoidal ochreous earthy masses. **Twinning:** None. **Varieties:** Bog ore, which occurs in bogs where it petrifies plant material; clay-ironstone, which has concretions and nodules and is mostly found in sandstone rocks.
OCCURRENCE Deposited near the surface after weathering of iron-rich minerals. Worldwide, but particularly in Canada and the USA.
USES Pigments and iron ore.

SPECIFIC GRAVITY 3.5–4.0 **HARDNESS** 5.0–5.5 **CRYSTAL SYSTEM** AMORPHOUS

OPAL

PROPERTIES There are four types of opal commonly used in jewelry: white, black, fire and water opal. Opal is one of the few non-crystalline, or poorly crystalline, gemstones. It is a hardened jelly made up of silica and water, and is found filling cavities in rocks, as stalagmites or replacing organic matter such as shell and bone. It has an uneven or conchoidal fracture. The play of color, or iridescence, is due to the interference of white light on minute silica spheres in the structure of opal.
OCCURRENCE Opal comes from Eastern Europe, Guatemala, Honduras and Mexico and, most importantly, from Queensland, Australia. It occurs in volcanic lava and in sedimentary and igneous rocks in veins, as lumps or in pipes. Other localities include Brazil, South Africa, Zimbabwe and the USA.
USES As gemstones. Fire opals are usually faceted, but other opals are cut *en cabochon* or carved. Opal has been imitated in several ways; one method is to place chips of colored plastic and opal behind a hollow-backed cabochon of rock crystal. Another is to cement iridescent shell to the back of a flat-based cabochon of rock crystal.

SPECIFIC GRAVITY 2.10 **HARDNESS** 6.0 **CRYSTAL SYSTEM** AMORPHOUS

RUTILE

PROPERTIES **Distinctive features:** Bright metallic coppery to reddish-brown needle-like crystals in quartz crystals or as darker, compact masses in acid to intermediate crystalline rocks. Sometimes in limestones, where deposited by mineralizing fluids. Transparent varieties have adamantine luster, but many specimens are opaque. **Color:** Coppery to reddish-brown. **Luster:** Metallic to adamantine. **Streak:** Pale brown. **Transparency:** Transparent to opaque. **Cleavage:** On 110 and 100. **Fracture:** Subconchoidal to uneven. **Tenacity:** Brittle. **Forms:** Often found as prismatic acicular crystals in quartz. Occasionally compact to massive. **Twinning:** On 101, sometimes with complex geniculation. **Varieties:** Ordinary rutile is brown-red to black, iron-rich rutile is black, while chromium-rich rutile is green.

OCCURRENCE In acid to intermediate crystalline rocks. Austria, Switzerland, France, Norway, Australia, Brazil and the USA.
USES Ore of titanium.

SPECIFIC GRAVITY 4.18–4.25 **HARDNESS** 6.0–6.5 **CRYSTAL SYSTEM** TETRAGONAL

CASSITERITE

PROPERTIES **Distinctive features:** Hardness, color, form and specific gravity. **Color:** Brown to black. **Luster:** Brilliant. **Streak:** White to brownish. **Transparency:** Nearly transparent to opaque. **Cleavage:** Poor on 100. **Fracture:** Subconchoidal to rough. **Tenacity:** Brittle. **Forms:** Dumpy pyramids and prismatic. **Twinning:** Interpenetrant, often on 101. Also elbow twins. **Varieties:** Tin stone, which is crystalline and massive; wood tin, which is botryoidal and reniform with a fibrous structure; toad's eye, which is the same as wood tin, but on a smaller scale; and stream tin, which is cassiterite in the form of sand, admixed with other mineral and rock grains.
OCCURRENCE Mostly in granitic rocks and associated pegmatites. Often associated with fluorite, apatite, topaz and wolframite deposited by mineralizing fluids. Malaysia, Indonesia, Bolivia, Congo, Mexico, England, Eastern Europe and the USA.
USES Principal ore of tin.

SPECIFIC GRAVITY 6.4–7.1 **HARDNESS** 6–7 **CRYSTAL SYSTEM** TETRAGONAL

CHROMITE

PROPERTIES **Distinctive features:** Streak, feebly magnetic. **Color:** Black. **Luster:** Submetallic. **Streak:** Brown. **Transparency:** Opaque. **Cleavage:** None. **Fracture:** Uneven to rough. **Tenacity:** Brittle. **Forms:** Octahedral. Massive to granular. **Twinning:** None.

OCCURRENCE In peridotites and serpentine and often associated with magnetite. The Urals, Austria, Germany, France, UK, South Africa, Iran, the USA and Canada.

USES Chromium ore, for hardening steel, chrome plating and chromium pigments.

SPECIFIC GRAVITY 4.1–4.9 **HARDNESS** 5.5 **CRYSTAL SYSTEM** ISOMETRIC

PYROLUSITE

PROPERTIES **Distinctive features:** Hardness and color of streak. **Color:** Iron black to dark steel gray; occasionally bluish. **Luster:** Metallic. **Streak:** Same as color. **Transparency:** Opaque. **Cleavage:** On 100 and 011. **Fracture:** Rough. **Tenacity:** Brittle. **Forms:** Commonly dendritic, granular to massive. **Twinning:** None. **Varieties:** Crystals, massive and the very pure form, which is called polianite.

OCCURRENCE Concentrated as a secondary ore deposit by circulating fluids, often in clays and siltstones. Brazil, Cuba, Germany, India, the Urals and the USA.

USES Ore of manganese; also used for coloring glass, in the preparation of chlorine, bromine and oxygen.

SPECIFIC GRAVITY 4.73–4.86 **HARDNESS** 2.0–2.5 **CRYSTAL SYSTEM** ORTHORHOMBIC

MAGNETITE

PROPERTIES **Distinctive features:** Heavy and magnetic, often with north and south poles. **Color:** Black. **Luster:** Metallic. **Streak:** Black. **Transparency:** Opaque. **Cleavage:** Indistinct. **Fracture:** Uneven. **Tenacity:** Brittle. **Forms:** Octahedral, massive to fine granular. **Twinning:** On 111. **Varieties:** Lodestone, which is strongly magnetic and has north and south poles.

OCCURRENCE Found in most igneous rocks, particularly those of basic composition, black beach sands, serpentines and metamorphic rocks. Sweden and Norway (largest deposits in the world), Siberia, Australia, Europe, Brazil, the USA, Cuba and Canada.

USES Iron ore.

SPECIFIC GRAVITY 5.17–5.18 **HARDNESS** 5.5–6.5 **CRYSTAL SYSTEM** ISOMETRIC

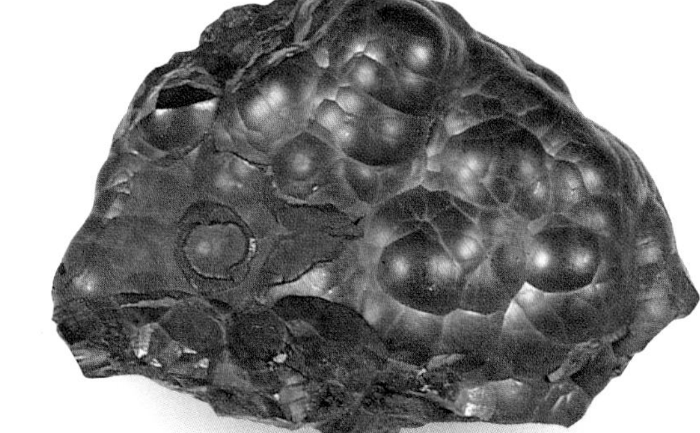

HAEMATITE

PROPERTIES **Distinctive features:** Streak, color, form, density. **Color:** Metallic gray to earthy red. **Luster:** Metallic to splendent. **Streak:** Bright red to Indian red. **Transparency:** Opaque. **Cleavage:** None. **Fracture:** Uneven to subconchoidal. **Tenacity:** Brittle, but elastic in thin plates. **Forms:** Tabular to thick crystals. **Twinning:** Interpenetrant on 0001 and 0112. **Varieties:** Specularite, which has splendent tabular crystals, often in brilliant masses; pencil ore, which is a fibrous compact form, often used in jewelry; kidney ore, which has botryoidal masses resembling kidneys; clay ironstone, which has deep red-brown compact masses, often in sedimentary rocks.

OCCURRENCE The Urals in Russia, Romania, Austria, Germany, Switzerland, France, Italy, UK, Ascension Island, Brazil, the USA and Canada.

USES Principal ore of iron.

SPECIFIC GRAVITY 4.9–5.3 **HARDNESS** 5.5–6.5 **CRYSTAL SYSTEM** HEXAGONAL

HALIDES

HALITE

PROPERTIES **Distinctive features:** Taste – it's the natural form of table salt – solubility, cleavage. *Note:* Specimens will absorb atmospheric water and deliquesce if not kept in a sealed container. **Color:** Colorless, white to yellowish-brown or shades of gray-blue. **Luster:** Vitreous. **Streak:** Same as color. **Transparency:** Transparent to translucent. **Cleavage:** Perfect on 100. **Fracture:** Conchoidal. **Tenacity:** Brittle. **Forms:** Cubes, often with sunken crystal faces. Massive, granular and compact. **Twinning:** Interpenetrant.
OCCURRENCE Worldwide as a main constituent of seawater. Commonly stratified up to 30m (33yd) in thickness in sedimentary rocks. Under pressure, the salt may flow upwards to produce huge salt domes at the surface. South-east Russia, Poland, Austria, Germany, Switzerland, France, UK, Iran, India, Peru, Colombia, the USA and Canada.
USES Principal source of common salt, but also in preparation of sodium compounds, glass and soap.

SPECIFIC GRAVITY 2.1–2.6 | HARDNESS 2.5 | CRYSTAL SYSTEM ISOMETRIC

FLUORITE

PROPERTIES Fluorite occurs in a wide range of colors including yellow, brown, green, blue, violet, pink and colorless. Crystals form as cubes, often with beveled edges. Twinning is common and cleavage is perfect octahedral. Luster is vitreous.

Most fluorite glows blue to violet under long-wave ultraviolet light, but blue John, a massive crystalline variety made up of curved bands of blue and purple, is inert under ultraviolet.
OCCURRENCE Some of the best crystals are found in the north of England and in Cornwall. Other localities include Switzerland, the USA, Canada, Germany, Eastern Europe, Italy and Norway. Blue John is only found in the lead mine at Castleton in Derbyshire, England.
USES Fluorite is too soft for jewelry and the perfect octahedral cleavage makes cutting difficult. Blue John has been carved into vases and other decorative objects since Roman times. Synthetic fluorite has been made.

SPECIFIC GRAVITY 3.01–3.25 | HARDNESS 4 | CRYSTAL SYSTEM ISOMETRIC

BORATES

SINHALITE

PROPERTIES Sinhalite varies from pale yellow-brown to dark greenish-brown in color. Until 1952 sinhalite was thought to be a brown-colored peridot, but it was noticed that the density was slightly higher, and X-ray crystallography showed that sinhalite was a different mineral. Sinhalite has distinct pleochroism, showing the colors pale brown, greenish-brown and dark brown.
OCCURRENCE Most gem-quality sinhalite is found as rolled pebbles in the gem gravels of Sri Lanka. A crystal has been known to have come from Burma, but this is particularly rare. Sinhalite has also been found in Warren County, New York (USA) but this is not of gem-quality.
USES Gem-quality sinhalite is faceted.

SPECIFIC GRAVITY 3.48 | HARDNESS 6.5 | CRYSTAL SYSTEM ORTHORHOMBIC

CARBONATES

MALACHITE

PROPERTIES Malachite is opaque and ranges in color from weak green to emerald-green and from deep, dark green to blackish-green. The color is due to the presence of copper. The compact monoclinic crystals, which occur in microcrystalline masses, are usually nodules with radiating bands. Malachite is usually found intergrown with the blue mineral azurite. It may also be found with turquoise and chrysocolla to give Eilat stone. When slabs of malachite are polished the distinctive banding of different shades of green give a very attractive ornamental stone with a silky luster.
OCCURRENCE Much of the older malachite used in jewelry was from copper mines in the Ural Mountains of Russia. Malachite suitable for cutting is also found in Australia, where it is found with azurite. Other localities include the USA and the copper-mining areas of Africa, including Zaire, Zambia and Zimbabwe.
USES The ancient Egyptians, Romans and Greeks all used malachite for jewelry. Malachite can be cut *en cabochon*, as beads for jewelry or carved.

SPECIFIC GRAVITY 3.80 mean	HARDNESS 4.0	CRYSTAL SYSTEM MONOCLINIC

AZURITE

PROPERTIES Azurite is blue due to the presence of copper. It is found as prismatic crystals which may form radiating, botryoidal or stalagmitic groups, or spheres with a silky luster. It may also occur in massive form. An alternative name for azurite is chessylite. It is doubly refractive.
OCCURRENCE Pure azurite is not usually tough enough to polish or use as a gemstone, but in 1971 some unusually tough azurite was recovered from an old abandoned mine near Las Vegas, USA. Other localities for azurite include Australia, Namibia, Romania and Siberia.
USES Azurite is usually found with malachite, which is an alteration product of azurite colored green by copper. The green and blue of malachite and azurite together in a rock give an attractively banded ornamental stone when polished. Azurite may also be cut *en cabochon*.

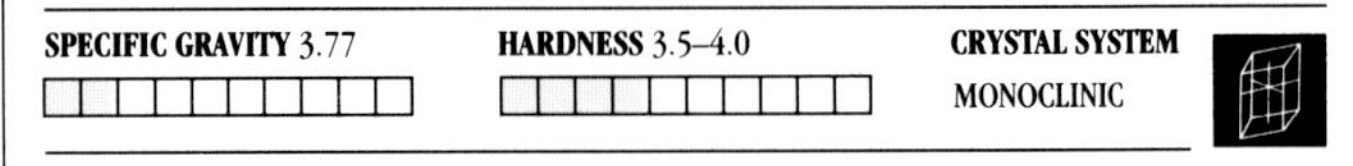

SPECIFIC GRAVITY 3.77	HARDNESS 3.5–4.0	CRYSTAL SYSTEM MONOCLINIC

CALCITE

PROPERTIES **Distinctive features:** Effervesces in dilute hydrochloric acid (take care doing this). Two excellent cleavages permit the mineral to break into perfect rhombohedrons and it fluoresces pale red under ultraviolet light, transparent forms being doubly refracting. **Color:** Colorless to white. Also any combination of colors, due to impurities, even to black. **Luster:** Vitreous to earthy. **Streak:** White to gray. **Transparency:** Transparent to opaque. **Cleavage:** Perfect on $10\bar{1}1$, giving rhombohedral-shaped fragments. **Fracture:** Difficult to obtain because of excellent cleavage. **Tenacity:** Brittle. **Forms:** Nail-head spa, dog-tooth spa. **Twinning:** On 0001, giving lamella twins. **Varieties:** Iceland Spar, which is transparent and doubly refracting. Calcite is the main component of limestone and varieties form in them – massive limestone, lithographic limestone, oolitic limestone, chalk, tufa, stalactites and stalagmites and marble.

OCCURRENCE Worldwide in limestone rocks, but particularly in Austria, Germany, France, UK, Iceland, Ireland, Mexico and the USA.
USES Many, including cement manufacture, making building blocks, ornamental, furnace flux, polarizing Nicol prisms, whitewash, agriculture.

SPECIFIC GRAVITY 2.7 | **HARDNESS** 3.0 | **CRYSTAL SYSTEM** HEXAGONAL

DOLOMITE

PROPERTIES **Distinctive features:** White to pale brownish saddle-shaped crystals that dissolve in dilute, warm hydrochloric acid (care is needed when doing this). **Color:** White when pure, otherwise brownish to reddish-brown or greenish to red, gray and black. **Luster:** Vitreous to pearly. **Streak:** Same as colour. **Transparency:** Translucent (the transparent form is rare). **Cleavage:** Perfect on $10\bar{1}1$. **Fracture:** Subconchoidal. **Tenacity:** Brittle. **Forms:** Rhombohedrons or curved, saddle-like crystals. Granular to massive (often full of tiny cracks). **Twinning:** On 0001 and $10\bar{1}1$.
OCCURRENCE Massive dolomite is formed by replacement of calcium in massive limestones by magnesium (hence alternative name of magnesium limestone). Czech Republic, Slovakia, Austria, Germany, Switzerland, Italy, Spain, England, Brazil, Mexico and the USA.
USES Ornamental, building blocks, cement manufacture, furnace linings.

SPECIFIC GRAVITY 3.0 | **HARDNESS** 3.5–4.0 | **CRYSTAL SYSTEM** HEXAGONAL

RHODOCHROSITE

PROPERTIES **Distinctive features:** Rose-red colored rhombohedral crystals in mineral veins, where it occurs as a secondary mineral. **Color:** Pale rose-red to dark red, though yellowish-grey forms are known. **Luster:** Vitreous to pearly. **Streak:** White. **Transparency:** Transparent to translucent.

Cleavage: Perfect on $10\bar{1}1$. **Fracture:** Uneven. **Tenacity:** Brittle. **Forms:** Rhombohedral, but also massive, compact, granular and botryoidal. **Twinning:** None.
OCCURRENCE As a secondary mineral associated with lead and copper veins rich in manganese. Rather rare mineral. Romania, UK, Germany and the USA.
USES Mineral collections.

SPECIFIC GRAVITY 3.5–3.6 | **HARDNESS** 3.5–4.5 | **CRYSTAL SYSTEM** HEXAGONAL

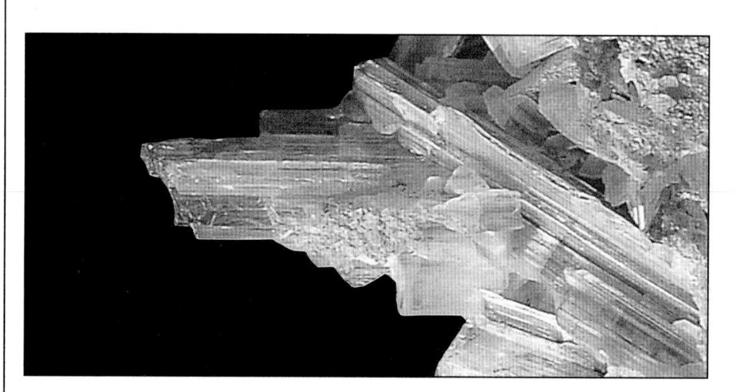

CERUSSITE

PROPERTIES **Distinctive features:** White, striated elongated prismatic crystals, often in small stellate groups. Reacts to nitric acid (take care doing this). **Color:** Mostly white, but may be greenish or dark bluish-gray. **Luster:** Adamantine. **Streak:** No color. **Transparency:** Translucent to, rarely, transparent. **Cleavage:** Good on 110 and 021. **Fracture:** Conchoidal (though this is difficult to see). **Tenacity:** Brittle. **Forms:** Tabular to elongated prismatic crystals, often in stellar-shaped groups. Occasionally stalactitic. **Twinning:** Common on 110 and 130.
OCCURRENCE In oxidized zones of lead-bearing veins, where lead ores have reacted with carbonate-rich water. Siberia, Austria, Germany, France, Scotland, Tunisia, Namibia, Australia and the USA.
USES Lead ore.

SPECIFIC GRAVITY 6.5–6.6 | **HARDNESS** 3.0–3.5 | **CRYSTAL SYSTEM** ORTHORHOMBIC

SILICATES

DIOPTASE

PROPERTIES The emerald green crystals of dioptase have a strong body color which masks their good "fire" and makes them translucent rather than transparent. Luster is vitreous.
OCCURRENCE Some of the best crystals of dioptase are from Russia. Other localities include the Congo, the copper deposits of the Atacama in Chile, and the USA, particularly Arizona.
USES Dioptase is too soft to be used as gemstones and it is only cut, either faceted or *en cabochon*, for the collector.

SPECIFIC GRAVITY 3.28–3.35 **HARDNESS** 5.0 **CRYSTAL SYSTEM** TRIGONAL

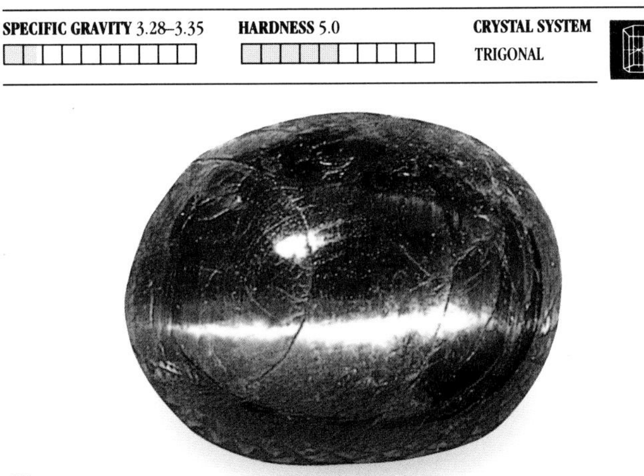

ENSTATITE

PROPERTIES Enstatite is one of the pyroxene minerals. Pyroxenes are a series of minerals with chemical compositions from magnesium silicate to iron silicate. The more iron present in the mineral, the darker the specimen. Too much iron makes the specimen almost opaque and too dark for faceting.
OCCURRENCE Crystals of enstatite are found as prisms, but gem-quality enstatite is usually found as rolled pebbles. Enstatite of a good green color is found with diamonds in the blue ground of the South African mines, especially the Kimberley mine. Brownish-green specimens are found in the Mogok area of Burma, and in Norway and California (USA).
USES Bronzite is a dark, iron-rich enstatite which comes from Austria and can be cut *en cabochon* to show the cat's-eye effect. Some Sri Lankan grey enstatite is also chatoyant.

SPECIFIC GRAVITY 3.27 **HARDNESS** 5.5 **CRYSTAL SYSTEM** ORTHORHOMBIC

DIOPSIDE

PROPERTIES Most diopside is bottle-green or light green, but colorless, brownish-green and violet-blue stones are also found. Crystals are fragile and have perfect prismatic cleavage. They are transparent to translucent with a vitreous luster. Crystals of a dark violet-blue diopside called violane are sometimes found, but it is more usual to find massive specimens. Star diopside from southern India shows a four-rayed star caused by needle-like inclusions of magnetite.
OCCURRENCE The best chrome diopside is found in the blue ground of the Kimberley diamond mines of South Africa. Gem-quality chrome diopside is also found in the gem gravels of Sri Lanka, Siberia and the Hunza region of Pakistan. The Hunza specimens often contain fibrous inclusions which give the crystals a cloudy appearance, but these can be cut *en cabochon* to give an attractive stone. The chrome diopside from Burma is chatoyant. Small, bright green crystals are found in California and smoky yellow crystals in Canada.
USES Massive specimens of violane diopside are polished as beads or used for inlay work. Transparent stones may be faceted, while those with inclusions are cut *en cabochon* to show the cat's-eye effect.

SPECIFIC GRAVITY 3.29 **HARDNESS** 5.0 **CRYSTAL SYSTEM** MONOCLINIC

SPHENE

PROPERTIES Gem-quality sphene is yellow, brown or green. Titanite is the correct mineralogical name for this gem. Crystals are found as wedge shapes and are often twinned. They are brittle and have a weak cleavage. Sphene has very high "fire" and the birefringence is high enough for doubling of the back facets to be seen with ease.
OCCURRENCE Major localities for sphene are the Austrian Tyrol and Swiss Grisons, and also Canada and Madagascar. Other sources include Burma, Baja California, Brazil and Sri Lanka.
USES Gemstones. Sphene is usually cut as brilliant or mixed-cut gems to show the "fire" to its best effect.

SPECIFIC GRAVITY 3.52–3.54 **HARDNESS** 5.5 **CRYSTAL SYSTEM** MONOCLINIC

BENITOITE

PROPERTIES Rare blue crystals of benitoite were discovered near San Benito in California (USA) in 1906 by a prospector looking for mercury and copper. He thought the crystals were sapphires but when they were sent to the University of California they were found to be a new mineral and were named after the locality. The crystals are small and resemble flattened triangles in shape. Benitoite has exceptionally strong "fire" (dispersion) which is almost as great as diamond but the blue color of the stone may mask this. Luster is vitreous. Benitoite can be distinguished from sapphire because of its obvious dichroism. On turning the stone the sapphire blue color is seen in one direction whilst the stone appears colorless when viewed from another. Benitoite is strongly birefringent.
OCCURRENCE Benitoite is very rare and is only found in the USA (California).
USES Blue benitoite has been faceted for collectors. Colorless crystals of benitoite are not uncommon but are not considered worth cutting.

SPECIFIC GRAVITY 3.65–3.68 **HARDNESS** 6.5 **CRYSTAL SYSTEM** HEXAGONAL

ZIRCON

PROPERTIES Zircon can be colorless, yellow, red, orange, brown, yellowish-green, bright green, dark green or sky blue. The crystals are usually square prisms with pyramidal terminations. There is imperfect cleavage and fracture is conchoidal. Stones may appear cloudy or have angular zoning and are occasionally chatoyant.

There are two types of zircon: "high type", which is used in jewelry, breaks down into "low type" as a result of radioactive decay. Heat can change the low type back to high type.

Zircon has a high birefringence and doubling of the back facets can easily be seen, but dichroism is rarely apparent. It has almost as much fire as diamond and is used as a diamond simulant. The characteristic absorption spectrum is due to uranium. Under ultraviolet light and X-rays, the stone varies from almost inert to strongly fluorescent.
OCCURRENCE Zircon can be found in igneous rocks worldwide. Much gem-quality zircon is found in Sri Lanka, Burma and Thailand. Rough zircon from Thailand is heat-treated to give blue, golden and colorless stones. Other localities are France, Norway, Tanzania and Australia.
USES As gemstones. Zircon is faceted, usually as round brilliants. Although it is moderately hard, the face edges are easily chipped when worn.

Synthetic blue zircon and colored glass is used to imitate other colors.

SPECIFIC GRAVITY 4.5–4.7 **HARDNESS** 6.5–7.5 **CRYSTAL SYSTEM** TETRAGONAL

UVAROVITE

PROPERTIES **Distinctive features:** Crystal shape, color, rock association. **Color:** Emerald green. **Luster:** Resinous to glossy. **Streak:** White. **Transparency:** Transparent to translucent to opaque. **Cleavage:** None. **Fracture:** Uneven and occasionally subconchoidal. **Tenacity:** Brittle. **Forms:** Dodecahedron and trapezohedrons. **Twinning:** None.
OCCURRENCE The Urals in Russia, Canada (Quebec), Spain, Scandinavia, West Africa.
USES Gemstone.

SPECIFIC GRAVITY 3.0–4.0 **HARDNESS** 6.5–7.2 **CRYSTAL SYSTEM** ISOMETRIC

RHODONITE

PROPERTIES Rhodonite has a rose-red color and is mostly opaque to translucent. The colour is due to the presence of manganese. Rhodonite has a distinct cleavage, uneven fracture and is brittle. It takes a good polish and makes an attractive decorative stone. It is doubly refractive.
OCCURRENCE Rhodonite is found in the Urals of Russia as massive material rather like marble. The pink is veined by black where manganese has been oxidized during weathering. Other localities include Sweden, USA, Mexico, South Africa, Australia and Cornwall in England.
USES Most translucent rhodonite is fashioned into beads and cabochons for ornamental articles and as inlay. Transparent rhodonite is rare, but has been faceted for collectors.

SPECIFIC GRAVITY 3.50–3.70 **HARDNESS** 6.0 **CRYSTAL SYSTEM** TRICLINIC

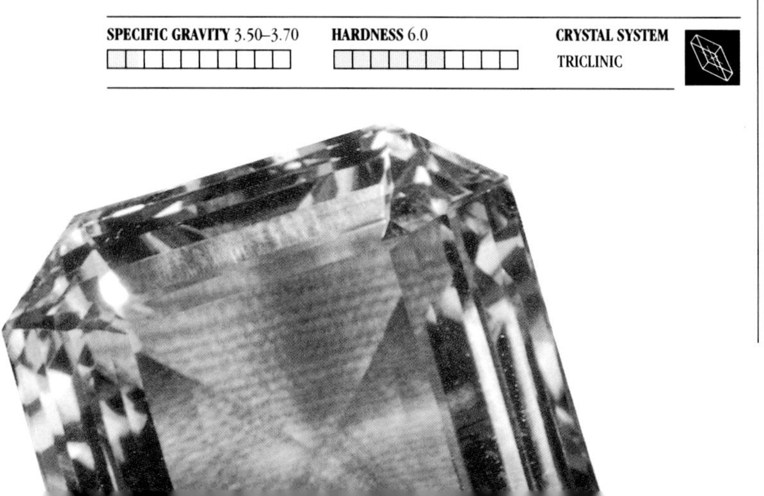

SCAPOLITE

PROPERTIES Scapolite is part of a continuous compositional series from calcium-rich to sodium-rich. Scapolite is found as white, pink, violet, blue and yellow stones. Crystals are prismatic with three directions of easy cleavage. Scapolite's luster varies from vitreous to resinous. The name scapolite comes from the Greek for "stick stone", which refers to the habit in which the crystal is usually found, i.e. as prismatic crystals.
OCCURRENCE Gem material was first found in the Mogok area of Burma as fibrous white, pink or violet stones. The pink and violet stones have strong pleochroism, showing dark blue and lavender blue, and can be cut *en cabochon* to show the cat's-eye effect. Yellow stones have been found in Brazil and Madagascar. These show strong pleochroism; the colors are three shades of yellow. An opaque massive yellow variety of scapolite which emits a brilliant yellow fluorescence under long-wave ultraviolet light is found in Quebec and Ontario, Canada. Colorless, purple and gem-quality yellow scapolite has been found in Kenya.
USES The Burmese scapolite is cut *en cabochon* to show the cat's-eye effect, while the Brazilian yellow scapolite is usually faceted.

SPECIFIC GRAVITY 2.60–2.70 **HARDNESS** 6.0 **CRYSTAL SYSTEM** TETRAGONAL

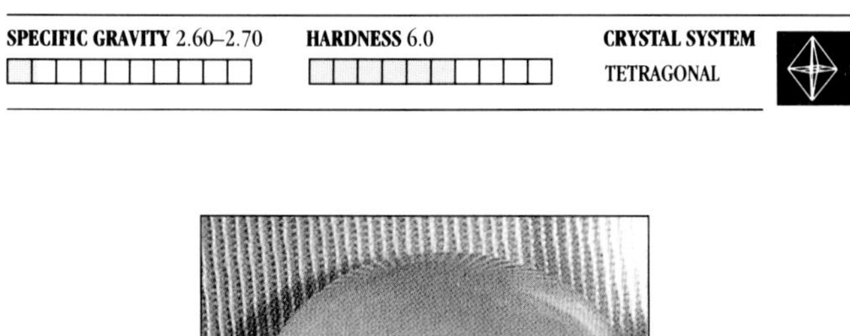

SERPENTINE

PROPERTIES Massive serpentine can be divided into those stones that can be carved, such as bowenite, and the softer types which are of little use as decorative stones. Colors vary and may be green, red, purple, brown, nearly black or white, and may be veined or spotted with as many colors.

Bowenite, which is a translucent green, is sometimes used as an alternative to jade. Williamsite is another variety. It is an oil-green color, softer than bowenite and contains black inclusions.

OCCURRENCE Italian serpentines vary from green to brownish-red in color and are often veined with white. In England the best known serpentine rock comes from Cornwall. Other sources include Wales, Scotland, Austria, France, Germany, South Africa and the USA.

USES China is the main exporter of figurines carved from yellowish-green bowenite. Dark green or bluish-green bowenite found in the South Island of New Zealand was used by the Maoris, who called it *tangiwai* meaning "tears", but little is found today. A coarser green bowenite from the USA was also used in the past. Bowenite is also found in Afghanistan.

SPECIFIC GRAVITY 2.58–2.59	HARDNESS 2.5	CRYSTAL SYSTEM MONOCLINIC

PERIDOT

PROPERTIES Peridot, or olivine, is green in colour due to the presence of iron. Crystals are found as vertically striated flattened prisms. Doubling of the back facets can be seen using a hand lens. There is little dispersion and the luster is vitreous and oily. Pleochroism is weak. Peridot has a distinctive absorption spectrum with three broad lines in the blue caused by the presence of iron. Inclusions are common. A stone with a single inclusion appears to have two, because the high double refraction shows a doubling of the outline.

OCCURRENCE The most important source of peridot was St John's Island in the Red Sea, but the island is no longer accessible for collecting. Gem-quality stones are found in the Mogok area of Burma. Crystals and rolled pebbles have been found in Norway, Australia and Brazil. Other localities include South Africa, New Mexico and Arizona (USA). Pebbles are found on the beaches of Hawaii. Peridot has been found in Antarctica and it has even been found in meteorites.

USES Gemstones. Peridot is usually cut in the step-cut style. Oval, pendeloque, round and mixed cuts are also used. Because of its softness, peridot is fashioned into brooches, pendants and earrings but is seldom used in rings or bracelets.

Glass and composite stones are used to imitate peridot but these lack the oily luster.

SPECIFIC GRAVITY 3.34	HARDNESS 6.5–7.0	CRYSTAL SYSTEM ORTHORHOMBIC

ANDRADITE

PROPERTIES Two varieties have been used in jewelry: opaque black melanite and green demantoid garnet, the color of which is due to the presence of chromium. Melanite crystals are usually dodecahedra or icositetrahedra or a mixture of both.

Demantoid is a rare variety of andradite. It has a higher dispersion than diamond, but the vivid green color masks this property. It is relatively soft and so is not commonly used in jewelry. Demantoid garnet looks red through the Chelsea color filter and has a characteristic absorption spectrum with a strong band in the red which is due to iron. It is inert under ultraviolet light and X-rays. Inclusions are groups of radiating asbestos fibers described as "horse-tails". Dermantoid is the only green mineral that has these horse-tails.

OCCURRENCE The main source for gem-quality demantoid is the Ural Mountains. It is also found in Zaire and Korea, although these are not of such good quality. Melanite is found in Italy and the Haute-Pyrenees of France.

USES Andradite garnet is faceted for use in jewelry.

SPECIFIC GRAVITY 3.85	HARDNESS 6.5	CRYSTAL SYSTEM ISOMETRIC

ANDALUSITE

PROPERTIES Andalusite varies in color from light yellowish-brown to green-brown, light brownish-pink, bottle green or grayish-green. Crystals are vertically striated prisms with an almost square cross-section and pyramidal terminations.

Andalusite is very pleochroic and appears yellow, green or red when viewed from different directions. Luster is vitreous. Chiastolite is a variety which has dark carbonaceous inclusions running across the plane of the prism. When these stones are cut and polished a cross can be seen. Chiastolite is found as long prisms and can be opaque, yellowish or gray.

OCCURRENCE Gem-quality andalusite is found as dull-green water-worn pebbles in Sri Lankan gem gravels and in Brazil. Other localities include Australia, Canada, Russia and the USA. Good examples of the chiastolite are found in Burma and Zimbabwe. Other localities for chiastolite include Australia, Bolivia, Chile, France, Spain and the USA.

USES Good-quality crystals, especially the greenish or reddish varieties, are faceted into gemstones. Chiastolite "cross-stones" are popular in the Pyrenees where they are worn in amulets and charms.

SPECIFIC GRAVITY 3.15 **HARDNESS** 7.5 **CRYSTAL SYSTEM** ORTHORHOMBIC

KYANITE

PROPERTIES **Distinctive features:** Translucent, pale blue, lath-shaped crystals. Hardness along length is less than across crystal. Often associated with staurolite in schists. **Color:** Pale cerulean blue, sometimes with white margins. **Luster:** Vitreous to pearly. **Streak:** None. **Transparency:** Translucent to transparent. **Cleavage:** Perfect on 100. **Fracture:** Not applicable. **Tenacity:** Brittle. **Forms:** Long, bladed or lath-shaped crystals. **Twinning:** None.

OCCURRENCE In mica schists resulting from regional metamorphism, often in association with staurolite, garnet and corundum. The Urals in Russia, European Alps and the USA.

USES In refractory materials for furnaces, because of its high melting point, and jewelry.

SPECIFIC GRAVITY 4 **HARDNESS** 4–7 **CRYSTAL SYSTEM** TRICLINIC

SILLIMANITE

PROPERTIES Sillimanite is pale blue or green and, as its alternative name, fibrolite, suggests, it is often fibrous. It has the same chemical composition as kyanite and andalusite and is therefore polymorphic. Crystals occur in parallel groups as long slender prisms which do not have distinct terminations. It has one direction of easy cleavage and shows strong pleochroism. The colors seen down the three principal optical directions are pale green, dark green and blue.

OCCURRENCE Violet-blue stones are found in Burma, grayish-green stones in Sri Lankan gem gravels and massive fibrous water-worn pebbles in Idaho (USA).

USES Gemstones. Sillimanite is commonly fashioned as baroque (irregular-shaped) stones by the tumbling process.

SPECIFIC GRAVITY 3.25 **HARDNESS** 7.5 **CRYSTAL SYSTEM** ORTHORHOMBIC

Spodumene

Properties Kunzite and hiddenite are both varieties of spodumene. Kunzite is lilac-pink in colour and has strong pleochroism, showing colorless and two shades of violet. Hiddenite is bright green, coloured by chromium, and pleochroic, showing bluish-green, emerald green and yellowish-green. It has a characteristic chromium absorption spectrum. Spodumene occurs as flattened prisms characterized by vertical striations and irregular terminations. The crystals exhibit strong cleavage in two directions.
Occurrence Spodumene was discovered in 1877 in Brazil. Emerald-green hiddenite and lilac-colored kunzite have been found in the USA. Other spodumene localities include Madagascar and Burma.
Uses Cutting is difficult because of the strong cleavage and the shape of the crystals. Because of the strong pleochroism, if used as gemstones the stones should be cut to show the best color through the front.

SPECIFIC GRAVITY 3.18 | **HARDNESS** 7.0 | **CRYSTAL SYSTEM** MONOCLINIC

Jadeite

Properties Jadeite is the rarer "jade". It is found in a large variety of colors, but it is the dark emerald green that is the most prized in jewelry. White, pink, brown, red, orange, yellow, mauve (due to manganese), blue, violet, black, shades of green and mottled green and white jadeites also occur. The presence of iron tends to give a dull green jadeite.

Jadeite is found as a mass of interlocking granular crystals. This causes a dimpled effect when polished. It is less tough than nephrite jade and has a characteristic absorption spectrum with a strong band in the blue. The white, mauve, yellow and pale green stones show a whitish glow under long-wave ultraviolet light and a strong violet-colored glow under X-rays, while the darker jadeite is inert. Green jadeite shows green under the Chelsea color filter.
Occurrence Burma is the most important source of jadeite. Burmese jadeite is found in metamorphic rocks and also as alluvial boulders, which have a brown skin due to weathering. Poorer quality jadeite is found in the USA and Japan.
Uses Jadeite is used mainly for carvings. Small pieces may be used to make beads, cabochons, ring stones, brooches and drop earrings. The boulder material with a brown skin can be used to make cameos or snuff bottles.

Jadeite has been imitated by bowenite, which is softer and can easily be scratched with a knife.

SPECIFIC GRAVITY 3.30–3.50 | **HARDNESS** 6.5–7.0 | **CRYSTAL SYSTEM** MONOCLINIC

Leucite

Properties **Distinctive features:** Distinctive trapezohedral crystals in recent lavas of trachytic to phonolitic composition. Some crystals fluoresce under ultraviolet light. **Color:** White to ash-white. **Luster:** Vitreous to dull. **Streak:** No color. **Transparency:** Usually opaque, sometimes translucent. **Cleavage:** Poor on 110. **Fracture:** Conchoidal. **Tenacity:** Brittle. **Forms:** Trapezohedral crystals. **Twinning:** None.
Occurrence In potassium-rich, silica-poor, igneous lavas, such as syenites and trachytes. Worldwide, but particularly in Italy, the USA and Canada.
Uses Mineral collections.

SPECIFIC GRAVITY 2.5 | **HARDNESS** 5.0–5.6 | **CRYSTAL SYSTEM** ISOMETRIC

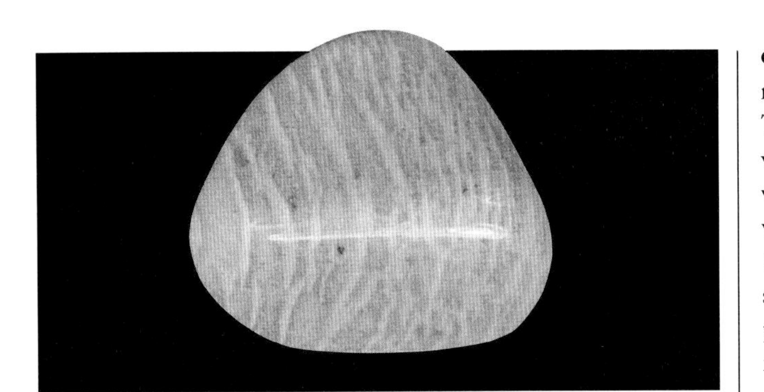

MICROCLINE

PROPERTIES **Distinctive features:** Pale turquoise to white, slightly streaked crystals. Similar to orthoclase in appearance, but with slightly lower specific gravity. **Color:** Pale turquoise to whitish-yellow, sometimes pale brick red. **Luster:** Vitreous. **Streak:** No color. **Transparency:** Usually translucent, rarely transparent. **Cleavage:** Perfect on 001. **Fracture:** Uneven. **Tenacity:** Brittle. **Forms:** Prismatic orthorhombic (like orthoclase), also massive to granular. **Twinning:** On 100 and 010.
OCCURRENCE Abundant in acid igneous rocks, such as granite. Good crystals may be obtained from granite pegmatites. Worldwide, but particularly the Urals in Russia, Italy, Scandinavia, Madagascar and the USA.
USES Jewelry, ornamental, in porcelain manufacture.

SPECIFIC GRAVITY 2.55 | **HARDNESS** 6.0 | **CRYSTAL SYSTEM** TRICLINIC

ORTHOCLASE

PROPERTIES In its purest form, orthoclase is transparent and colorless and is a collector's gemstone. There are two directions of easy cleavage, at about 90° to each other. Yellow orthoclase owes its color to iron. It is doubly refractive.
OCCURRENCE Orthoclase commonly occurs in intrusive, magmatic and metamorphic rocks where it has cooled slowly. The best examples of yellow orthoclase are found in Madagascar, where the cat's-eye variety is also found, and Germany. Other varieties are distributed widely around the world, including western Europe and the USA.
USES Yellow orthoclase is usually faceted as step-cut stones. It shows a cat's-eye effect when cut *en cabochon*. Colorless and pinkish-brown stones have also been cut. Orthoclase is also used in the manufacture of porcelain.

SPECIFIC GRAVITY 2.56 | **HARDNESS** 6.0–6.5 | **CRYSTAL SYSTEM** MONOCLINIC

MOONSTONE

PROPERTIES Moonstone is a variety of orthoclase which has a blue schiller (sheen) caused by the reflection of light from the internal structure of alternate layers of albite and orthoclase feldspar. Thicker layers give a white schiller rather than the most attractive blue schiller. There is no characteristic absorption spectrum. Luminescence is usually bluish under long-wave ultraviolet light and a weak orange under short-wave ultraviolet light, with a whitish to violet glow under X-rays (this may help to distinguish moonstone from its imitations). It is doubly refractive.
OCCURRENCE Each locality may have characteristic inclusions. Sri Lankan moonstone usually has straight lath-like "stress cracks" which run parallel to the vertical axis of the crystal and from which there are branching cracks which appear to taper off. Indian moonstone is characterized by the variations in body colour from white to reddish-brown or plum-blue and even green. Other localities include Madagascar, Burma, Tanzania and the USA.
USES To show the sheen of moonstone to its best advantage, the stone should be cut *en cabochon* with the base of the cabochon parallel to the plane of the layers.

Heat is used to give synthetic white spinels a schiller to imitate moonstone. White chalcedony may also be cut *en cabochon* to imitate moonstone and may show a blue moon effect.

SPECIFIC GRAVITY 2.57 | **HARDNESS** 6.0–6.5 | **CRYSTAL SYSTEM** MONOCLINIC

ADULARIA

PROPERTIES **Distinctive features:** Bladed to prismatic, white to transparent crystals with a pearly appearance. Occurs in crystalline schists. **Color:** Clear to white. **Luster:** Pearly. **Streak:** White. **Transparency:** Transparent to translucent. **Cleavage:** Perfect on 001, good on 010. **Fracture:** Uneven. **Tenacity:** Brittle. **Forms:** Bladed to prismatic crystals with elongated 110 faces. **Twinning:** Fairly common on 021.

OCCURRENCE Adularia is the purest form of orthoclase found in granites, granitic gneisses and schists. It occurs in open druses and pegmatite veins, where it is associated with other granite minerals. Switzerland, Austria, Italy.

USES Mineral collections.

SPECIFIC GRAVITY 2.56 | HARDNESS 6.0 | CRYSTAL SYSTEM MONOCLINIC

PLAGIOCLASE

PROPERTIES **Distinctive features:** White to grey rhombic to tabular crystals in which the polysynthetic twinning may show as fine parallel striations on crystal faces. Present in almost all igneous and metamorphic rocks. **Color:** White to grayish-blue or reddish. **Luster:** Vitreous to pearly. **Streak:** No color. **Transparency:** Mostly translucent, but some forms are transparent. **Cleavage:** On 001 and 010 at 90°. **Fracture:** Uneven. **Tenacity:** Brittle. **Forms:** Tabular. **Twinning:** Polysynthetic twins are common. **Varieties:** Albite, oligoclase, andesine, labradorite, bytownite and anorthite. A continuous compositional series from sodium-rich albite to calcium anorthite in which varieties can be distinguished only by specialized testing.

OCCURRENCE Abundant and important rock-forming mineral of nearly all igneous rocks, but good crystals are only found in pegmatites and similar cavities and veins. Worldwide.

USES In porcelain manufacture, jewelry.

SPECIFIC GRAVITY 2.6–2.7 | HARDNESS 6.0 | CRYSTAL SYSTEM TRICLINIC

MUSCOVITE

PROPERTIES **Distinctive features:** Shiny, silvery, platy mineral. The plates are flexible and can easily be prised off with a knife blade or pin. Common in granites and related rocks. **Color:** Colorless to pale brown or green or yellow. Pale red varieties are also known. **Luster:** Vitreous to pearly. **Streak:** No color. **Transparency:** Transparent to translucent. **Cleavage:** Perfect on 010. **Fracture:** Tends to bend without breaking. **Tenacity:** Flexible, elastic. **Forms:** Usually tabular; may occur as tapering book of tabular crystals. **Twinning:** On 001 (easily cleavable).

OCCURRENCE An important component of many igneous and metamorphic rocks, especially acid igneous rocks, schists and gneisses. Occurs in granite pegmatites as large book-like masses. Worldwide.

USES Electrical insulators, furnace and stove windows.

SPECIFIC GRAVITY 2.7–3.0 | HARDNESS 2.5–3.0 | CRYSTAL SYSTEM MONOCLINIC

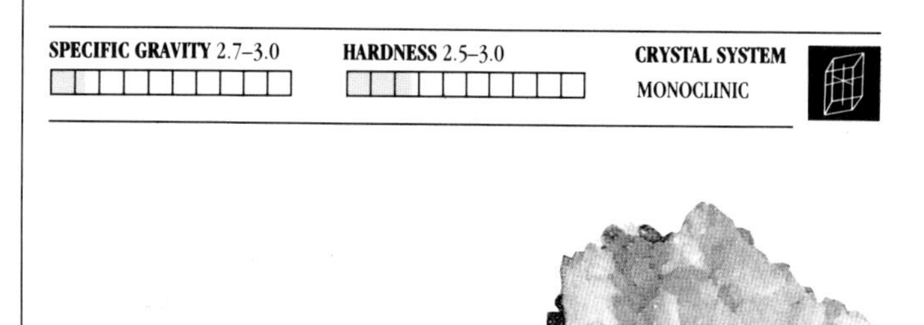

EMERALD

BERYL VARIETY

PROPERTIES Emerald is the best-known variety of beryl. The green color is due to a trace of chromium and usually some iron. Emerald crystallizes as hexagonal prisms with two flat terminations. Cleavage is poor and parallel to the basal plane. Luster is vitreous.

Emerald has distinct dichroism, showing blue-green and yellowish-green. Most stones show bright red through the Chelsea color filter.

OCCURRENCE The world's finest emeralds are from the Chivor and Muzo mines in Colombia. The crystals are found in cracks or pockets within the rock and often have three-phase inclusions. Color and inclusions may give clues as to a stone's source. Brazilian emeralds are often pale yellowish-green with two-phase inclusions; Russian emeralds are often cloudy; Australian emeralds are pale and often badly flawed; South African stones often contain brown mica plate inclusions. Indian emeralds have characteristic "comma" inclusions. Other localities include Austria, Norway, Pakistan, Tanzania, the USA, Zambia and Zimbabwe.

USES The best-quality gemstone emeralds are cut in the step-cut style. Poorer stones are cut *en cabochon* or as beads. Almost all are oiled to fill cracks. Composites using garnet, quartz, spinel or glass are used as imitations. Most imitations show green through the Chelsea color filter.

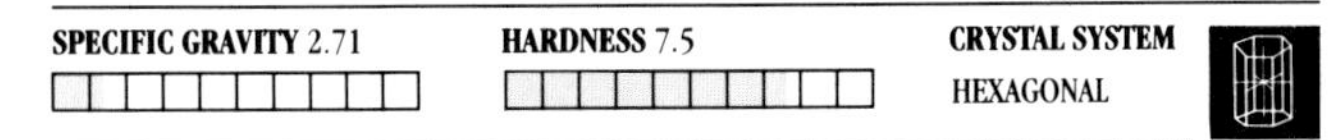

SPECIFIC GRAVITY 2.71 **HARDNESS** 7.5 **CRYSTAL SYSTEM** HEXAGONAL

AQUAMARINE

BERYL VARIETY

PROPERTIES The hexagonal crystals are often large and flawless and may be striated or tapered due to erosion. Luster is vitreous and there is a weak, basal cleavage. Aquamarine is dichroic, showing colorless and deep blue. The absorption spectrum is weak and there is no luminescence. A strong greenish-blue color is seen through the Chelsea color filter. Some stones show chatoyancy when cut *en cabochon*.

OCCURRENCE The best gem-quality aquamarines come from Minas Gerais, Brazil, where crystals are found as alluvial deposits. The Russian Urals are also known for their fine aquamarines. Other localities include Argentina, Burma, China, India, Namibia, Northern Ireland, Madagascar, Norway, Tanzania, the USA and Zimbabwe.

USES Gemstones. A step cut is normally used because of the pale color. The size of the stone is kept large to give a fairly strong color and the table facet is cut parallel to the length of the prismatic crystals.

Aquamarine is imitated by synthetic spinel colored with cobalt. This appears bright red through the Chelsea color filter. Pale blue glass imitating aquamarine is only singly refractive.

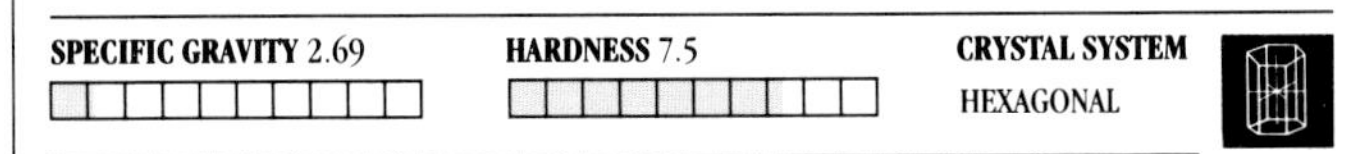

SPECIFIC GRAVITY 2.69 **HARDNESS** 7.5 **CRYSTAL SYSTEM** HEXAGONAL

MORGANITE

BERYL VARIETY

PROPERTIES The pink, rose and peach colors of morganite are due to manganese. Morganite is usually found as tubular prisms. It is dichroic, the two colors being pink and a deeper bluish-pink. There is no characteristic absorption spectrum and luminescence under ultraviolet light is weak. Under X-rays there is an intense red glow.

OCCURRENCE A pure pink morganite is found in Minas Gerais, Brazil and also in Madagascar. Pale rose-colored beryl is found around San Diego, California (USA). Deposits also occur in Mozambique, Namibia and Zimbabwe.

USES Morganite is usually faceted as step-cut stones in order to give a strong color. It is often heat-treated to drive off any yellow tinge. Morganite is imitated by pink topaz, kunzite, natural and synthetic pink sapphire and spinel. Garnet-topped doublets and pastes are also made in a pink color.

SPECIFIC GRAVITY 2.80 **HARDNESS** 7.5 **CRYSTAL SYSTEM** HEXAGONAL

YELLOW BERYL

BERYL VARIETY

PROPERTIES Yellow beryl, or heliodor, varies in color from a pale yellow to a rich golden color. Its physical properties are like those of aquamarine. The absorption spectrum is weak and the presence of iron, which gives rise to the golden-yellow color, dulls any luminescence. Although many heliodors, morganites and aquamarines are virtually flawless, inclusions in the form of slender, parallel tubes can occur which reduce the stones' transparency and luster.
OCCURRENCE Yellow beryls are found in all the aquamarine localities, particularly Madagascar, Brazil and Namibia. They are also found in the USA (Connecticut).
USES Gemstones. The step cut is the most usual cut for yellow beryls as they need the depth to give a strong color.

SPECIFIC GRAVITY 2.68	HARDNESS 7.5	CRYSTAL SYSTEM HEXAGONAL

PYROPE

PROPERTIES Pyrope is usually red. It is colored by iron and sometimes also by chromium. Pyrope does not fluoresce under ultraviolet light due to its iron content, but red spinel, which is similar, does. Pyrope is moderately magnetic and this can also be used to separate it from red spinel. The pyrope absorption spectrum is characterized by three dark bands. The bright red stones from Czechoslovakia, Arizona (USA) and Kimberley (South Africa) have a typical chromium spectrum with a narrow doublet in the red and a broad band. Pyrope rarely has inclusions. When they are present they are usually small rounded crystals with irregular outlines.
OCCURRENCE Pyrope from Czechoslovakia is found in conglomerates, volcanic rocks and in various alluvials, but rarely as good crystals. Most pyrope now used is found in the diamond mines of South Africa. Russian pyrope is also of good quality. Other localities include Argentina, Australia, Brazil, Burma and Tanzania.
USES Most pyrope is faceted for setting in jewelry and was particularly popular in the nineteenth century.

SPECIFIC GRAVITY 3.70–3.90	HARDNESS 7–7.5	CRYSTAL SYSTEM ISOMETRIC

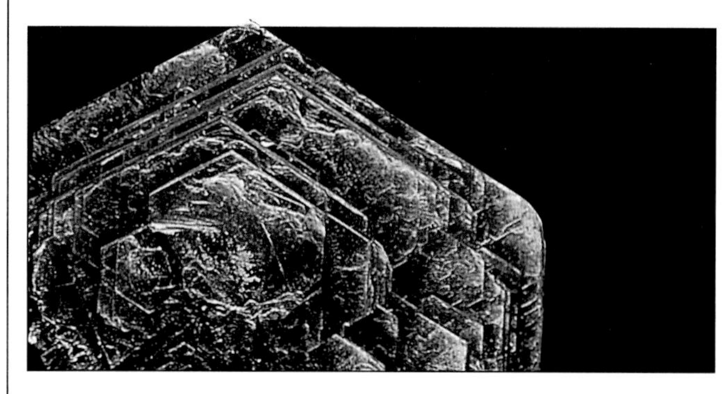

PHLOGOPITE

PROPERTIES **Distinctive features:** Shiny, coppery-brown, patchy black, platy mineral. The plates are flexible and easily prised off with a knife point or pin. Flakes often show a starlike figure in transmitted light. **Color:** Coppery-brown to yellowish-brown, with much darker patches. **Luster:** Pearly and sometimes slightly metallic. **Streak:** No color. **Transparency:** Transparent to subtransparent. **Cleavage:** Perfect on 001. **Fracture:** Bends without breaking. **Tenacity:** Flexible, elastic. **Forms:** Tabular, scaly masses. Often seen as small flakes in acid igneous rocks. **Twinning:** On 001, along which it is easily cleaved.
OCCURRENCE A product of metamorphism. Occurs in serpentine, granular limestones and dolomites. Romania, Switzerland, Italy, Scandinavia, Finland, Sri Lanka, Madagascar, the USA and Canada.
USES Mineral collections.

SPECIFIC GRAVITY 2.8–3.0	HARDNESS 3.0	CRYSTAL SYSTEM MONOCLINIC

GROSSULAR

PROPERTIES Grossular garnets are usually opaque and have little use in jewelry, but there are some varieties which are transparent or semi-opaque and may be cut as gemstones. Hessonite garnets are a yellowish-brown to orange-red variety which have characteristic inclusions that give a treacle-like appearance. Pure grossular is colorless. "Transvaal jade", a massive grossular garnet from South Africa, is also green or gray, blue or pink.

OCCURRENCE Hessonite is found in the gem gravels of Sri Lanka and in Brazil, Canada, Russia and the USA. Green grossular garnet has been found in Tanzania and Kenya.

USES Grossular garnets may be faceted or cut *en cabochon*. "Transvaal jade" makes an attractive stone when carved.

SPECIFIC GRAVITY 3.65 **HARDNESS** 7–7.5 **CRYSTAL SYSTEM** ISOMETRIC

ZOISITE

PROPERTIES The best gem-quality zoisite crystals are called tanzanite. The transparent blue crystals with vitreous luster are the most attractive for use in jewelry. Blue, green, yellow, pink or brown zoisite all change color to blue when heated. Zoisite has one perfect plane of cleavage and shows distinct pleochroism. Thulite is a massive pink variety of zoisite.

OCCURRENCE Tanzanite and a massive green chrome-rich variety of zoisite, which contains hexagonal rubies, are found in Tanzania. Thulite is found in Norway, the Austrian Tyrol, Western Australia and the USA (North Carolina).

USES Zoisite found with parallel fibres shows a cat's-eye effect when cut *en cabochon*. Massive green zoisite has been fashioned complete with rubies as ashtrays and small objects. Thulite is used as an ornamental stone.

SPECIFIC GRAVITY 3.35 **HARDNESS** 6.5 **CRYSTAL SYSTEM** ORTHORHOMBIC

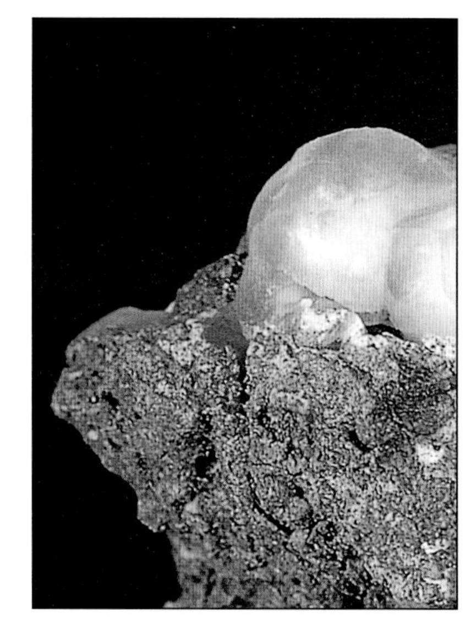

PREHNITE

PROPERTIES **Distinctive features:** Pale green botryoidal or reniform masses of small tabular crystals. Often stalactitic or in radiating clusters. **Color:** Pale green to whitish-gray, the color fading on exposure to air. **Luster:** Vitreous. **Streak:** No color. **Transparency:** Usually translucent, rarely subtransparent. **Cleavage:** Not applicable. **Fracture:** Uneven to rough. **Tenacity:** Brittle. **Forms:** Tabular, often barrel-shaped crystals; often globular or in radiating clusters. **Twinning:** None.

OCCURRENCE Mostly as a secondary mineral in basic igneous rocks and gneisses. Austria, Italy, Germany, France, UK, South Africa and the USA.

USES Mineral collections.

SPECIFIC GRAVITY 2.9 **HARDNESS** 6.0–6.5 **CRYSTAL SYSTEM** ORTHORHOMBIC

LABRADORITE

PROPERTIES Labradorite has a brilliant play of color with blue, green, red, yellow and purple flashes in a gray background. This schiller is only seen on a polished surface or near a cleavage plane and is due to the interference of light at the fine layers that are produced by repeated twinning. Platy inclusions of magnetite probably give labradorite the gray color.
OCCURRENCE A transparent labradorite from the USA, Mexico and Australia may be almost colorless or pale yellow and does not show a play of color. A transparent labradorite with a blue flash and needle-like inclusion is found in Madagascar. Other sources include Newfoundland, Quebec and the Ural Mountains. The variety spectrolite comes from Finland and is similar to the material from Labrador.
USES Labradorite is used in ornamental masonry when it occurs as a monominerallic rock or is carved into decorative boxes, cameos and other *objets d'art*. Smaller specimens are sometimes made into beads, brooches or ring stones.

SPECIFIC GRAVITY 2.70	HARDNESS 6.0–6.5	CRYSTAL SYSTEM TRICLINIC

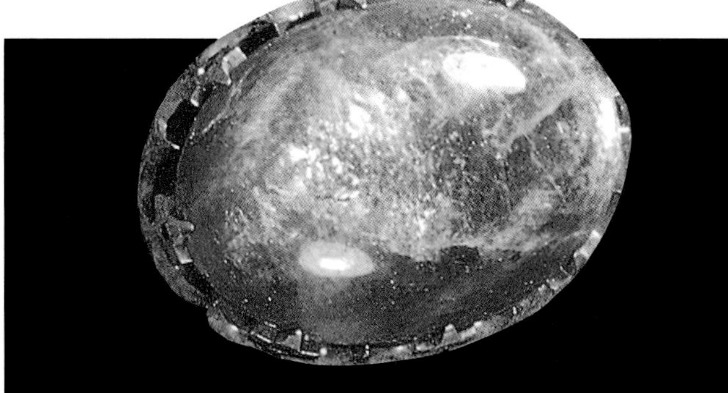

OLIGOCLASE

PROPERTIES **Distinctive features:** Oligoclase is a member of the plagioclase feldspar group. It may be gray, white, greenish, yellowish, reddish, brown or colorless, and has a white streak. The variety shown here, sunstone, has reflective inclusions of red, orange or green thin platy crystals of haematite or goethite within an almost colorless oligoclase base. Luster is vitreous and repeated twinning is common. Sunstone is inert under ultraviolet light but shows a whitish glow when irradiated with X-rays.
OCCURRENCE The USA, Canada, Norway, India and Russia. The best sunstone is found in Norway, where it is found as irregular masses in veins of white quartz in gneiss. In the USA, sunstone is found in the states of Maine, New Mexico, New York, North Carolina, Pennsylvania and Virginia.
USES As a gemstone, sunstone is cut *en cabochon*.

SPECIFIC GRAVITY 2.64	HARDNESS 6.0–6.5	CRYSTAL SYSTEM TRICLINIC

STILBITE

PROPERTIES **Distinctive features:** Waisted, tabular, white crystals filling cracks or lining cavities in basaltic lavas. **Color:** White to brownish-red. **Luster:** Vitreous to silky. **Streak:** No color. **Transparency:** Transparent to translucent. **Cleavage:** Perfect on 010. **Fracture:** Uneven. **Tenacity:** Brittle. **Forms:** Tabular crystals compounded into sheaflike aggregates, giving them a waisted appearance. **Twinning:** Often on 001, sometimes interpenetrant or cruciform.
OCCURRENCE Filling or lining cracks or cavities in basaltic lavas. Iceland, UK, India, Canada and the USA.
USES Mineral collections.

SPECIFIC GRAVITY 2.0	HARDNESS 3.5–4.0	CRYSTAL SYSTEM MONOCLINIC

Spessartine

PROPERTIES Spessartine garnets are orange-pink, orange-red, red-brown or brownish yellow. They have a characteristic absorption spectrum which is partly due to the presence of manganese. Spessartine is inert under ultraviolet light and X-rays. Characteristic lace- or feather-like inclusions can only be detected by experts. Hessonite garnet is similar in color but has quite different inclusions which give it a treacly appearance.
OCCURRENCE Gem-quality examples are rare. Most of the crystals found in Germany and Italy are too small to be used in jewelry, but good examples are found in Australia (New South Wales), Burma, Madagascar, Norway and the USA (Virginia and California). Some gem-quality spessartine is found in Brazil, but the majority is too dark to be of use in jewelry.
USES Spessartine may be faceted or cut *en cabochon* for use as a gemstone.

SPECIFIC GRAVITY 4.16	HARDNESS 7.0	CRYSTAL SYSTEM ISOMETRIC

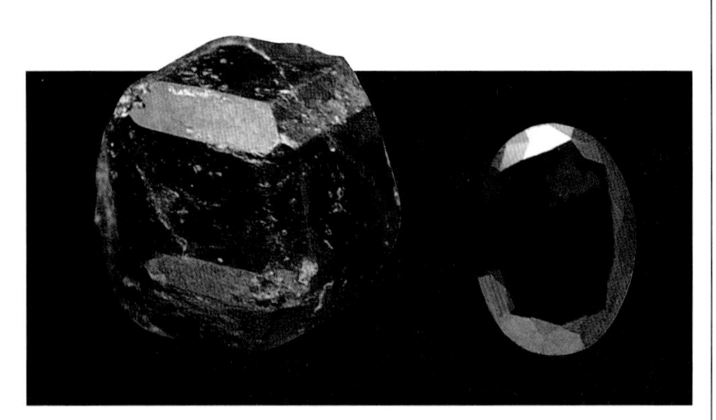

Almandine

PROPERTIES Red almandine and pyrope are the most widely used of all garnets. Almandine is usually a darker red than the blood-red of pyrope. Cut crystals have a brilliant luster, but their transparency is sometimes marred by excessive depth of color. Inclusions such as "zircon haloes" and orientated needle-shaped or rod-like crystals of minerals such as hornblende (which give the stones a silky luster) are seen in Sri Lankan almandine garnets.
OCCURRENCE Almandine is found worldwide in metamorphic rocks such as garnet mica schists. India is a good source of gem-quality almandine. Other localities include Central and South America (in particular Brazil), Madagascar, Tanzania and Zambia. There are many deposits in Brazil and gem-quality almandine has been found in Austria.
USES Almandine is usually faceted in the mixed-cut style or occasionally the step-cut style. Star-stones, and those too dark to facet, are cut *en cabochon*. Irregular-shaped pieces may be fashioned by tumbling to be used as beads. Almandine cabochons are called "carbuncles".

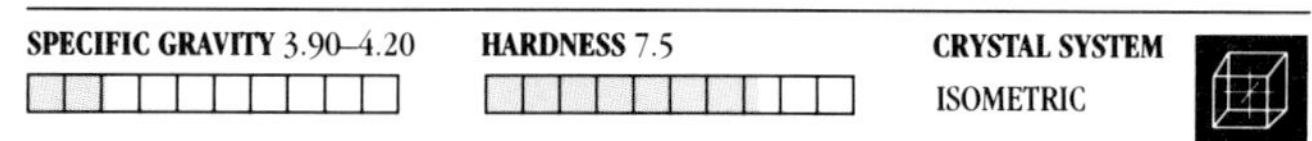

SPECIFIC GRAVITY 3.90–4.20	HARDNESS 7.5	CRYSTAL SYSTEM ISOMETRIC

Cordierite

PROPERTIES Cordierite, or iolite, is pale to dark grayish-blue, greenish, yellowish or brown and may be transparent or translucent. The crystals are usually short, pseudohexagonal prismatic twins with vitreous luster. It is often strongly pleochroic, showing brownish-yellow, light blue and dark blue. The best blue color is seen when the crystal is viewed down the length of the prism. Inclusions may be present. Sri Lankan cordierite sometimes contains so many thin platelets of haematite and goethite that they give the stone a red color. This has been called "bloodshot iolite".
OCCURRENCE Mostly in acid igneous rocks in Scandinavia, Austria, Greenland, Sri Lanka and the USA. Most gem-quality iolite is found as water-worn pebbles in gem gravels in Burma, Sri Lanka, Madagascar, India and Canada.
USES Used as gemstones when transparent. Most iolite is faceted, although massive grey iolite makes a decorative stone for carving.

SPECIFIC GRAVITY 2.57–2.66	HARDNESS 7.0	CRYSTAL SYSTEM ORTHORHOMBIC

Staurolite

PROPERTIES **Distinctive features:** Mostly opaque to deep red stumpy prisms or cruciform twins in mica schists resulting from regional metamorphism. Often associated with kyanite, garnet and quartz. Crystal surfaces often rough. **Color:** Deep wine red to brown or yellow. **Luster:** Resinous to poorly vitreous. **Streak:** No color. **Transparency:** Mostly opaque, but sometimes translucent. **Cleavage:** Good on 010. **Fracture:** Subconchoidal, but this is difficult to see because the crystals are small. **Tenacity:** Brittle. **Forms:** Stumpy or flattened prismatic crystals and cruciform twins. **Twinning:** Cruciform twins on 032.
OCCURRENCE In schists of regionally metamorphosed zones. Associated with kyanite, garnet, quartz and tourmaline. Worldwide, but particularly in Switzerland, France and the USA.
USES Rarely as a gemstone.

SPECIFIC GRAVITY 3.6–3.8 **HARDNESS** 7.0–7.5 **CRYSTAL SYSTEM** ORTHORHOMBIC

Biotite

PROPERTIES **Distinctive features:** Shiny black tabular scales, which are flexible and can be easily prised off with a knife or pin. **Color:** Black to greenish-black and brown. **Luster:** Splendent to submetallic. **Streak:** White. **Transparency:** Transparent to opaque. **Cleavage:** Perfect on 001. **Fracture:** Tends to bend before breaking. **Tenacity:** Flexible, elastic. **Forms:** Usually tabular. **Twinning:** On 001, along which it is also easily cleaved.
OCCURRENCE Important component of most igneous rocks, from granite to gabbro and their fine-grained equivalents. Found in granite pegmatites as large book-like masses. Worldwide.
USES Mineral collections.

SPECIFIC GRAVITY 2.6–3.0 **HARDNESS** 2.4–3.1 **CRYSTAL SYSTEM** MONOCLINIC

Epidote

PROPERTIES **Distinctive features:** Deep green to black, elongated and striated, prismatic crystals occurring in fibrous or granular masses in contact-metamorphosed limestones. **Color:** Emerald green to pistachio green to reddish or yellow. **Luster:** Vitreous to resinous. **Streak:** None. **Transparency:** Subtransparent to opaque (transparent varieties rare). **Cleavage:** Perfect on 001. **Fracture:** Uneven. **Tenacity:** Brittle. **Forms:** Elongated and striated clusters of prismatic crystals. Also massive. **Twinning:** Common on 100. **Varieties:** Crystals, fibrous, massive. Withamite, which is bright red to pale yellow, and chrome epidote, which is emerald green to lemon yellow.
OCCURRENCE In contact-metamorphic zones, in regionally metamorphosed rocks, such as gneisses and schists. Worldwide, but particularly the Urals in Russia, France, Norway and the USA.
USES Mineral collections.

SPECIFIC GRAVITY 3.3–3.5 **HARDNESS** 6.0–7.0 **CRYSTAL SYSTEM** MONOCLINIC

Augite

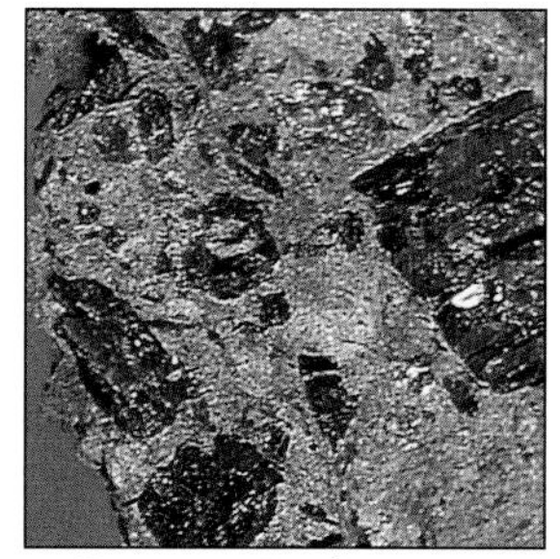

PROPERTIES **Distinctive features:** Dark color, crystalline shape, rock association, 90° cleavage. **Color:** Green to brownish-black. **Luster:** Vitreous to resinous. **Streak:** White to gray to greenish. **Transparency:** Transparent to opaque. **Cleavage:** Perfect on 110 at 90°, often seen only in basal thin sections. **Fracture:** Conchoidal to uneven. **Tenacity:** Not applicable. **Forms:** Fat, prismatic crystals, sometimes tabular on 100. **Twinning:** Contact twins on 100 common. **Varieties:** Aegirine-augite, which is green to yellow, and fassaite, which is deep green.
OCCURRENCE Worldwide in most basic igneous rocks, but ankaramite often yields large specimens up to 8cm (3in).
USES As important rock-forming mineral in nature.

SPECIFIC GRAVITY 3.2–3.6 **HARDNESS** 5–6 **CRYSTAL SYSTEM** MONOCLINIC

NEPHRITE

PROPERTIES Nephrite is made up of an aggregate of fibrous crystals which form a very tough interlocking structure. Color ranges from a creamy color ("mutton fat" jade) to dark green; the greater the iron content and smaller the magnesium content the darker the stone.

Nephrite has a distinct absorption spectrum with a doublet in the red and a sharp line in the green. It shows no luminescence under ultraviolet light and looks green through the Chelsea color filter.

OCCURRENCE Most of the early Chinese jade carvings are of nephrite, which was probably imported from Central Asia. Siberian nephrite is found as dark green boulders which may have black spots. The dark green nephrite of New Zealand is found as pebbles in glacial deposits and used by Maoris to fashion ornaments. Considerable amounts of black nephrite are produced in South Australia. European localities include northern Italy, the Harz mountains of Germany and also Poland, where nephrite is a creamy white to sand color with green patches. American nephrite is found in several states, including California, in a variety of colors. Large boulders of yellow green to dark green nephrite have been found in Canada. Other locations include eastern Turkestan, Brazil, Taiwan, the USA, Canada and Zimbabwe.

USES Nephrite is mainly carved, although some Alaskan nephrite and some from the Rocky Mountains of the USA can be cut *en cabochon* to show the cat's-eye effect.

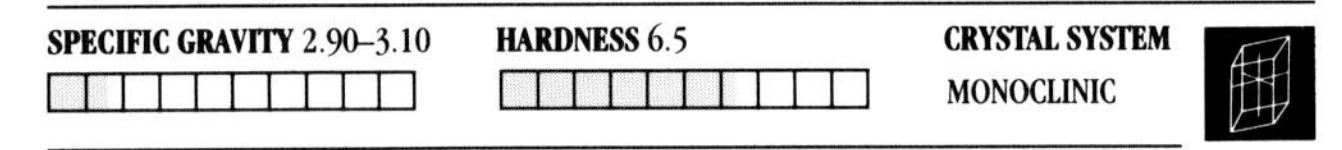

HORNBLENDE

PROPERTIES **Distinctive features:** Common mineral in igneous rocks, where it occurs as black to dark green stubby, prismatic crystals, although elongated forms are not uncommon. Distinguished in basal section from augite by its two cleavages that intersect at 120°. **Color:** Black to green-black and dark brown. **Luster:** Vitreous, but often dull. **Streak:** No color.

Transparency: Opaque. Occasionally subtransparent. **Cleavage:** Perfect on 110 directions. Intersect at 120°. **Fracture:** Subconchoidal. **Tenacity:** Brittle. **Forms:** Stubby, prismatic crystals. Fibrous, granular and massive. **Twinning:** Common on 100. **Varieties:** Hornblende is the most common member of the amphibole group of minerals. Other forms in the group include common hornblende, which is black; basaltic hornblende, which is deep green; riebeckite, which is dark blue-black; and asbestos, which is a fibrous-flaxy form in various colors.

OCCURRENCE An important component of many igneous rocks. Indeed, the classification of these rocks is based on the presence or absence of hornblende. Worldwide in igneous and metamorphic rocks.

USES Mineral collections.

SPECIFIC GRAVITY 3.0–3.5 HARDNESS 5.0–6.0 CRYSTAL SYSTEM MONOCLINIC

TOPAZ

PROPERTIES Topaz is colorless, blue, green, sherry-yellow, port-red or, very rarely, pink. It is found as prismatic, deeply striated crystals, usually terminated at one end only. Cleavage is basal and the crystals show a distinctive lozenge shape when viewed down their length. The high birefringence causes a doubling of the back facets in the cut stone. Luster is vitreous and topaz has a characteristic slippery feel.

There is distinct pleochroism, showing no color and a weak and a stronger shade of the body color. When gently heated or rubbed, topaz becomes electrically charged. Inclusions are tear-shaped cavities.

OCCURRENCE Topaz occurs in cavities with rocks such as granite or rhyolite and in pegmatite dykes. Much is found as water-worn pebbles in alluvial deposits, especially in Brazil. Other localities include Australia, the USA, many of the countries of Africa, Sri Lanka, Burma and Japan.

USES As gemstones. Often cut as oval or pendeloque stones using the mixed-cut style. Dark-colored stones may be step cut. Pale pink topaz may be backed by a red foil to enhance the color.

SPECIFIC GRAVITY 3.50–3.60 HARDNESS 8.0 CRYSTAL SYSTEM ORTHORHOMBIC

SODALITE

PROPERTIES Sodalite has a rich blue color and is one of the components of the rock lapis lazuli. It is a darker blue color and has a lower density than lapis lazuli and it rarely contains the brassy specks of the mineral pyrite that are found in lapis lazuli.
OCCURRENCE Sodalite was found in Canada during a Royal visit and was called "Princess Blue". It is also known as "Canadian Blue Stone" or just "Bluestone". The major commercial source in Canada is in Hastings County, Ontario, Sodalite is also found in Norway, the USA, Brazil and Namibia.
USES Sodalite is fashioned as cabochons and beads, and is cut and polished into slabs for use as inlays in clock cases, cigarette boxes and other items.

SPECIFIC GRAVITY 2.15–2.35 **HARDNESS** 5.5–6.0 **CRYSTAL SYSTEM** ISOMETRIC

KORNERUPINE

PROPERTIES Kornerupine is a rare mineral which may be green, brownish-green or yellow. It was first found in Greenland, where it is scarce and of no use as a gemstone. The strong pleochroism is a characteristic feature and the two colors are green and reddish-brown.
OCCURRENCE Kornerupine is found as rolled pebbles, in gem gravels for example, rather than crystals. Gem-quality green stones were found in 1912 in Madagascar and in 1936 brownish-green stones were found in Sri Lanka. Green kornerupine has been found in the Mogok area of Burma. The fine green color of kornerupine found in Kenya and Tanzania is due to the presence of a small amount of the element vanadium.
USES To obtain the best color the stones should be cut with the table facet parallel to the length of the crystal. Small dark chatoyant stones, which are cut *en cabochon*, are found in Sri Lanka. Gem-quality kornerupine is rare but has been faceted for collectors of the unusual.

SPECIFIC GRAVITY 3.32 **HARDNESS** 6.5 **CRYSTAL SYSTEM** ORTHORHOMBIC

TOURMALINE

PROPERTIES Tourmaline comes in a wide range of colors. Varieties include rubellite (red and pink), indicolite (blue), achroite (colorless), dravite (brown), siberite (violet) and schorl (black). It may also be parti-colored. The crystals are usually long thin prisms with vertical striations and a characteristic rounded triangular section when viewed down their length. Fracture is uneven and there is no cleavage. Luster is vitreous and transparency varies from opaque to transparent. Birefringence is high and a doubling of the back facets should be apparent in cut stones.

Dichroism is more obvious in the darker stones. The absorption spectrum is weak and luminescence not distinctive. Inclusions are black patches or fluid-filled cavities. When heated, lighter-colored tourmaline becomes electrically charged.
OCCURRENCE Tourmaline is found in schists and pegmatic rocks with cavities or in alluvial deposits. Gem-quality stones are found in the Urals and Madagascar. Other localities include Sri Lanka, Burma, Brazil, Tanzania, Namibia, South Africa, Zimbabwe, Mozambique, Kenya and the USA.
USES As gemstones. The mixed cut (step-cut pavilion and brilliant-cut crown) and the step cut are used. Flawed tourmaline is used to make beads or small figurines. When cut *en cabochon* it may show the cat's-eye effect.

SPECIFIC GRAVITY 3.06 **HARDNESS** 7.5 **CRYSTAL SYSTEM** TRIGONAL

Lazurite

PROPERTIES The color of lazurite, or lapis lazuli, varies from a greenish-blue to a rich purple blue. A dark intense blue is the most prized color. It is translucent and usually occurs in massive form, although rarely dodecahedral crystals and cubes are found. Luster is dull or vitreous and streak is blue.

OCCURRENCE Afghanistan is the most famous source of lazurite, where it is found in black and white limestone high up in the mountains. Other localities include Russia, Chile, Burma, Angola, Pakistan and Canada.

USES In jewelry, mosaics and paint. As a gemstone, lazurite is usually cut *en cabochon* or used for beads or small carved objects. It is also used as an inlay material. Imitations can be recognized by the lack of a whitish glow under ultraviolet light.

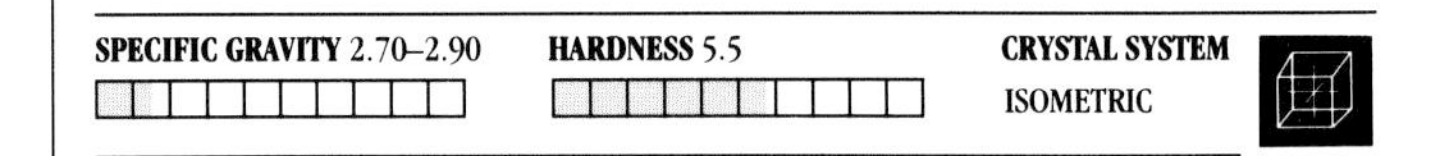

PHOSPHATES

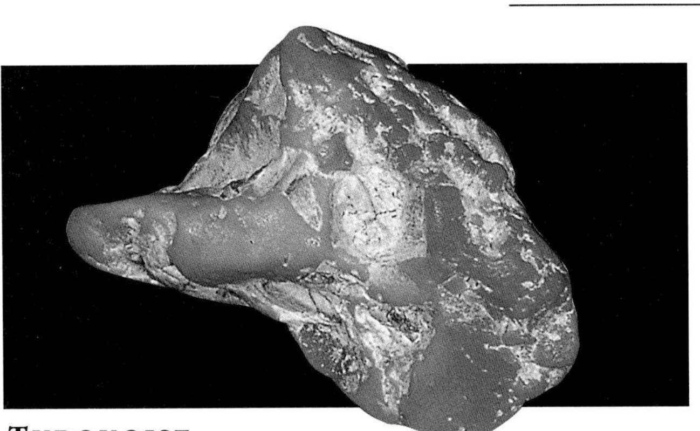

Turquoise

PROPERTIES Turquoise forms as a porous blue cryptocrystalline aggregate and is found as encrustations, nodules or botryoidal masses or in veins within rocks in arid regions. The blue color is due to copper and/or iron. It may fade with excess sunlight and alter to a green color, possibly due to dehydration. Turquoise is semi-translucent, and the absorption spectrum has a characteristic pattern of weak bands. Under long-wave ultraviolet light it appears a greenish-yellow to bright blue. It is inert under short-wave ultraviolet light, whereas some imitations show a strong blue color.

OCCURRENCE The best turquoise is the sky-blue form from Iran, although good-quality turquoise is also found in Colorado, Nevada, Arizona and New Mexico in the USA, Tibet, Egypt and Mexico. The turquoise from the USA is lighter in color and more porous than that of Iran and Mexico. Other localities include Russia, Cornwall in England, Chile and Australia.

USES Turquoise has a wax-like luster and takes a good polish. It can be carved, cut *en cabochon* or cut flat for inlay work. Natural minerals which resemble turquoise include lazulite, wardite and odontolite (blue-colored fossil tooth or bone).

SPECIFIC GRAVITY 2.60–2.80 HARDNESS 6.0 CRYSTAL SYSTEM TRICLINIC

Apatite

PROPERTIES Apatite may be colorless, yellow, green, blue or violet. Small gem-quality crystals are found as transparent hexagonal prisms which may be tabular. The crystals are fragile with cleavage parallel to the base. They tend to be transparent to opaque with a vitreous luster. Some lose their color when heated and others will fluoresce a bright yellow under ultraviolet light. Apatite has a characteristic absorption spectrum with intense narrow lines due to rare-earth elements.

OCCURRENCE Although apatite is found worldwide, the gem-quality material comes mainly from Burma. Blue Burmese apatite is strongly dichroic, showing blue and colorless. Other locations include Sri Lanka, Brazil, Norway, Mexico, the USA and Canada.
USES Fibrous blue crystals from Burma and Sri Lanka show the cat's-eye effect when cut *en cabochon*. A massive apatite variety, which is sky-blue in color, has been polished as an ornamental stone. Apatite is faceted for collectors, but is easily scratched.

SPECIFIC GRAVITY 3.17–3.23 **HARDNESS** 5.0 **CRYSTAL SYSTEM** HEXAGONAL

PYROMORPHITE

PROPERTIES **Distinctive features:** Small, yellowish-green, six-sided, prismatic crystals filling rock cavities in mineralized zones rich in lead. **Color:** Pale yellowish-green usually, but also various shades of brown and yellow. **Luster:** Resinous. **Streak:** White to pale yellow. **Transparency:** Subtransparent to translucent. **Cleavage:** None. **Fracture:** Irregular. **Tenacity:** Brittle. **Forms:** Six-sided prismatic or tabular crystals. Sometimes botryoidal, fibrous or granular. **Twinning:** None. **Varieties:** According to form, e.g. fibrous pyromorphite.
OCCURRENCE A sporadic secondary mineral in lead mineralized zones. Germany, France, Spain, UK, Australia and the USA.
USES Source of lead.

SPECIFIC GRAVITY 7.0 **HARDNESS** 3.5–4.0 **CRYSTAL SYSTEM** HEXAGONAL

MIMETITE

PROPERTIES **Distinctive features:** Small, yellow to brownish-orange six-sided crystals with flat (0001) terminations found in areas where there are lead-rich metalliferous veins. **Color:** Yellow to yellowish-brown to orange and, rarely, white. **Luster:** Resinous. **Streak:** White. **Transparency:** Translucent, occasionally transparent. **Cleavage:** Poor on 10$\bar{1}$1. **Fracture:** Subconchoidal, but difficult to see because of small size of the crystals. **Tenacity:** Brittle. **Forms:** Usually six-sided prismatic crystals, but sometimes as mammillated or globular forms encrusting rocks. **Twinning:** None. **Varieties:** Campylite, which has yellowish-brown-red crystals – found only in UK.
OCCURRENCE Associated with lead carbonates and limonite in areas of lead-rich veins. Austria, Siberia, Czechoslovakia, Germany, UK, France, Namibia, Mexico and the USA.
USES Source of lead.

SPECIFIC GRAVITY 7.0 **HARDNESS** 3.5 **CRYSTAL SYSTEM** HEXAGONAL

VANADINITE

PROPERTIES **Distinctive features:** Six-sided prismatic red to straw-colored crystals associated with areas of secondary lead deposits. **Colour:** Various shades of red to yellowish-brown. **Luster:** Resinous to adamantine. **Streak:** White to yellow. **Transparency:** Subtransparent (darker colors are opaque). **Cleavage:** None. **Fracture:** Uneven. **Tenacity:** Brittle. **Forms:** Six-sided prismatic crystals. The 0001th face is often hollow. Also found as rock encrustations. **Twinning:** None.
OCCURRENCE Rather rare mineral, found in areas of secondary lead deposits. Mexico, Argentina, the Urals in Russia, Austria, UK, Zaire and the USA.
USES Source of vanadium and lead.

SPECIFIC GRAVITY 6.5–7.0 **HARDNESS** 2.7–3.0 **CRYSTAL SYSTEM** HEXAGONAL

SULPHATES

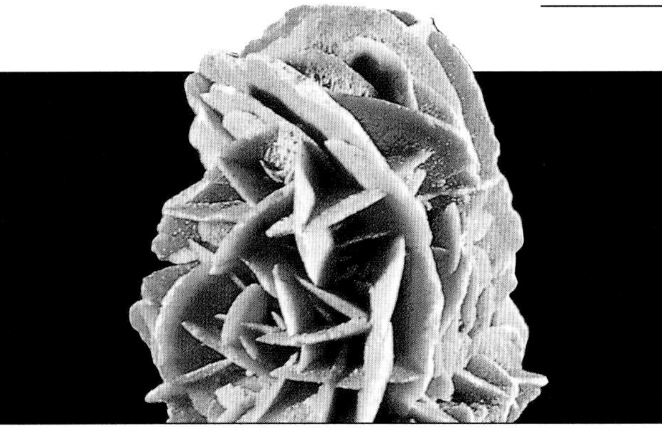

GYPSUM

PROPERTIES **Distinctive features:** Soft enough to be scratched by a finger nail. When it is heated in an open tube, it gives off water. There is no reaction to acid. **Color:** White to pale grey and shades of pinkish-red. **Luster:** Pearly to glistening or dull and earthy. **Streak:** White. **Transparency:** Transparent to opaque. **Cleavage:** Excellent on 010. **Fracture:** Conchoidal, sometimes fibrous. **Tenacity:** Crumbly. **Forms:** Massive, flat or elongated, generally prismatic, crystals. Swallow-tailed twins are common and distinctive. **Twinning:** Good on 100, giving swallow-tailed twins. **Varieties:** Selenite, which has transparent, distinct, bladed crystals; satin spar, which has pearly, fibrous masses; and alabaster, which is fine-grained and slightly colored.
OCCURRENCE As beds, sometimes massive, in sedimentary rocks, such as limestones, shales and clays. UK, France, Russia and the USA.
USES Medical (source of plaster of Paris), for manufacturing wall plaster used in building trade, ornamental carvings made from alabaster.

SPECIFIC GRAVITY 2.3 **HARDNESS** 1.5–2.0 **CRYSTAL SYSTEM** MONOCLINIC

BARYTES

PROPERTIES **Distinctive features:** High density, pale greenish-white to pale brownish tabular crystals. Also appears as desert roses of radiating pale brown crystals. Hardness. **Color:** White to greenish-white or pale brownish-red. **Luster:** Vitreous to resinous. **Streak:** White. **Transparency:** Transparent to opaque. **Cleavage:** Perfect on 001 and 110. **Fracture:** Uneven. **Tenacity:** Brittle. **Forms:** Often occurs as groups of tabular or bladed crystals. Also massive, encrusting, banded, mammillary and fibrous. **Twinning:** None.
OCCURRENCE In veins and beds associated with ores of lead, copper, zinc and iron. Common gangue mineral in metalliferous veins. It is associated with fluorite, quartz, calcite, dolomite and stibnite. Czechoslovakia, Romania, France, Spain, England and the USA.
USES Barium ore, for refining sugar, for drilling mud in the oil industry, for medical barium meals for X-ray, as pigment, in the paper industry.

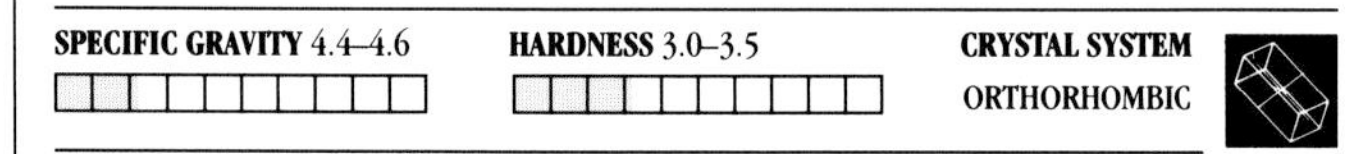

SPECIFIC GRAVITY 4.4–4.6 **HARDNESS** 3.0–3.5 **CRYSTAL SYSTEM** ORTHORHOMBIC

CHROMATES

CROCOITE

PROPERTIES **Distinctive features:** Pinkish-red elongated prismatic crystals, often in masses. **Color:** Shades of pinkish-red to bright saffron-coppery pink. **Luster:** Adamantine to vitreous. **Streak:** Yellowish-orange. **Transparency:** Transparent. **Cleavage:** Good on 110. **Fracture:** Uneven, sometimes conchoidal. **Tenacity:** Sectile. **Forms:** Elongated, prismatic crystals. Also columnar or granular. **Twinning:** None.
OCCURRENCE Secondary minerals deposited by mineralizing waters that have leached lead from adjacent veins. The Urals in Russia, Romania, Tasmania, the Philippines and the USA.
USES Mineral collections.

SPECIFIC GRAVITY 5.9–6.1 **HARDNESS** 2.5–3.0 **CRYSTAL SYSTEM** MONOCLINIC

MOLYBDATES

WULFENITE

PROPERTIES **Distinctive features:** Usually as thin, tabular brownish-yellow to orange crystals, associated with lead ore deposits. **Color:** Bright orange to brownish-yellow to brown. **Luster:** Resinous to adamantine. **Streak:** White. **Transparency:** Subtransparent to translucent. **Cleavage:** Good on 111. **Fracture:** Subconchoidal, but difficult to see with the naked eye. **Tenacity:** Brittle. **Forms:** Usually thin, square, tabular to octahedral or prismatic crystals, but granular and compact forms also occur. **Twinning:** None.

OCCURRENCE A secondary mineral, found in upper (oxidized) zones rich in lead ore deposits. Eastern Europe, Austria, Morocco, Congo, Australia, Mexico and the USA.

USES Molybdenum ore.

SPECIFIC GRAVITY 6.5–8.0 **HARDNESS** 2.5–3.0 **CRYSTAL SYSTEM** TETRAGONAL

TUNGSTATES

WOLFRAMITE

PROPERTIES **Distinctive features:** Well-formed, tabular or prismatic, silvery black crystals in metalliferous sulphide and pegmatite veins in granites. **Color:** Black to very dark gray. **Luster:** Submetallic. **Streak:** Black. **Transparency:** Opaque. **Cleavage:** Good on 010. **Fracture:** Uneven to rough. **Tenacity:** Brittle. **Forms:** Mostly as tabular crystals, but prismatic forms also occur. **Twinning:** None.

OCCURRENCE In metalliferous veins, cavities and pegmatites in granites, where it is associated with cassiterite and copper ores. Worldwide, China, UK, Malaya, Australia, Portugal, Burma, Bolivia and the USA.

USES Source of tungsten.

SPECIFIC GRAVITY 7.0 **HARDNESS** 4.0–4.5 **CRYSTAL SYSTEM** MONOCLINIC

NATURAL GLASS

OBSIDIAN

PROPERTIES Natural glasses do not belong to any of the seven crystal symmetry systems since they are amorphous, i.e. do not have a crystalline structure. Obsidian is the best known of the natural glasses. It may be brown, black or gray and, very rarely, green, red or blue. Inclusions of gold or silver-colored minerals give a metallic sheen and other colors show as iridescence. Obsidian itself has a vitreous luster. Crystallites are crystalline inclusions. Obsidian may have white marks like snowflakes ("snowflake obsidian"), contain bubbles, or have red or brown banding.
OCCURRENCE Obsidian is found throughout the world where volcanic activity occurs or has occurred in the past (for instance Hawaii, Japan, Iceland and the Lipari islands off Italy). It is formed by the rapid cooling of volcanic lava which allows no time for crystals to form. There is no cleavage, but fracture is shell-like (conchoidal). Most of the obsidian used in jewelry comes from the USA and South America (Mexico, Guatemala and Equador). Arizona, Colorado and Nevada have deposits of obsidian, and California has many sites where the material has been quarried from ancient times. Glassy, pebble-like solid lumps of obsidian are found in New Mexico and are called "Apache tears".
USES Obsidian is carved or cut *en cabochon*. Iridescent obsidian from Oregon was used by the American Indians to make arrowheads. In Mexico, the Incas used obsidian for weapons, mirrors, masks and earrings.

SPECIFIC GRAVITY 2.33–2.42	HARDNESS 5.0	CRYSTAL SYSTEM AMORPHOUS

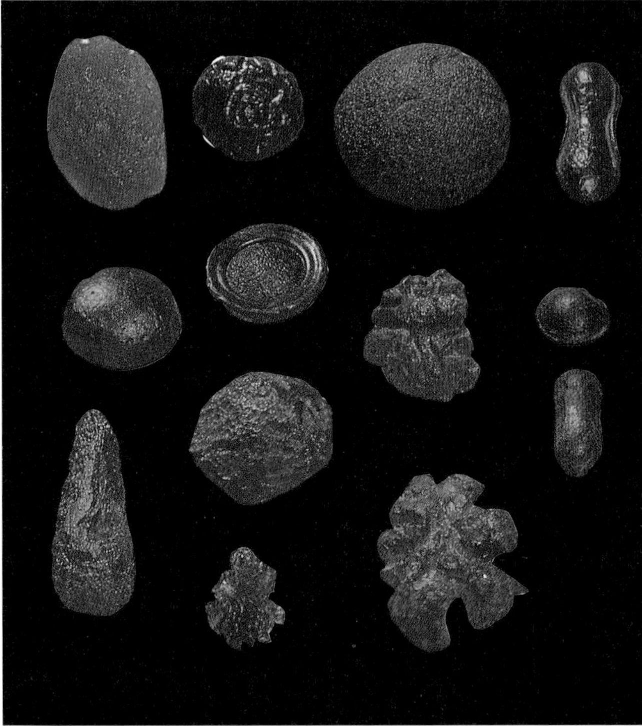

TEKTITES

PROPERTIES Tektites are natural glasses of unknown origin. Tektites are transparent green, greenish-brown or brown in color, and have a bobbly or craggy surface. One theory suggests that the characteristic shape of tektites is due to the fact that they were still molten as they traveled through the atmosphere from outer space. Alternatively, tektites may be the scattered drops of molten rock thrown out by the impact of a large meteorite[1].
OCCURRENCE Moldavites are a type of tektite named after the river in Czechoslovakia where these glassy pieces were first found in 1787. Pieces of tektite from other localities have also been named after the place where they were found. For example, billitonites from Billiton Island, in Indonesia, australites from Australia and georgiaites from Georgia in the USA.
USES Moldavites have been faceted as gemstones and look similar to the bottle-green mineral peridot. They contain round or torpedo-shaped bubbles and characteristic swirls like treacle. These are easily distinguished from the swirls in paste (glass) since there are no crystalline inclusions as there are in volcanic obsidian. Other forms of tektites are carved into small decorative objects.

SPECIFIC GRAVITY 2.34–2.39	HARDNESS 5.0	CRYSTAL SYSTEM AMORPHOUS

[1]The name comes from the Greek word *tektos* meaning molten.

ORGANICS

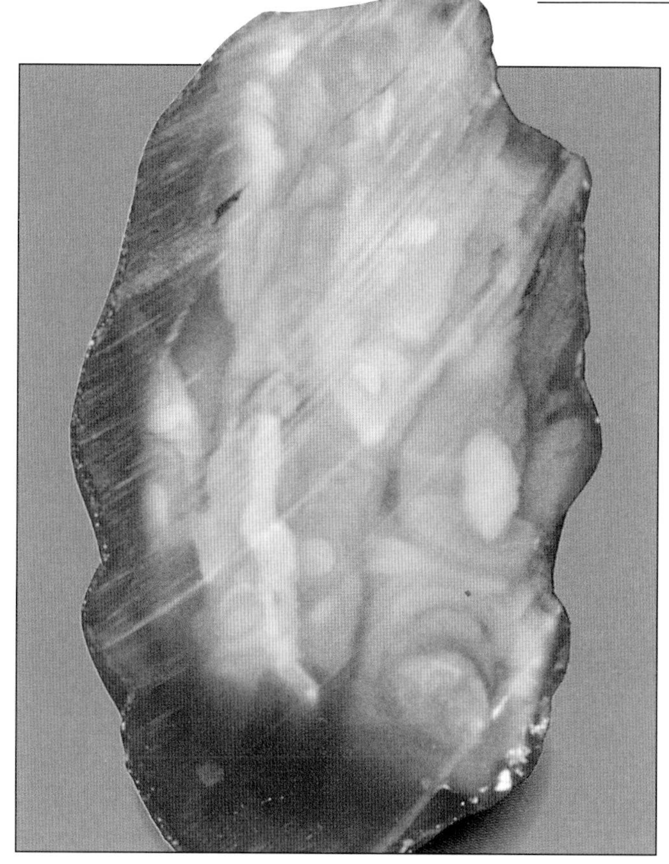

AMBER

PROPERTIES Amber is a fossil resin thought to have come from pine trees. Rubbing it produces a negative charge which attracts small particles. Amber is transparent to translucent and has a greasy luster. Its color is typically yellow or brown but it may have a red or white tinge and it is often cloudy, due to air spaces. Heating cloudy material in oil fills the air spaces and clears the amber. Insects, pieces of moss, lichens and pine needles can be found trapped in amber, which was once a soft, sticky resin.

OCCURRENCE The main localities for amber are along the Samland Coast near Kaliningrad, Russia. Pit amber is obtained by open-pit mining. The amber is separated from the soft sandy deposits using strong jets of water. Sea amber, washed out from the sea bed, floats on water and is carried by the tides and currents to the shorelines of the Baltic, Norway, Denmark and England. Amber is also found in Burma, Sicily, the Dominican Republic, Romania, Czechoslovakia, Germany, Canada and the USA.

USES Amber is valued for jewelry and ornaments since it is readily carved and takes a high polish. Pieces that are too small to work are pressed together under gentle heat to form a larger piece which is called ambroid.

Amber can be imitated by plastic, glass and resin.

SPECIFIC GRAVITY 1.08 **HARDNESS** 2.5 **CRYSTAL SYSTEM** AMORPHOUS

JET

PROPERTIES Jet is a variety of coal. It is a fossil wood which formed when wood rotted in stagnant water and was then flattened by the pressure of burial over millions of years. It smells like coal when burnt or when touched with a hot needle. Some jet may induce electricity when rubbed and for this reason it is sometimes known as "black amber".

OCCURRENCE There is evidence that jet was mined as early as 1400BC and during the Roman occupation of the British Isles jet was shipped to Rome. It was a popular gem during Victorian times when it was used for mourning jewelry. Jet for use in jewelry has also been mined in Asturias, Spain. Other sources include Aude in France, Utah in the USA, Germany and Russia, but these have not been systematically worked.

USES Jet has an intense black color and can take a good polish. Beads, pendants and charms made of jet have been found in early burial mounds which pre-date written history.

Coal, rubber, glass, obsidian, black stained chalcedony and plastics have all been used to imitate jet. "Paris jet" is a black glass.

SPECIFIC GRAVITY 1.30–1.35 **HARDNESS** 2.5–4.0

Part II ROCKS

Rocks, essentially, are "collections" of different minerals in solid form, although some consist of just one mineral, such as limestone and sandstone. There are three types of rocks: sedimentary, igneous and metamorphic.

Sedimentary rocks are generally stratified, fine-grained or composed of fragments of older rocks from which these were derived, such as pebbles, sand, angular fragments of older rocks, broken shells, rounded mineral grains and alteration minerals such as clays. Limestones are easily identified because they effervesce in dilute hydrochloric acid. Many sedimentary rocks also contain fossils.

Igneous rocks, on the other hand, are non-stratified intrusions or extrusions. They can be extremely coarse-grained (granite), fine (andesite) or glassy (obsidian). They are composed of minerals that have crystallized from molten rock.

Metamorphic rocks are sedimentary or igneous rocks that have been altered by heat and/or pressure. As they are derived from previously existing igneous, sedimentary or even metamorphic rock, their appearance is variable. They are identified by the types of minerals they contain and their texture. Thermally metamorphosed rocks occur bordering igneous intrusions, which altered the surrounding rock originally because of their intense heat, resulting also in the formation of new minerals, such as andalusite and garnet. Regionally metamorphosed rocks occur in the roots of mountain ranges, where intense pressures and high temperatures formed platy minerals (e.g. micas) and high-pressure minerals (e.g. staurolite).

ABOVE *Igneous rocks, such as granite, are usually coarse-grained.*

PROPERTIES

Field specimens of rocks are identified according to their composition, texture and mode of origin. Each major rock type has its own range of textures.

SEDIMENTARY ROCK TEXTURES

Clastic Consisting of broken and weathered fragments of pre-existing rocks and/or minerals and/or shell fragments, clastic rocks may have their individual components cemented together by calcite, iron oxide, etc.

Crystalline Consisting of crystals that have been precipitated from solution, which are locked together like the pieces of a three-dimensional jigsaw puzzle, thus giving the rock great strength without cementing material (e.g. limestone).

Organic Mainly composed of well-preserved organic debris, such as plants, shells or bones (e.g. coal, shelly limestone).

IGNEOUS ROCK TEXTURES

Granular Consisting of crystal grains that are large enough to be easily seen by the naked eye, the grains varying in size from 1/32in in andesites to over 1/4in in granites.

ABOVE *Sandstone is a medium-grained clastic sedimentary rock with grains cemented by iron oxide.*

IDENTIFICATION TABLE FOR IGNEOUS ROCKS							
TEXTURE	ORTHOCLASE		PLAGIOCLASE				NO FELDSPAR
	+quartz	−quartz	+quartz	−quartz	pyroxene		+olivine
	+mica	+leucite nepheline	−biotite and/or hornblende		−olivine	+olivine	
GRANULAR	granite	syenite	grano-diorite	diorite	gabbro	olivine gabbro	picrite peridotite
FINELY GRANULAR	micro-granite	porphyry			dolerite	olivine dolerite	
APHANITIC	rhyolite	trachyte phonolite	dacite	andesite	basalt	olivine basalt	
GLASSY	obsidian (massive) pumice (frothy glass) pitchstone (bituminous)			glass	tachylite (like obsidian but not translucent)		
PYROCLASTIC volcanic deposits	ash (unconsolidated air-falls <4mm (⅛in)), volcanic bombs tuff (consolidated air-falls/ash flows <4mm (⅛in)) breccia (angular rock fragments >4mm (⅛in))						

NOTE: gradations may occur between all types.

Aphanitic Made up of tiny crystals, which can only be identified using a microscope or powerful hand lens, they give the rock a flow texture (e.g. basalt) when aligned.

Glassy Composed of volcanic glass, sometimes the glass may be streaky, due to aphanitic bands, and may often contain micro crystals of feldspar (e.g. obsidian).

Pyroclastic These are volcanic rocks in which the magma has been shattered by an explosive eruption and so may consist of tiny slivers of volcanic glass, fragments of pumice, crystals or fractured rock; they may be unconsolidated or cemented together when fresh and altered to clays by weathering when not.

Porphyritic Larger crystals – phenocrysts – are embedded in a finer ground mass; some of the large crystals best being described as megacrysts that have grown in nearly solid rock by means of the replacement of other minerals – a common feature in many granites.

Foliated Minerals are arranged in parallel bands, sometimes contorted as a result of the way the rock flowed while it was still hot and plastic (e.g. flow-banded rhyolite).

METAMORPHIC ROCK TEXTURES

Slaty Finely crystalline rock in which minerals, such as mica, are aligned parallel to one another, which means that the rock splits readily along the mica cleavage planes (e.g. slate).

Schistose Minerals such as mica, chlorite and hornblende are aligned in easily visible parallel bands and, because of their platy alignment, the rock splits easily (e.g. schist).

Gneissose Characterized by a coarse foliation with individual bands several inches across – indeed, the foliation may wrap around larger crystals, as in Augen gneiss – and all the minerals are coarsely granular and readily identifiable (e.g. gneiss).

Granoblastic Mainly large mineral grains that have crystallized at the same time and, therefore, penetrate each other, the grains remaining large enough to be identified easily (e.g. grauwacke or greywacke).

Hornfels Compact, finely grained rock that shatters into sharply angular fragments (e.g. hornfels).

Banded Components occur in well-defined bands (e.g. gneiss).

SYMBOLS USED

The symbols that accompany each rock are common symbols used to represent the rock-type on a geological diagram or map.

SEDIMENTARY ROCKS

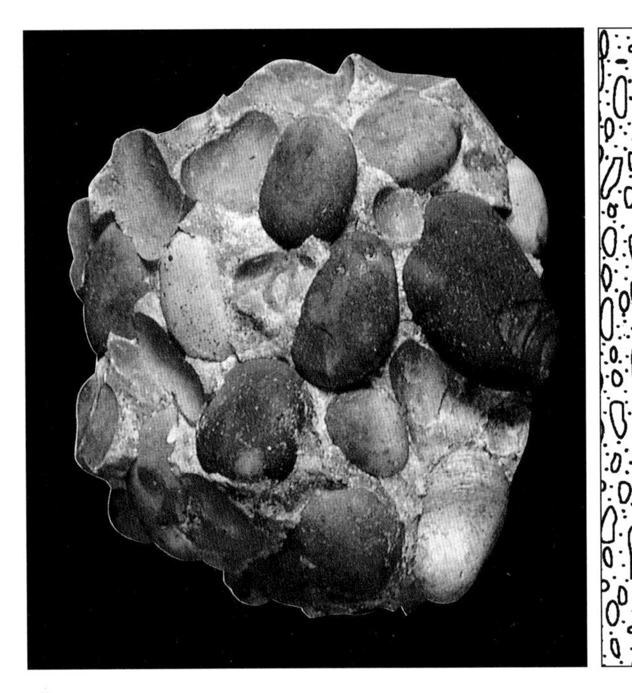

CONGLOMERATE

PROPERTIES **Distinctive features:** Boulders, pebbles or shingle, set in fine-grained matrix, sometimes resembling coarse concrete. **Color:** Variable, depending on the type of rock fragments. **Texture and granularity:** Variable. **Composition:** Rounded rock fragments set in a fine-grained matrix. **Field associations:** Derived from beach, lake and river deposits of boulders, pebbles and gravel. Often found near deposits of sandstone and arkose.
OCCURRENCE Worldwide.
USES Aggregate, ornamental when highly compacted forms are cut and polished.

BRECCIA

PROPERTIES **Distinctive features:** Similar to conglomerate, but rock fragments are angular and set in fine-grained matrix. Distinguished from agglomerate (volcanic equivalent) by its sedimentary origin. **Color:** Variable, depending on type of rock fragments. **Texture and granularity:** Angular fragments of rock set in fine-grained matrix. **Composition:** Fragmented rocks of any kind can form breccia. The matrix is normally fine sand or silt, cemented by secondary silica or calcite. **Field associations:** Derived from screes and fault zones. Often found near conglomerate, arkose and sandstone. **Varieties:** Named according to rock type of which it is composed.
OCCURRENCE Worldwide.
USES Aggregate, ornamental when highly compacted.

SANDSTONE

PROPERTIES **Distinctive features:** Sand in which the grains are cemented together by secondary silica or calcite. May be loosely cemented and soft or well cemented and hard. **Color:** Buff to brownish; sometimes reddish, due to presence of iron oxides, or greenish, due to presence of iron oxides, or greenish, due to presence of glauconite. **Texture and granularity:** Sandy, with grains up to 1/16in. in diameter. **Composition:** Sand grains (quartz), cemented by secondary silica or calcite. **Field associations:** Compacted and/or cemented ancient beach, river, delta, lake and desert deposits. Occurs as thick, stratified beds in sedimentary sequences, often showing current or dune bedding. **Varieties:** Quartz sandstone, which has cemented rounded or angular quartz grains; greywacke (*see* Greywacke); arkose (*see* Arkose); and calcareous sandstone, which has a high proportion of calcite, usually as cement.
OCCURRENCE Worldwide.
USES Construction industry.

Arkose

Properties **Distinctive features:** Sandstone rich in feldspars. Bedding is sometimes present, but fossils are rare. It effervesces slightly in dilute hydrochloric acid, which indicates calcite cement. **Color:** Buff to brownish-grey or pink. **Texture and granularity:** Usually medium-grained 1⁄16in. on average), but can be fine-grained. Mineral grains do not interlock. **Composition:** Quartz sandstone containing over a quarter feldspar with calcite or iron oxide cement. Micas may also be present. **Field associations:** Derived from rapid weathering, transportation and deposition of granitic rocks.
Occurrence Worldwide.
Uses Building stone, millstones for grinding corn.

Greywacke

Properties **Distinctive features:** Poorly sorted dark gray to greenish, fine-grained sandstone. **Color:** Various shades of dark gray to dark greenish-gray. **Texture and granularity:** Granular, fine-grained. **Composition:** Quartz, plagioclase and tiny rock fragments set in a matrix of microscopic quartz, feldspar, clay and other minerals that are too small to determine without a microscope. **Field associations:** Formed at bottom of ocean trenches bordering continents by avalanches of submarine sediments. Occurs in association with black shales of deep sea origin. **Varieties:** Feldspathic greywacke, which is rich in feldspar; and lithic greywacke, which is rich in tiny rock fragments.
Occurrence Worldwide, but especially bordering ancient fold mountain ranges.
Uses None of any importance.

Shale

Properties **Distinctive features:** Splits easily into thin plates along well-defined planes parallel to the original stratification. Buff to grey very fine-grained silty rock. **Color:** Buff to various shades of grey. **Texture and granularity:** Fine-grained. **Composition:** Complex mixture of microscopic clay minerals, plus mica and quartz. **Field associations:** Derived from ancient mud deposits, it occurs in most sedimentary sequences with fine sandstone and limestone. **Varieties:** Probably mudstone.
Occurrence Worldwide.
Uses Source of fossils.

Limestone

Properties **Distinctive features:** Whitish compact rock that effervesces in dilute hydrochloric acid. Often rich in fossils. **Color:** White to yellowish or gray. Black varieties are rich in hydrocarbons. **Texture and granularity:** Variable; compact, oolitic, crystalline, earthy-granular, pisolitic, shelly. **Composition:** Mostly calcium carbonate. **Field associations:** Deposited in ancient seas by precipitation or by the accumulation of calcite-rich shells etc., coral reefs, around hot springs. **Varieties:** Crystalline limestone, which has granoblastic calcium carbonate crystals; crinoidal limestone, which is rich in fragments of fossil crinoids; oolitic limestone, which has tiny ooliths of calcium carbonate; pisolite, which has large (up to 1⁄8in.) ooliths; and reef limestone, which is rich in coral reef fossils.
Occurrence Worldwide.
Uses Source of cement, building construction (locally), blackboard chalk.

Chalk

PROPERTIES **Distinctive features:** White, porous rock that effervesces in dilute hydrochloric acid. Often contains bands of flint nodules and is rich in fossils. **Color:** White to yellowish or gray. **Texture and granularity:** Fine-grained, earthy, crumbly, porous rock. **Composition:** Mostly calcium carbonate, with minor amounts of fine silt. Often contains flint and pyrite nodules. **Field associations:** Deposited in ancient seas by the accumulation of tests (tiny shells) of microscopic marine organisms.
OCCURRENCE UK, France, Denmark.
USES As a source of cement.

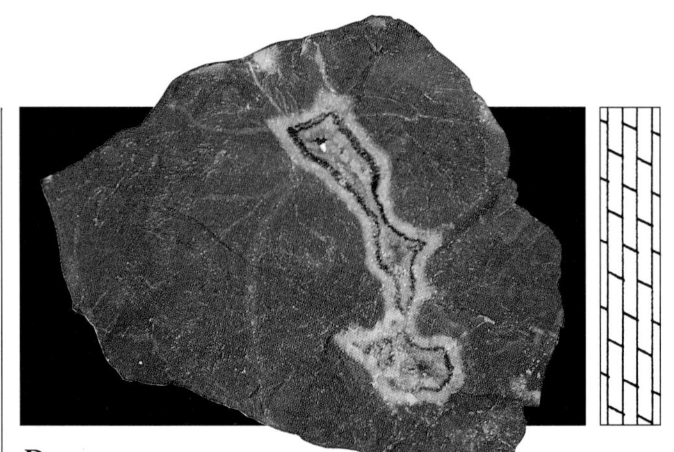

Dolomite

PROPERTIES **Distinctive features:** Pale-coloured massive limestone that often contains small cavities. Sometimes associated with evaporite deposits of gypsum and halite. **Color:** Creamy white to pale brown. **Texture and granularity:** Coarse- to fine-grained. Often compact. **Composition:** Magnesium carbonate with, at times, small amounts of silica and other derived minerals. **Field associations:** Often interbedded with calcite-rich limestones, but may form thick massive deposits. **Varieties:** Sometimes known as magnesium limestone.
OCCURRENCE Worldwide.
USES Aggregate.

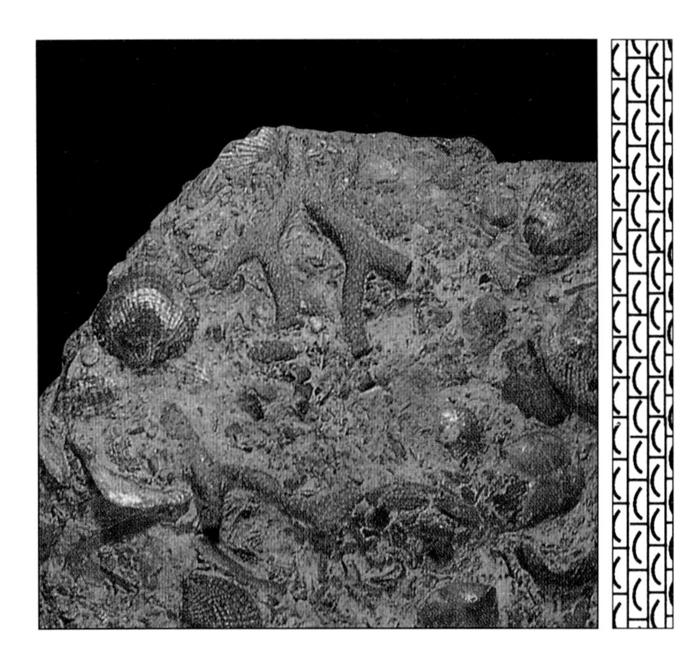

Shelly limestone

PROPERTIES **Distinctive features:** Pale gray highly fossiliferous rock. Effervesces in dilute hydrochloric acid (care!). **Color:** Grayish-white to buff or yellowish-grey. **Texture and granularity:** Shelly. **Composition:** Mostly entire and broken fossilized shells cemented by calcium carbonate. **Field associations:** Represents a thick accumulation of marine shells and other calcite-rich organisms deposited in shallow water.
OCCURRENCE Worldwide.
USES Source of fossils.

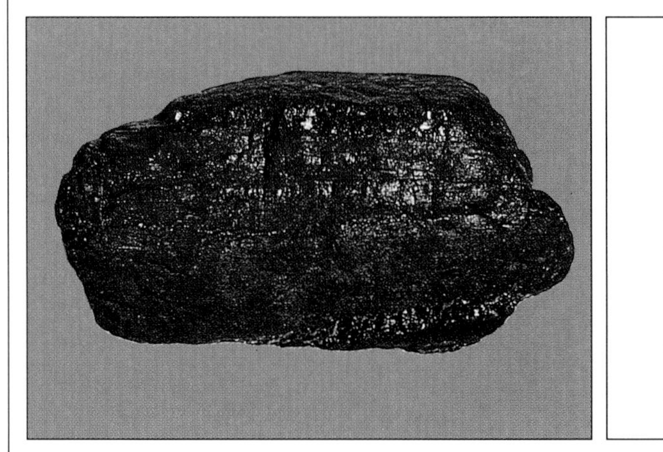

Coal

PROPERTIES **Distinctive features:** Black, dirty, hard to crumbly rock. Burns with a bright yellow flame. **Color:** Dull, earthy black to glistening submetallic black. **Texture and granularity:** Massive, brittle. **Composition:** Highly compacted plant debris. **Field associations:** Represents remains of ancient forests that flourished mainly on tropical deltas. Occurs mostly as thick beds in rocks of Carboniferous age, although some thin coal bands are found in rocks of other ages. **Varieties:** Cannel coal, which is a soft brownish-black; coal, which is brittle, black, sometimes with glistening bands; and anthracite, which is brittle, black, glistening.
OCCURRENCE USA (Pennsylvania), southern Russia, Ukraine, UK, China, Africa.
USES Domestic and industrial fuel.

SEPTARIAN NODULES

PROPERTIES **Distinctive features:** Ball-like structures, often enclosing shell fragment or other nuclei. Composed of sandstone or clay cemented by calcite or silica, the internal shrinkage cavities, usually filled with calcite, may be seen when the nodule is cut or broken. **Color:** Variable: gray to buff to dark brown with white-yellow calcite filling the interior, radiating cracks and cavities. **Texture and granularity:** Usually fine-grained. **Composition:** Variable, depending on origin. Sand, silt or clay together with calcite. **Field associations:** Fine-grained or clay sediments.

OCCURRENCE Worldwide.

USES Ornamental when cut and polished.

IGNEOUS ROCKS

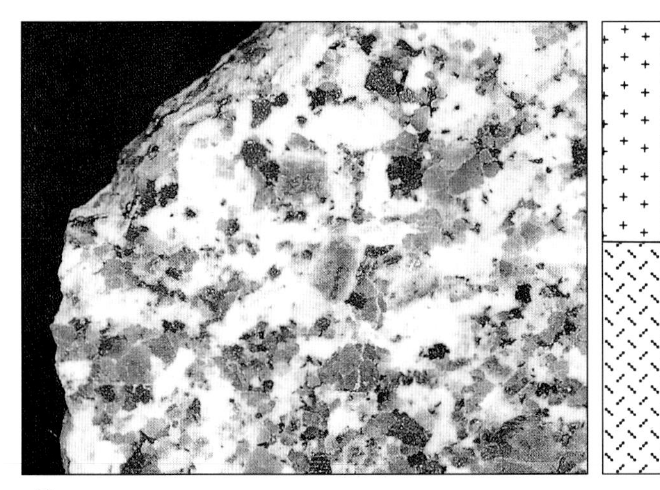

GRANITE

PROPERTIES **Distinctive features:** Granular, composed of feldspars and quartz, with accessory biotite and muscovite. One feldspar may be flesh coloured, while the other is white. The white feldspar may show twinning striations characteristic of plagioclase; the other feldspar is almost certainly orthoclase. The quartz appears as grey glassy grains. Biotite is black and muscovite is white or silvery and both shine or sparkle by reflected light. **Color:** As above. **Texture and granularity:** Granular, coarse-grained, often porphyritic with feldspar crystals up to 4in. **Composition:** Orthoclase feldspar is always greater than plagioclase. If plagioclase is dominant the rock is probably a quartz diorite. White to salmon pink orthoclase feldspar megacrysts, set in a ground mass of glassy quartz, white/pink orthoclase, white plagioclase, black biotite and silvery muscovite. Accessory minerals include gold-colored pyrites and silvery black magnetite. **Field associations:** Associated with fold mountains (e.g. Himalayas, Andes, Urals, Appalachians and Rockies). Granites often mark position of ancient fold mountain systems. **Varieties:** Numerous. Immense variation in granularity and color – extremely coarse pegmatite, fine-grained microgranite, saccharoidal oplite. Orbicular has composite minerals arranged in ovoid or spherical bodies.

OCCURRENCE Worldwide.

USES Roadstone, building blocks, but has poor resistance to fire as it crumbles when exposed to intense heat.

SYENITE

PROPERTIES **Distinctive features:** Texture and granularity and its composition. **Color:** White, pinkish-gray to gray. **Texture and granularity:** Granular – coarse to very coarsely grained. **Composition:** Orthoclase more dominant than plagioclase (if plagioclase is dominant, the rock is probably diorite). Quartz is absent but there are small amounts of hornblende, mica, augite and magnetite, which are easily seen in coarse examples. Nepheline and leucite may also be present. **Field associations:** Uncommon rocks that may be associated with nearby granites, but generally from magma chambers underlying trachytic (the fine-grained equivalent of syenite) volcanoes. **Varieties:** Syenite, which contains more orthoclase than plagioclase and no quartz; nepheline syenite, which has orthoclase and nepheline; and anorthosite, which is mostly plagioclase (labradorite).

OCCURRENCE Worldwide, but particularly in the Alps, Germany, Norway, Azores, Africa, Russia, USA (New England, Arkansas, Montana and other states).

USES Building industry, superior to granite because of its fire-resisting qualities.

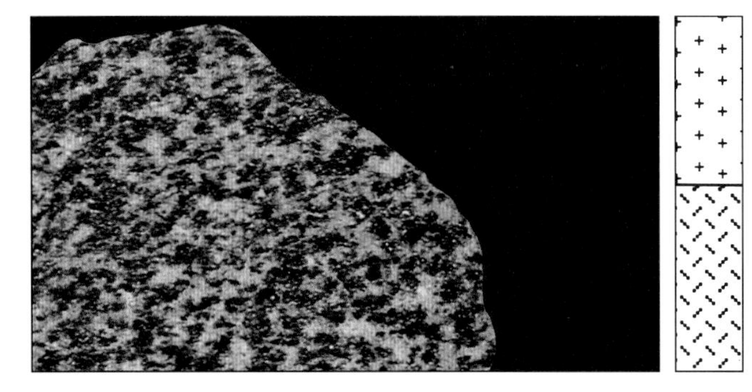

GRANODIORITE

PROPERTIES **Distinctive features:** Texture, color and the ratio of plagioclase to orthoclase as well as the presence of quartz (polysynthetic twinning sometimes seen as fine striations on plagioclase phenocrysts). Association with granitic masses. **Color:** Pale to medium gray. **Texture and granularity:** Granular, coarse-grained, often with phenocrysts of feldspar, hornblende or mica. **Composition:** More plagioclase than orthoclase, plus quartz. Minor quantities of biotite, hornblende, apatite and sphene are also present. **Field associations:** Found in association with granitic batholiths. Forms large intrusive masses in the roots of mountain ranges. **Varieties:** Hornblende biotite granites, but these are really granodiorites.
OCCURRENCE Worldwide, but particularly in Scandinavia, Brazil, Canada, USA (California has 3500 square miles of granodiorite).
USES Roadstone aggregate.

DIORITE

PROPERTIES **Distinctive features:** Texture and granularity, composition, occurrence. **Color:** Dark gray, dark greenish-gray to black, depending on the percentage of dark minerals present. **Texture and granularity:** Granular, though not particularly coarse. Hornblende crystals may give it the appearance of a porphyritic texture. **Composition:** There is more hornblende than feldspar and more plagioclase then orthoclase. The presence of quartz is uncommon; but if it is present the rock is then granodiorite (quartz diorite) rather than diorite. **Field associations:** Associated with both granite and gabbro intrusions, into which they may subtly merge. **Varieties:** Granodiorite, when minor amounts of quartz are present.
OCCURRENCE Worldwide, but particularly in the eroded roots of fold mountains.
USES Ornamental – capable of taking a high polish.

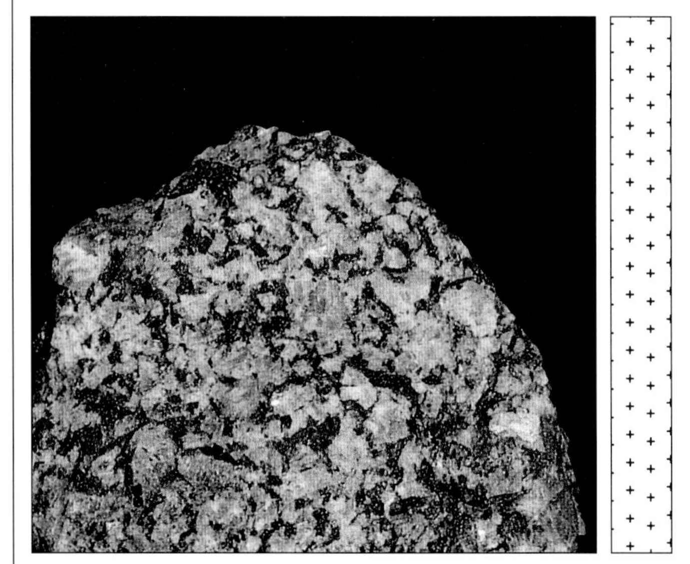

GABBRO

PROPERTIES **Distinctive features:** Color, granularity, predominance of pyroxene and, often, olivine. May appear to be porphyritic because of the size of the pyroxenes. **Color:** Dark gray, dark greenish-gray to black. **Texture and granularity:** Coarsely granular, but rarely porphyritic. Sometimes bonded, resembling gneiss. **Composition:** Mainly pyroxene and plagioclase, with greater amounts of pyroxene than plagioclase or equal amounts of both. Olivine is often present, as well as grains of iron ore (magnetite and/or ilmenite) and bronze-coloured biotite. **Field associations:** As plutons and similar large bodies, but not as large as those of granites. Also as large sheets, often containing valuable ore deposits (e.g. Lake Superior deposits). **Varieties:** Olivine gabbro, which is like gabbro, but also has olivine phenocrysts.
OCCURRENCE Scotland, Scandinavia, Canada, England, Germany, USA (New England, New York, Minnesota, California and lesser amounts in other states).
USES Building industry, monumental since it takes a high polish, as a source of iron, nickel and copper ores (e.g. Sudbury ores in Ontario, Canada).

PERIDOTITE (and other ultra basic rocks)

PROPERTIES **Distinctive features:** Greenish color when fresh, medium brown when weathered. Texture and composition. **Color:** Olive green when fresh, but weathering to dark ochre brown due to the formation of iron oxides. **Texture and granularity:** Granular – saccharoidal. **Composition:** Made up almost entirely of small grains of olivine, or pyroxene may be present in appreciable amounts. **Field associations:** As small intrusions, sills and dykes. Often brought to the surface from a great depth by volcanic activity (olivine nodules in basalt). **Varieties:** Dunite, which is composed of olivine only and is a pistachio green color, and picrite, which is composed of olivine plus subordinate amounts of plagioclase and is pale green. *Note:* Pyroxenite, which consists only of pyroxene, is black and has a 90 degree cleavage, and hornblendite, which consists only of hornblende, is black and has a 120 degree cleavage.
OCCURRENCE Worldwide, but particularly in New Zealand, USA (New York, Kentucky, Georgia, Arkansas, Carolina and lesser amounts in other states).
USES As a source of valuable ores and minerals, including chromite, platinum, nickel and precious garnet. Diamonds are obtained from mica-rich peridotite (kimberlite) in South Africa.

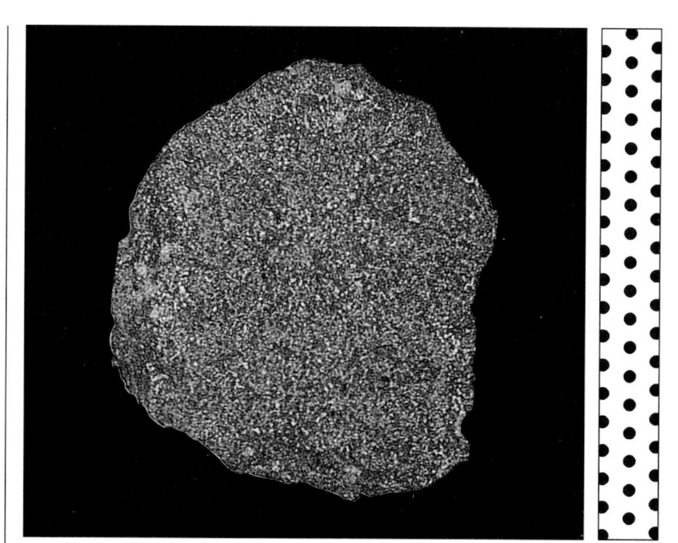

DOLERITE

PROPERTIES **Distinctive features:** Color, texture. Difficult to distinguish between the hornblende and pyroxenes because of their small grain size. The plagioclase occurs as thin laths. Pyrite, bronze biotite and iron oxide may be seen using a hand lens. **Color:** Medium gray to black. **Texture and granularity:** Granular to fine grains. Occasionally porphyritic. **Composition:** Pyroxene and plagioclase with larger amounts of pyroxene than plagioclase or equal amounts of both. Olivine is also often present, as well as grains of iron ore (magnetite and/or ilmenite) and bronze-colored biolite. **Field associations:** As dykes and sills, often of great thickness. It may pass into gabbro at depth (dolerite is the medium-grained equivalent of gabbro). **Varieties:** Olivine dolerite, which is dolerite, plus olivine phenocrysts.
OCCURRENCE Worldwide, but particularly in Canada (Lake Superior), UK, USA (eastern states – notably Palisades Sill – and western states as lava flows that merge into basalts).
USES Monumental, masonry, paving slabs, aggregate for roadstone.

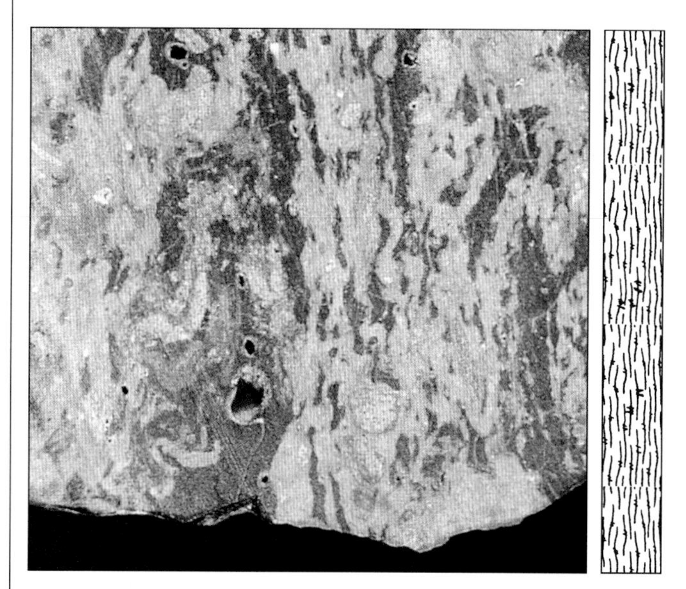

RHYOLITE

PROPERTIES **Distinctive features:** Aphanitic, buff to grayish flow-banded rock, often containing spherulites or phenocrysts of quartz and feldspar. **Color:** Buff to grayish, banded. **Texture and granularity:** Aphanitic to very fine-grained. **Composition:** Same as granite, but the crystals too small to see without using a microscope. **Field associations:** As thick lava flows from acidic volcanoes. **Varieties:** Spherulitic rhyolite, which contains rounded bodies (spherules) of microcrystalline quartz and feldspar.
OCCURRENCE Worldwide.
USES Aggregate.

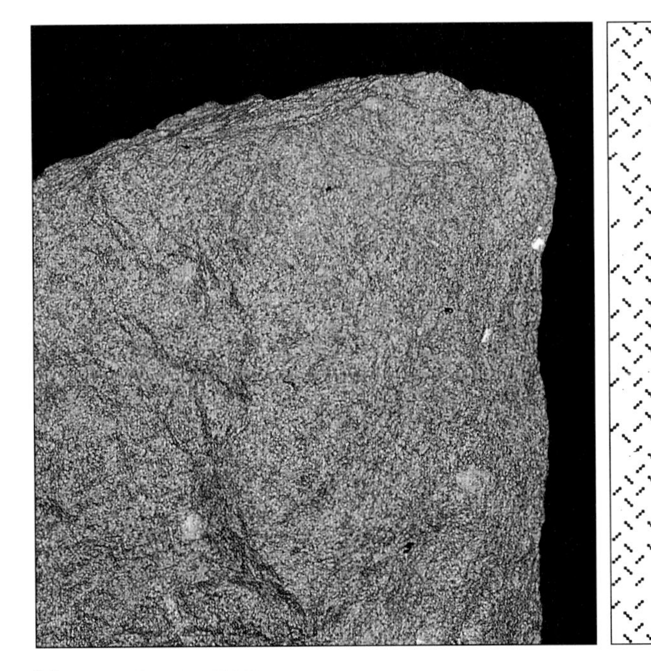

MICROSYENITE

PROPERTIES **Distinctive features:** Texture and granularity and composition. **Color:** White to pinkish-gray. **Texture and granularity:** Granular – fine-grained to aphanitic. **Composition:** Orthoclase appears in greater quantities than plagioclase and there is no quartz. The small amounts of hornblende, mica, augite and magnetite that are present can only be seen in thin sections with the aid of a microscope. Nepheline and leucite may also be present. **Field associations:** This is an uncommon rock, associated with syenite masses.
OCCURRENCE Worldwide, but particularly in the Alps, Germany, Norway, Azores, Africa, Russia, USA (New England, Arkansas, Montana and lesser amounts in other states).
USES Aggregate.

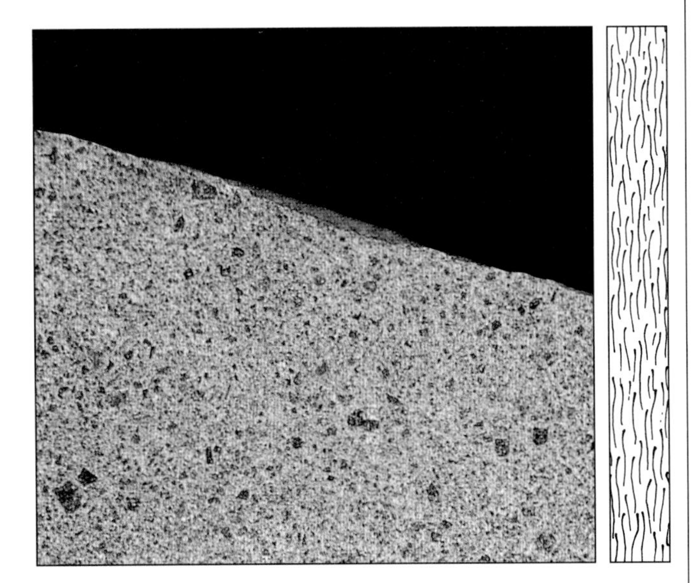

ANDESITE

PROPERTIES **Distinctive features:** Color and texture. Often flow-banded and porphyritic and plagioclase phenocrysts occur as thin laths. Biotite, hornblende and pyroxenes may be seen with the aid of a hand lens, but they can be difficult to identify because they are small. **Color:** White to black, but mostly medium gray. **Texture and granularity:** Aphanitic to finely granular, porphyritic and flow-banded. **Composition:** Fine-grained ground mass of plagioclase, with smaller amounts of hornblende, biotite and augite, which may occur as small phenocrysts. **Field associations:** Lava flows and small intrusions associated with volcanic mountain ranges. **Varieties:** Hornblende augite andesite, which is andesite with phenocrysts of hornblende and augite.
OCCURRENCE Abundant in continental collision zones, such as the Andes, Cascades, Carpathians, Indonesia, Japan and other western Pacific volcanic islands.
USES Roadstone aggregate.

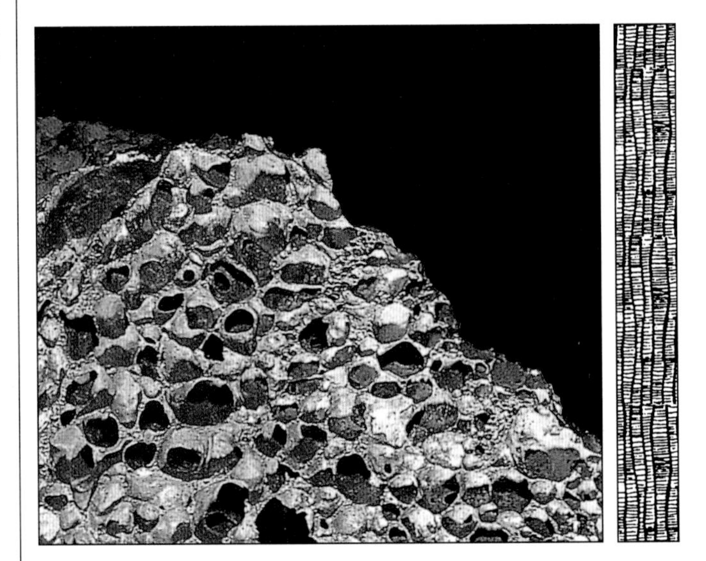

BASALT

PROPERTIES **Distinctive features:** Texture, color, denseness and often contorted by flow on eruption or cindery. **Color:** Dark greenish-gray to black. **Texture and granularity:** Aphanitic with crystals that are too small to identify with the naked eye unless they occur as phenocrysts (e.g. augite and/or olivine). Fine-grained equivalent of gabbro. **Composition:** Pyroxene and plagioclase, with pyroxene appearing in greater amounts than plagioclase or equal amounts. Olivine is also often present, as well as grains of iron ore (magnetite and/or ilmenite) and bronze-coloured biotite. It may contain olivine or pyroxene nodules brought up from depth. **Field associations:** As lava flows, sills and dykes associated with volcanoes. **Varieties:** Olivine basalt, which is basalt plus olivine phenocrysts, and quartz basalt, which is basalt plus scarce quantities of quartz.
OCCURRENCE Worldwide, but particularly in Canada (Lake Superior has vast copper deposits), Greenland, India (Deccan traps), Iceland, Scotland, USA (Montana, western states).
USES Roadstone aggregate, source of iron ore, sapphires and native copper.

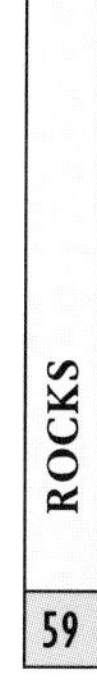

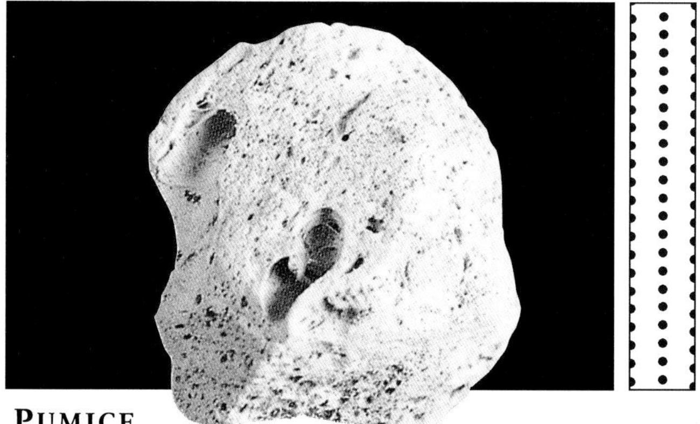

PUMICE

PROPERTIES **Distinctive features:** White or creamy white highly vesicular rock, but weathers to a pale brown on its surface. Very low density. **Color:** Creamy white when fresh, but turns pale brown on surface when weathered. **Texture and granularity:** Vesicular. **Composition:** Composed principally of glass froth of granitic to granodioritic composition. **Field associations:** Chiefly on rhyolitic to dacitic volcanoes.
OCCURRENCE Worldwide.
USES Abrasive, cleansing powders.

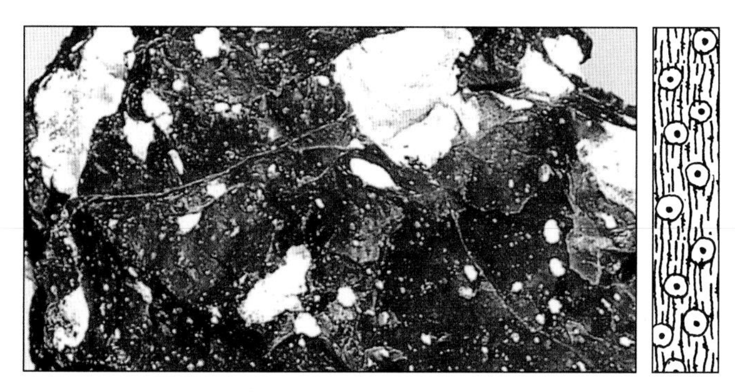

PITCHSTONE

PROPERTIES **Distinctive features:** Black, opaque volcanic glass that may contain irregular, whitish clusters of minerals. Resembles pitch in appearance. **Color:** Dull black. **Texture and granularity:** Glassy and breaks to produce poorly defined conchoidal fracture. **Composition:** Glass with the same chemical composition as granite, syenite or granodiorite. Microscopic crystals of pyroxene may appear as whitish flecks. Microscopic iron ores oxidize, giving reddish colors. **Field associations:** Pitchstone originates from a rapidly chilled lava flow and is therefore always associated with volcanoes. **Varieties:** Obsidian, which is bright black glass with no phenocrysts; pumice, which is highly vesiculated glass; and vitrophyre, which is glass with tiny phenocrysts.
OCCURRENCE Worldwide, but particularly in Iceland, Italy, Lipari, Japan, Mexico, New Zealand, Russia, USA (Yellowstone Park, California, Oregon, Utah, New Mexico, Hawaii and lesser amounts in other states).
USES Aggregate.

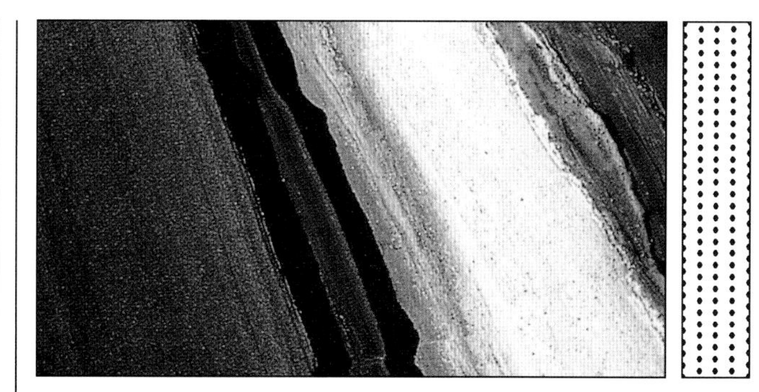

ASH (and related rocks)

PROPERTIES **Distinctive features:** Unconsolidated or poorly consolidated white to black cindery ash of varying grain size. **Color:** Ranging from pure white to black. **Texture and granularity:** Pyroclastic. Unconsolidated when fresh, but consolidating to form hard volcanic tuff. **Composition:** Dependent on the composition of the source magma. Mostly basaltic (black) to trachytic (white). **Field associations:** As stratified beds of air-fall material ejected by volcanic eruptions, sometimes unstratified when formed from ash flows. **Varieties:** Basaltic ash, which is coarse, cindery to fine black ash; trachytic (syenitic) ash, which is coarse, cindery to fine creamy white ash; and tuff, which is dense, varying from cream to yellow.
OCCURRENCE Worldwide and always associated with volcanoes.
USES Prefabricated building blocks, road surfacing, abrasives.

IGNIMBRITE

PROPERTIES **Distinctive features:** Fine-grained to aphanitic, buff to dark brown compact rock with parallel streaks or lenticles of black gass. **Color:** Pale cream to brownish to dark red-brown. **Texture and granularity:** Fine-grained to aphanitic and flow foliation is often present. **Composition:** Usually trachytic/phonolitic to andesitic. **Field associations:** Exclusively produced by violently explosive volcanoes. **Varieties:** Sillar, which is poorly consolidated rock of same origin as ignimbrite but in which pumice blocks have *not* collapsed to form plates of black glass and which is poorly sorted.
OCCURRENCE Worldwide – associated with andesitic to phonolitic/trachytic volcanoes.
USES Local building construction, aggregate.

ECLOGITE

PROPERTIES **Distinctive features:** Generally coarse, green (reddish when weathered) pyroxene in which are set red garnets. **Color:** Pistachio green when fresh, but mottled with red when weathered. **Texture and granularity:** Granular – coarse- to medium-grained. **Composition:** Omphacite (green pyroxene), green hornblende and pyrope–almandine garnet. Kyanite and diamond sometimes occur. **Field associations:** Metamorphosed gabbro, or basic magma crystallized at high pressure at great depth. **Varieties:** Coarse- and medium-grained varieties only.
OCCURRENCE As blocks in the "blue ground" that fills diamond pipes in Kimberley, South Africa, Norway, Scotland, USA, Asia.
USES Scientific.

PYROCLASTICS and miscellaneous volcanic products

VOLCANIC BOMB Rounded or spindle-shaped rock of mainly basaltic composition ejected during eruptions.
BREADCRUST BOMB Rounded, smooth-surfaced pumice block with cracked surface resembling cracked crust of bread, hence the name.
ACHNELITH Small, glassy volcanic bomb, sphere, dumbbell and droplet shapes resulting from very liquid magma.
PAHOEHOE LAVA Vesicular, basaltic lava with ropy surface texture.
RETICULITE Lightest rock known. A basaltic pumice in which the walls of the vesicles have collapsed, leaving a network of fine, interconnecting glass threads.
PALAGONITE Submarine lava flow altered to yellowish-brown color by the formation of the gel mineral palagonite.

METAMORPHIC ROCKS

SLATE

PROPERTIES **Distinctive features:** Grayish, very fine-grained, foliated rocks that split into thin sheets. Sometimes contain well-formed pyrite crystals. Found in metamorphic environments. **Colour:** Usually shades of medium to dark gray, but sometimes a buff colour. **Texture and granularity:** Slaty and very fine-grained. **Composition:** Mica, quartz and other minerals that can be determined only by X-ray. **Field associations:** In areas of regionally metamorphosed shale or volcanic tuff.
OCCURRENCE Worldwide.
USES Roofing sheets.

SCHIST

PROPERTIES **Distinctive features:** Schistose and mostly composed of biotite, muscovite and quartz. Sometimes contains green chlorite or garnets or staurolite and kyanite. **Color:** Streaky, silvery, black, white or green. **Texture and granularity:** Schistose with mineral grains that are platy or aligned. **Field associations:** Zones of contact or regional metamorphism. **Varieties:** Greenschist, mica schist, garnet mica schist, staurolite–kyanite schist, and amphibolite schist.
OCCURRENCE Worldwide.
USES Source of minerals for collectors.

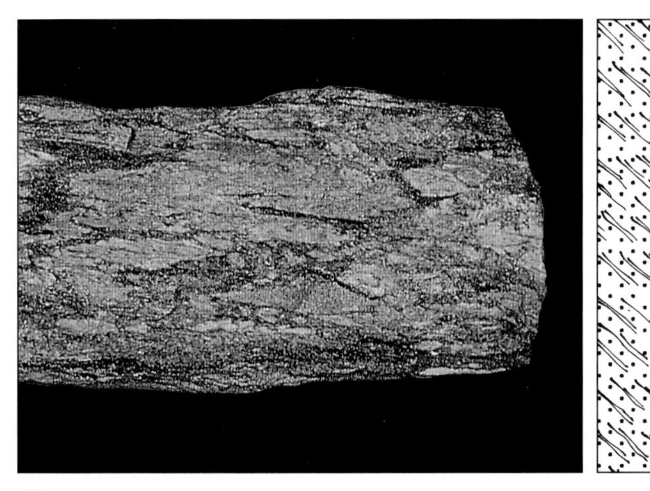

Gneiss

PROPERTIES **Distinctive features:** Coarse-grained, pale-colored gneissose rock, containing abundant feldspar. **Color:** Whitish to dark gray – the darker varieties containing more biotite. **Texture and granularity:** Gneissose, coarse-grained. **Composition:** Mostly feldspar, with quartz, mica, hornblende and garnet. **Field associations:** In roots of eroded fold mountain systems. **Varieties:** Depends on the source rock. Granitic gneiss is the most common, but basic varieties also occur.

OCCURRENCE Worldwide, but always in roots of fold mountain systems.

USES Construction, ornamental, aggregate.

Quartzite

PROPERTIES **Distinctive features:** Compact, hard, very fine-grained rock, which breaks into sharp angular fragments. Quartzite is always associated with other metamorphic rocks, while cemented sandstone is always associated with other sedimentary rocks. **Color:** White to creamy white. **Texture and granularity:** Granoblastic and very fine-grained. **Composition:** Interlocking sand (quartz) grains, often with silica cement. **Field associations:** In zones of regionally metamorphosed sandstones. **Varieties:** Local varieties based on colour.

OCCURRENCE Worldwide.

USES Aggregate, monumental.

Hornfels

PROPERTIES **Distinctive features:** Hard, compact rock that breaks into splintery fragments. Mineral content is variable. Found in zones of contact metamorphism. **Color:** Dark to medium gray. **Texture and granularity:** Hornfelsic and fine-grained, sometimes with porphyroblastic crystals. **Composition:** Dependent on parent rock. **Field associations:** Zone or aureole of contact metamorphism bordering granitic intrusions. **Varieties:** Cordierite hornfels, which contains crystals of cordierite; andalusite hornfels, which contains crystals of andalusite; pyroxene hornfels, which contains crystals of pyroxene; and sillimanite hornfels, which contains crystals of sillimanite.

OCCURRENCE Worldwide.

USES Aggregate.

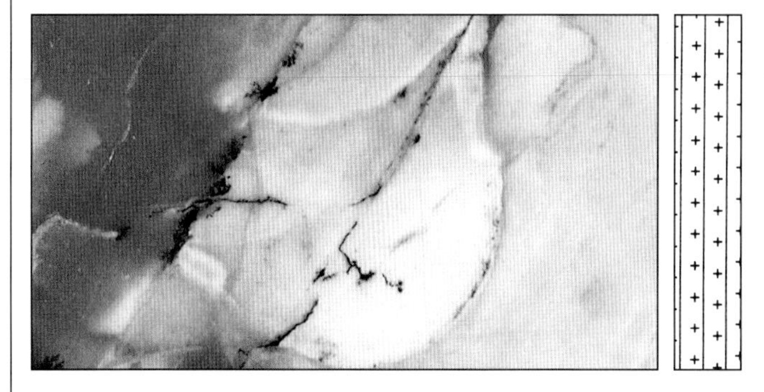

Marble

PROPERTIES **Distinctive features:** Fine- to coarse-grained granoblastic that effervesces in dilute hydrochloric acid. Often banded with various colors and sometimes veined. **Color:** Variable: white, cream, gray, red, green and often streaky with light and dark patches. **Texture and granularity:** Fine- to coarse-grained, granoblastic. **Composition:** Calcium carbonate. **Field associations:** In zones of regionally metamorphosed limestone. **Varieties:** Many, depending on the color and banding, e.g. Connemara marble, which is pale green.

OCCURRENCE Worldwide.

USES Building and ornamental.

Part III SHELLS

Man has used both shells and the animals that produce them for over 6000 years, and their remains have been found in archeological sites dating from at least 4000BC. The remains of shells such as limpets, oysters and land snails have been found in Bronze Age settlements, and the Romans are known to have farmed oysters for food. Bronze Age sites in Africa have yielded bivalve shells that were clearly used as scrapers. Museums throughout the world contain evidence of the early use of shells in the production of items as diverse as drinking utensils and fish-hooks, but traces of shells such as cowries and conches and fragments of mother-of-pearl suggest that shells were also esteemed for their decorative qualities.

Shells are produced by animals belonging to the phylum Mollusca. This is a diverse and widespread group made up of five major classes – Gastropoda, Bivalvia, Polyplacophora, Cephalopoda and Scaphopoda – and it is useful for the shell collector to understand something of their biology.

MOLLUSCAN BIOLOGY

Molluscs are found in a wide variety of habitats, from the deepest ocean basins to the highest mountain tops, and there is great diversity of form not only among classes but also among species of the same family.

LEFT
A seventeenth-century carved pearly nautilus shell mounted in silver-gilt and coral, probably made in Holland or Germany.

LEFT
A characteristic Victorian decorative ornament, c1880, made by wiring shells together to form flowers.

GASTROPODA

This class contains over three-quarters of living molluscs. Gastropods have a soft body and large foot, which are normally enclosed in a hard, protective shell. Although gastropod shells are often spirally coiled, some species have dome-, cap- or cone-shaped shells. The spiral shells

ABOVE *A live example of the painted top,* Calliostome zizyphinum, *which is widely distributed in shallow rocky areas throughout western Europe.*

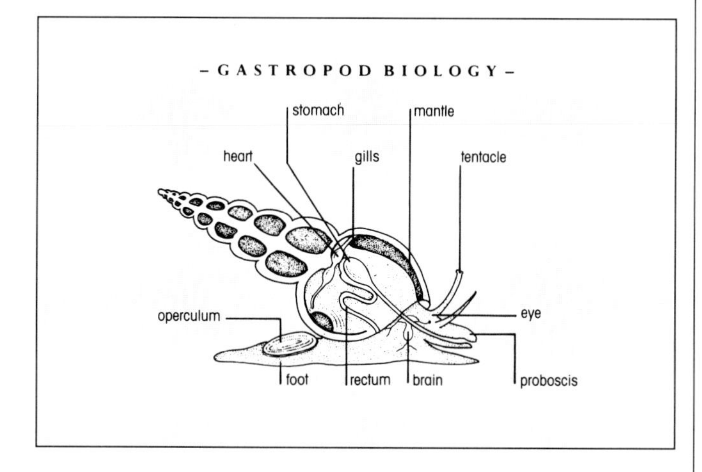

are usually coiled into a helix, but some are formed into a flat plane, while others open out into an irregular, twisted shape. Most gastropods are active and highly mobile, and they are found in the sea, in freshwater and on land. There are approximately 30 000 described species, including limpets, top shells, cowries, cones and volutes.

In some species of gastropod the shell is reduced, internal or absent; in others various organs are reduced or absent – the operculum, for example, is not always present.

Many gastropods possess a radula, a rasping tongue that is used in feeding from vegetable or animal matter. In some specialized species, the radula is used to bore a hole in the shell of prey. The radular teeth of cone shells, members of the Conidae family, are modified to form hollow, harpoon-like barbs through which a poison is shot into the prey. The species with the largest apertures are thought to be most dangerous, and several human deaths are reported to have been caused by careless handling of live specimens.

Respiration is normally by means of gill-like filaments, although in terrestrial forms these are modified to form a lung-like chamber.

The sexes are usually separate, although in some species the creature may be both sexes, either simultaneously or changing from one sex to the other through age or in response to environmental factors. Development may be from eggs, from which free-swimming, intermediate-stage larvae known as veligers emerge, or direct.

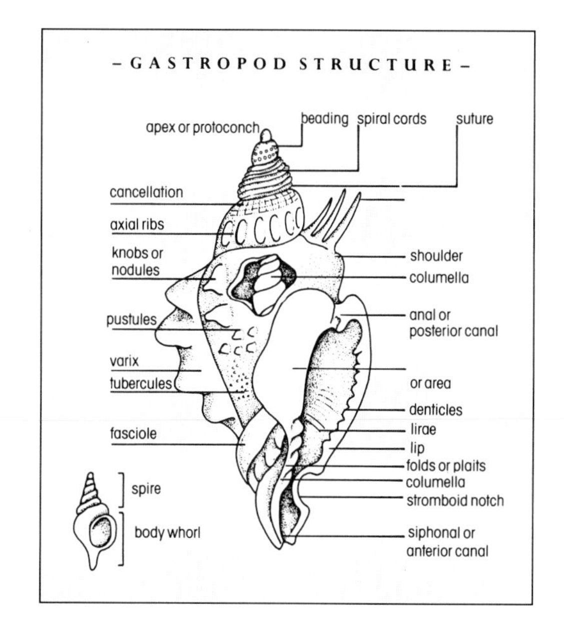

BIVALVIA

The shells of bivalves are composed of two valves which vary considerably, but in all species they are joined along their dorsal surface by an elastic ligament, which causes the valves to open. To counteract this, the valves are held together by strong muscles that are attached to the inner shell surface and that produce the characteristic scars. The hinge structure may or may not have interlocking, tooth-like projections.

The animal lacks a true head and radula and feeds by trapping organic particles as they pass over its gills. The tongue-like foot, which protrudes from the front end, is often comparatively large and is used for locomotion, although species such as oysters become permanently

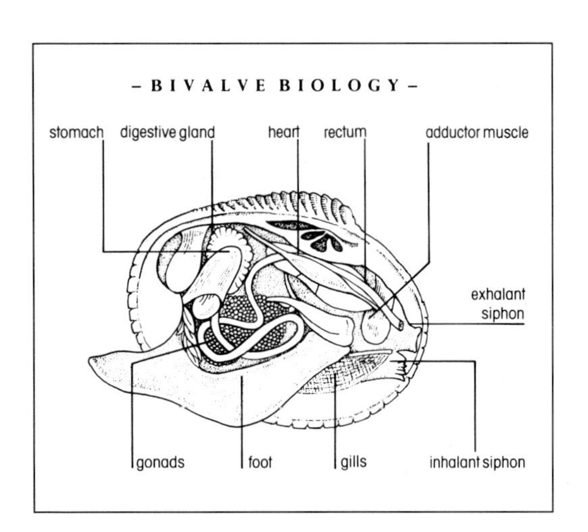

attached to the substrate by means of silky threads produced by a byssal gland in the foot. Inhalant and exhalant siphons, in varying degrees of complexity, are situated at the posterior end.

In most species the sexes are separate, but some species are hermaphrodite, and some change sex over time. Eggs and sperm may be liberated into the surrounding water via the exhalant siphons, and the fertilized eggs develop into free-swimming veligers, which develop into bivalves. In some species, eggs are brooded within the shell cavity.

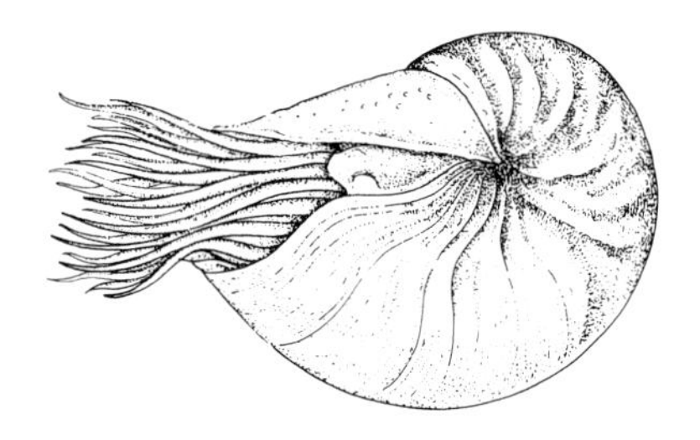

CEPHALOPODA

This group contains creatures with a well-developed head with eyes. They have eight or ten sucker-bearing arms or tentacles and a horny, beak-like structure, which is used for tearing their prey. All are carnivorous. The class includes octopuses and squids, but only the Nautilidae and Argonautidae are of interest to shell collectors. The head and foot are united, and there are gills and sensory organs. In most species the sexes are separate and there is no free-swimming larval or veliger stage. Instead, the fully developed embryo emerges from the egg.

Nautilids have external shells. Argonauts, on the other hand, are octopus-like creatures that do not have true shells. The "shell", which is produced by the female of the species, is only loosely attached to the body and its main function is to hold the eggs.

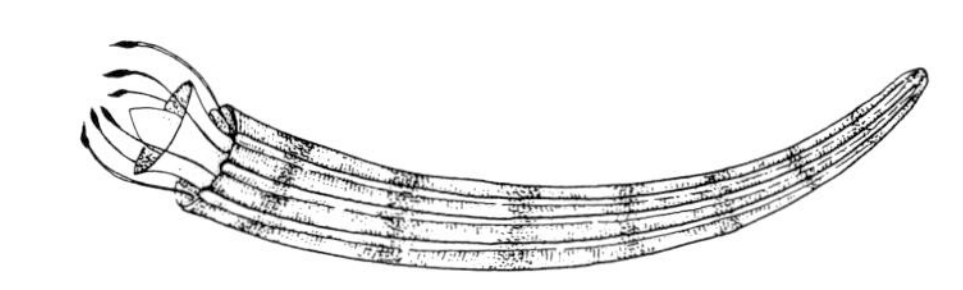

SCAPHOPODA

The members of this class are commonly known as tusk shells, and they are found throughout the world in temperate to tropical seas. There are over 1000 species. They have hollow, tubular, tusk-shaped shells, which are open at both ends. Some species have a notch or slit in the posterior portion of the shell or a small terminal "pipe". The shell tapers along its length, and the creature's foot emerges from the larger, lower opening.

Scaphopods live buried in sand inside their tubular shells. The animal feeds by sucking in water bearing organic particles through the smaller open end of the shell, which protrudes above the sand's surface. There is no distinct head, eyes or gills, but the foot is large and there is a well-developed radula. They feed mainly on protozoa and other microscopic organisms. The sexes are separate, and the larval form has a pair of valve-like structures that fuse together to produce the adult shell. These are usually deep-water species, and living specimens are seldom seen. However, the empty shells are regularly washed up on beaches.

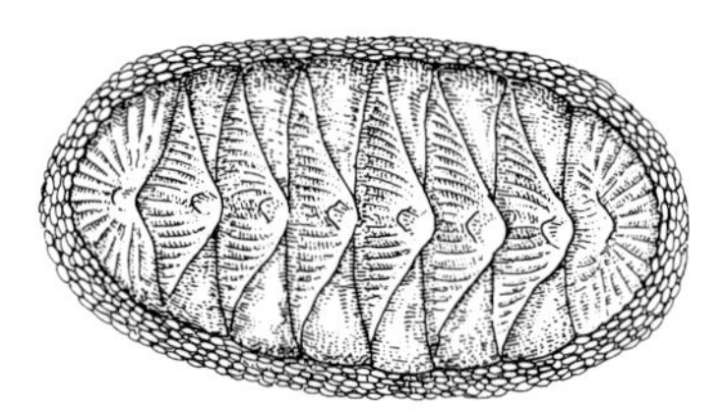

POLYPLACOPHORA

This class, also known as Amphineura, contains the chitons or coat-of-mail shells, whose strange, segmented shells of eight plates are held together by a leathery band or girdle and which resemble woodlice when they curl up for protection. There are believed to be between 600 and 1000 species, all of which are vegetarians.

These species live in the intertidal zone and in offshore waters, generally in rock crevices or beneath rocks. They possess a well-developed radula, a large foot but no tentacles or eyes. The sexes are separate. A few species have free-swimming veliger, but in most species the mother protects her young until they are capable of fending for themselves.

HABITAT AND DISTRIBUTION

Marine molluscs occur throughout the world and in almost any environment where the water offers an adequate supply of food. Most species, including the most highly colored and patterned, live in shallow waters, many thriving in sand or muddy habitats, or burrowing into sandy substrates.

The habitat in which a shell is discovered is often an important clue to its identity. In this book shell habitats are described as **intertidal**, which refers to the area between the extreme high-tide and extreme low-water marks, or as **subtidal**, which is in the shallow water from below the extreme low-water mark down to the edge of the continental slope. Deep-water species are known as **abyssal**.

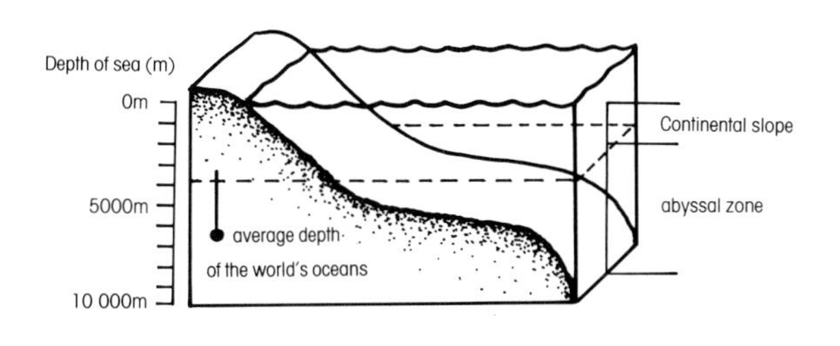

COLLECTING

CLEANING AND STORAGE

Shells purchased from dealers or obtained through exchange will normally be ready to be placed directly into your collection. Specimens that you have collected yourself may require further treatment.

The soft body parts of live-collected material must be preserved or removed before they begin to decompose and putrefy. If you wish to preserve the animal, it should be drowned by being placed in freshly boiled water, which will cause it to relax and come out of its shell, and then placed in a preservative. Suitable preservatives are a 10 per cent solution of formalin mixed with a few drops of glycerine, industrial methylated spirits or 70 per cent alcohol, although this last is difficult to obtain unless you have access to a laboratory. Animals can be removed by being boiled for a short time. Bivalves are easily removed from their shells, but you will need a pin to deal with gastropods. Take care to remove and preserve the operculum if one is present. This should be kept separately or stuck to a piece of cotton wool and inserted into the shell aperture.

Encrustations on the shell can be removed with a wire brush or in a weak solution of acetic acid (white wine vinegar). Some collectors prefer to retain such "blemishes", since they provide additional information about the animal's habitat.

Storage will depend on your personal taste and also on any limitations imposed by space and finances. Closets or cabinets with shallow drawers are preferable, and individual shells can be kept in plastic- or glass-topped boxes, tubes or cardboard trays. Each shell should be numbered and accompanied by a label bearing all the relevant information, including the scientific and common names, the date and place of collection, the name of the collector, the name of the identifier, preservation methods and any other appropriate information. This information should, ideally, also be kept in a loose-leaf file or notebook.

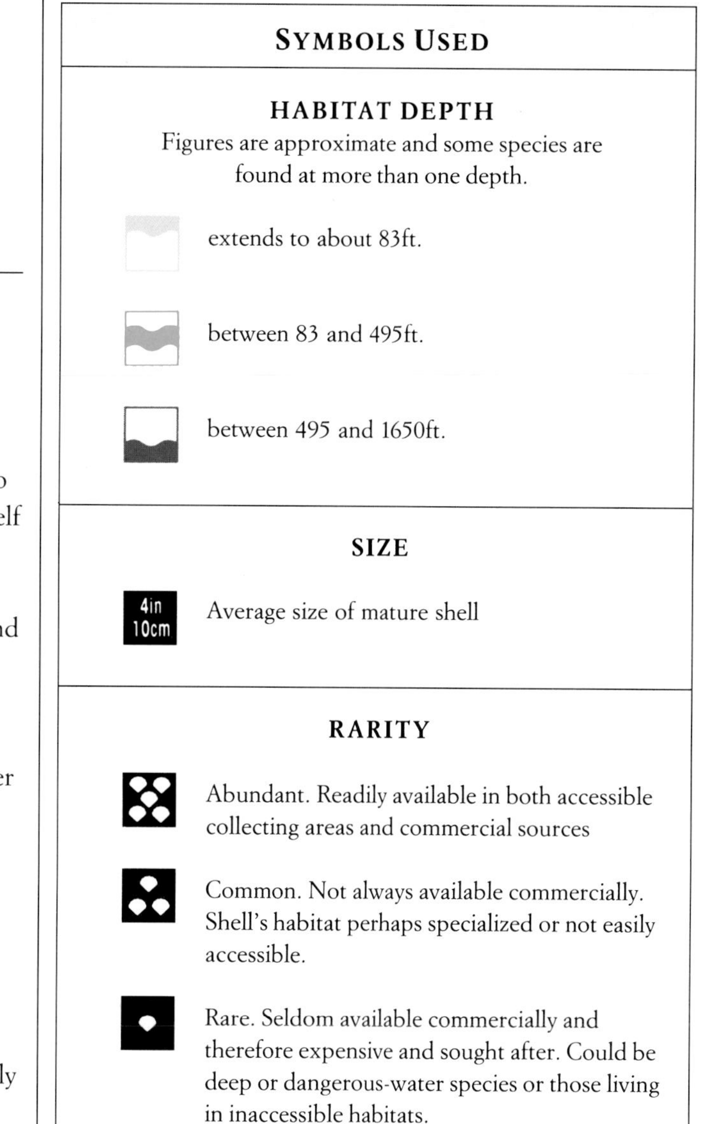

SYMBOLS USED

HABITAT DEPTH

Figures are approximate and some species are found at more than one depth.

extends to about 83ft.

between 83 and 495ft.

between 495 and 1650ft.

SIZE

4in 10cm — Average size of mature shell

RARITY

Abundant. Readily available in both accessible collecting areas and commercial sources

Common. Not always available commercially. Shell's habitat perhaps specialized or not easily accessible.

Rare. Seldom available commercially and therefore expensive and sought after. Could be deep or dangerous-water species or those living in inaccessible habitats.

Class GASTROPODA

Superfamily PLEUROTOMARIOIDEA

Family PLEUROTOMARIIDAE Slit shells

The ancestors of this ancient molluscan family occur as Cambrian fossils, formed some 600 million years ago, and they too possessed the characteristic slit on the body whorl and a horny operculum. All recent species are vegetarians, and they normally inhabit waters to depths of 600m (2000ft), for which reason they are rarely seen in amateur collections. The shells are comparatively large and usually round or conical.

PEROTROCHUS WESTRALIS

WEST AUSTRALIAN SLIT SHELL

GENERAL DESCRIPTION This recently described species has a large, top-shaped shell with eight or nine whorls; the body whorl has the characteristic slit. The shell is a pale beige color, decorated with a few faint orange streaks. It is sometimes trawled off west Australia at depths of 1500ft.

Another recently described and closely related species, *Perotrochus tangaroana*, has been dredged to a depth of about 2000ft. from Lau Ridge and the North Cape Rise off New Zealand.

OCCURRENCE West Australia.

2in 5cm

Family HALIOTIDAE Abalones

Abalones, which are also known as ormers or sea ears, are vegetarians. There are about 100 species distributed throughout the world from low-tide level to depths of several hundred metres. The shells are flattened, ear shaped and have a series of holes on the body whorl through which water and waste products are passed. The pearly interior, which bears a single, central muscle scar, is often used as a source of mother-of-pearl. The animal lacks an operculum. Abalones are often used as food, and the larger species from California are farmed for this purpose.

HALIOTIS RUBER

RUBER ABALONE

GENERAL DESCRIPTION The spire of *Haliotis ruber* is often eroded, exposing the white, highly iridescent pearly layer beneath. The upper surface is a pale red color. It is perhaps the best known Australian abalone, and it is commonly found on rocks and in crevices from extreme low-tide level downwards throughout the shallow waters off south Australia.

OCCURRENCE South Australia; Tasmania.

6in 15cm

Superfamily FISSURELLOIDEA

Family FISSURELLIDAE Keyhole limpets

The members of this family are commonly known as keyhole limpets because there is a hole at the apex of the conical shell in the majority of species. They are found throughout the world on rocky shores and among coral. They are fairly primitive molluscs with no operculum. All the members of the family are vegetarians.

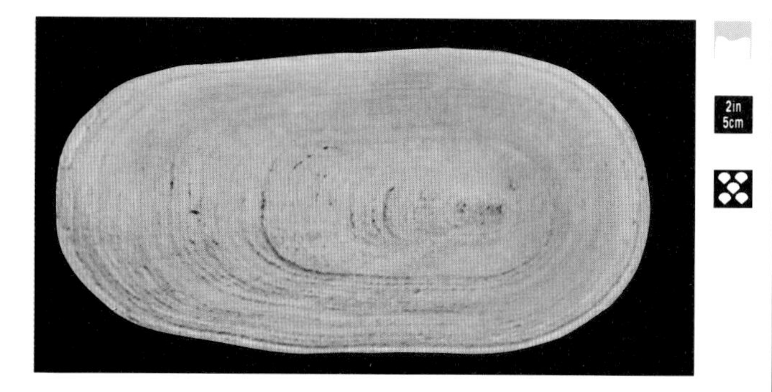

SCUTUS ANTIPODES

ROMAN SHIELD LIMPET

GENERAL DESCRIPTION The Roman shield limpet is atypical of the family because it does not have an apical hole. Its generic and common names derive from the shell's supposed resemblance to a Roman shield, *scutum*. It is common on rocks in the intertidal zone of New Zealand and grows on average to 2in., although specimens up to 3½in. have been found. The ribbed exterior, which clearly reveals the shell's growth stages, is yellowish-beige; the interior is white.
OCCURRENCE South Australia; north New Zealand.

FISSURELLA BARBADENSIS

BARBADOS KEYHOLE LIMPET

GENERAL DESCRIPTION The Barbados keyhole limpet, with its oval shape, pale green interior and characteristic figure-of-eight apical hole, is well known to collectors. The outer shell surface is often coated with lime deposits, which can obscure the delicate radiating ridging. It is common on intertidal rocks from south Florida to Brazil, and is, as its name suggests, especially abundant in the West Indies.
OCCURRENCE South Florida to Brazil; West Indies.

Superfamily PATELLOIDEA

Family ACMAEIDA and LOTTIIDAE True limpets

The members of these two families have limpet-like shells with a horseshoe-shaped muscle scar on the porcellaneous interior, which is often brightly colored. Most species occur intertidally on rocky shores, but they may also be discovered on seaweed or even on other shells. They are found throughout the world but are particularly common on the Pacific coasts of North America.

LOTTIA GIGANTEA

GIANT OWL LIMPET

GENERAL DESCRIPTION The upper surface of this large, flattened, oval shell is patterned with irregular blotches and is normally heavily encrusted. The interior exhibits an oval, pale blue or white muscle scar, which is surrounded by the uniform deep brown and glossy inner surface, which is, in turn, edged by a black marginal band. The species occurs on rocks just below the high-tide mark.
OCCURRENCE California to Mexico.

PATELLOIDEA ALTICOSTATA

HIGH RIBBED LIMPET

GENERAL DESCRIPTION This widespread species is usually found in association with the green seaweed *Ulva,* on which it feeds. The upper surface has about 20 radial ridges, but these are often hidden beneath encrusting algae. The inside is white or off-white with a pale brown, central muscle scar. Some shells also have a black marginal border.
OCCURRENCE South Australia.

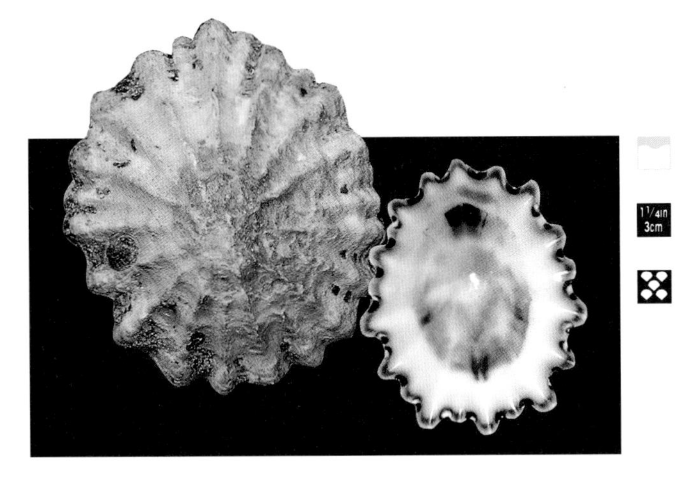

1¼in
3cm

Superfamily TROCHOIDEA

Family TROCHIDAE Top shells

The hundreds of species in this family have a worldwide distribution. The small to large conical shells are covered by a skin or periostracum and often have radial or spiral sculpture. The inner shell layer is pearly, and the animal has a corneous operculum. Top shells feed on seaweed and occur in large numbers on coral reefs or among seaweed on rocky shores.

CALLIOSTOMA ANNULATUM

RINGED TOP SHELL

GENERAL DESCRIPTION Has long been a collector's item, and specimens were fetching $3–4 even in the 1800s. The shell's exquisite appearance results from each whorl being sculptured by coloured spiral beading to produce red and white dots, which contrast with a spiral band of lavender above the suture. The background is yellowish-brown. It occurs offshore at depths from 3 to 60ft.
OCCURRENCE Alaska to southern California.

1in
2.5cm

CITTARIUM PICA

MAGPIE SHELL

GENERAL DESCRIPTION This well-known species, with its thick, heavy shell traversed by striking, wavy black and cream bands, has a wide umbilicus. It has a circular, greenish-black, horny operculum. The species is found in subtidal rocky areas, where it is collected as an ingredient for soup.
OCCURRENCE Caribbean.

3in
7cm

LISCHKEA IMPERIALIS

IMPERIAL TOP SHELL

GENERAL DESCRIPTION This is an extremely rare species. The thin, rather dirty-looking beige outer surface contrasts with the highly iridescent pearly interior. The five or six whorls are decorated by four or five rows of spiny nodules. It occurs at depths between 200 and 1000ft. and is sometimes caught in fish or lobster traps. The shell illustrated was obtained from off Carlisle Bay, Barbados, at a depth of 1000ft.
OCCURRENCE Off Florida and the Caribbean.

2in
5cm

Family TURBINIDAE Turban shells

Turban shells contain several hundred species, which are divided into three subfamilies, the dolphin shells or Angariinae, the true turbans or Turbininae and the star shells or Astraeinae. In general the shells are medium to large, and are solid and top shaped. They may or may not bear long, curved spines. The interior is pearly, and the columella is smooth. The operculum is normally solid and calcareous. The species are herbivores, and they occur in warm inter- and subtidal waters among seaweed or on rocky or coral reefs.

ANGARIA TYRIA

TYRIA DELPHINULA

GENERAL DESCRIPTION The tyria delphinula belongs to the dolphin shells and, like the other members of the subfamily, it has a thin and corneous operculum. The shells are highly variable in form, but they have well-developed spines. This species is found on shallow coral reefs. The larger of the shells illustrated was obtained from off north-west Australia; the smaller one probably comes from the Philippines.
OCCURRENCE South-west Pacific; Australia.

3in
7cm

Families PHASIONELLIDAE and TRICOLIIDAE Pheasant shells

Pheasant shells possess smooth, brightly colored exteriors, which occur in a wide range of patterns and colors. They differ from trochids and turbans in having a porcellaneous, non-pearly interior. The pear-shaped aperture has a chalky but smooth operculum. Most species are vegetarian, and are widely distributed in temperate and warm waters.

PHASIANELLA AUSTRALIS

AUSTRALIAN PHEASANT

GENERAL DESCRIPTION The Australian pheasant shell, which is also sometimes known as the painted lady, exhibits considerable variation in color and pattern, as can be seen from the examples illustrated. The early apical whorls are not normally patterned. This, the largest and perhaps most attractive of the pheasant shells, is worthy of a place in any collection. The species may be found among seaweed in shallow waters around south Australia and Tasmania.
OCCURRENCE South Australia; Tasmania.

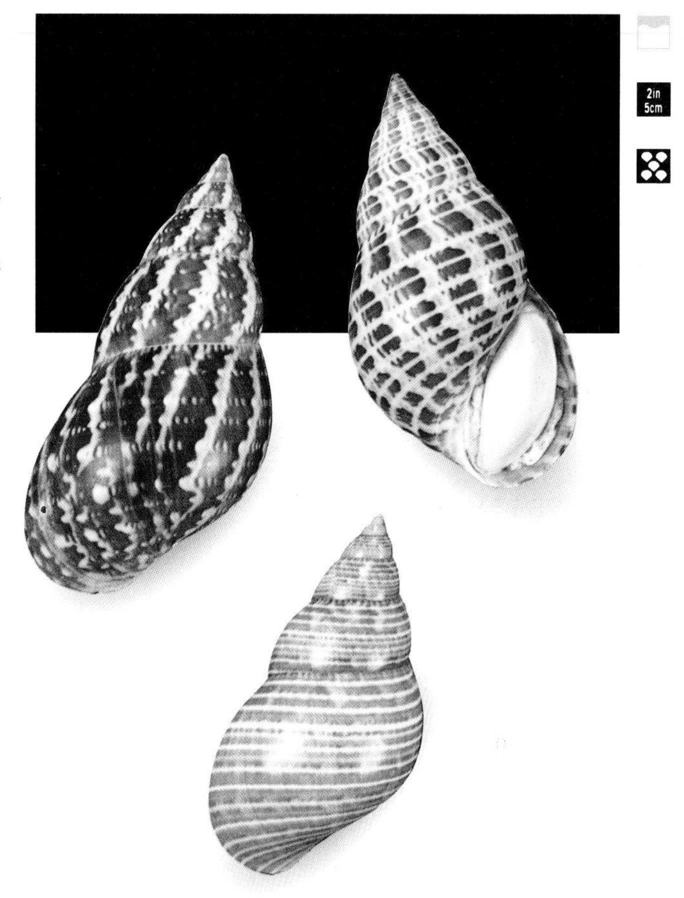

2in
5cm

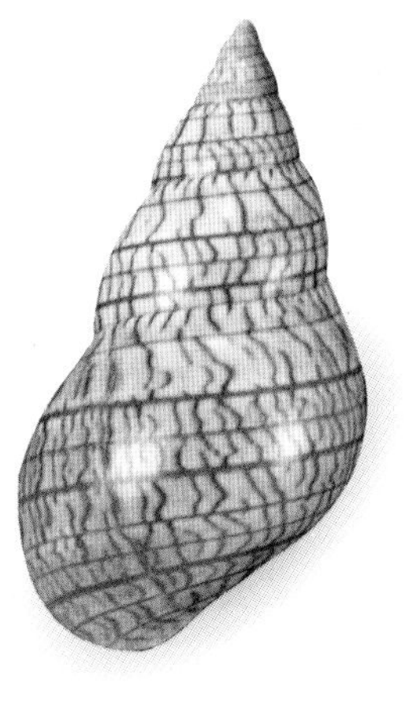

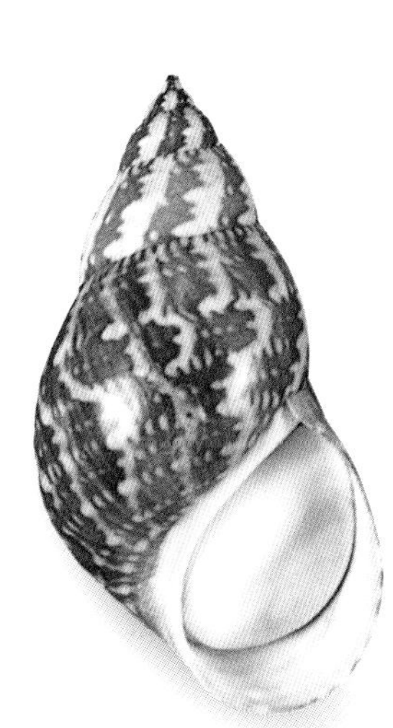

Superfamily NERITOIDEA

Family NERITIDAE Nerites

These small to medium, thick and rather short-spired shells have a thickened outer lip, which is often toothed. The umbilicus is absent. They have a calcareous operculum, which has a tooth-like projection on its inner surface. They are herbivorous. Nerites are mostly found in the intertidal zone, with some species occurring in brackish or fresh water. There are about 50 species in all.

SMARAGDIA VIRIDIS

EMERALD NERITE

GENERAL DESCRIPTION This minute species is deservedly popular among collectors, for its bright green coloration is attractively crossed by numerous fine white axial lines. The spire is low, and the body whorl is greatly enlarged. It lives in shallow water, especially on eel-grass beds.
OCCURRENCE South-east Florida; West Indies; Bermuda.

¼in 0.7cm

Superfamily LITTORINOIDEA

Family LITTORINIDAE Periwinkles

Periwinkles are small to medium-sized shells that are found throughout the world. There are at least 50 species, although some authorities say there are 100. They have a circular, thin, horny operculum but no umbilicus. All are vegetarians, feeding on seaweed and other algae. The sexes are separate, the females shedding their eggs directly into water or laying gelatinous egg masses.

1in 2.5cm

LITTORINA LITTOREA

COMMON PERIWINKLE

GENERAL DESCRIPTION The common periwinkle has a robust, rounded shell, with a rather short spire. It is gray in color and may exhibit fine spiral striations. The aperture and columella are white and smooth, and the corneous operculum is dark brown. It occurs among seaweed on rocky shores and is in great demand for food.
OCCURRENCE West Europe; north-east North America.

1in 2.5cm

LITTORINA SCABRA ANGULIFERA

ANGULATE PERIWINKLE

GENERAL DESCRIPTION This species appears to have two color forms. Shells that come from the Caribbean are generally yellowish or white and are mottled with light and dark brown streaks. Australian specimens, such as the examples from Yeppoon, Queensland, illustrated here, tend to be uniform browns, pinks or yellows, and they are lighter in weight with sharp spiral ribs.
OCCURRENCE South-east United States to Brazil; Bermuda; Queensland, Australia.

Superfamily CERITHIOIDEA

Family CERITHIIDAE Cerith shells

All species are vegetarian. The small to medium, elongated shells are often spirally striated or nodular. The aperture is set at an oblique angle and extends as a recurved siphonal canal. The thin, horny operculum is subcircular and has only a few whorls. Ceriths are mainly distributed in the tropics in intertidal and shallow subtidal areas, where they are found on seaweed or among coral debris, feeding on algae and detritus. A few species are found in the cooler waters off Europe.

CERITHIUM CUMINGI

CUMMING'S CERITHIUM

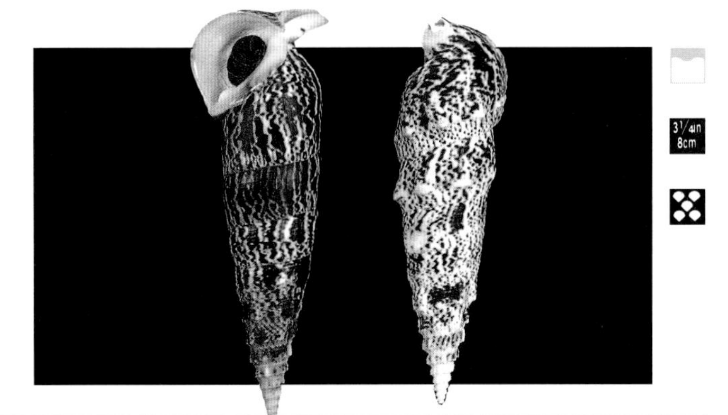

3¼in
8cm

GENERAL DESCRIPTION This species has a rather weakly nodulose shell, and the beige background is overlaid by flecks of darker brown. The shells can be locally common on sand or mud in shallow water. The two specimens shown here come from Port Hedland, on the west coast of Australia, and the right-hand example illustrates the typical cerithid aperture and operculum.
OCCURRENCE Indo-Pacific islands; north and west Australia.

Family CAMPANILIDAE Bell clappers

The bell clapper is the sole survivor of a formerly large family, which included over 700 species, including one species found in the deposits of the Paris Basin, *Campanula giganteum*, which grew to a length of at least 20in.

CAMPANILE SYMBOLICUM

BELL CLAPPER

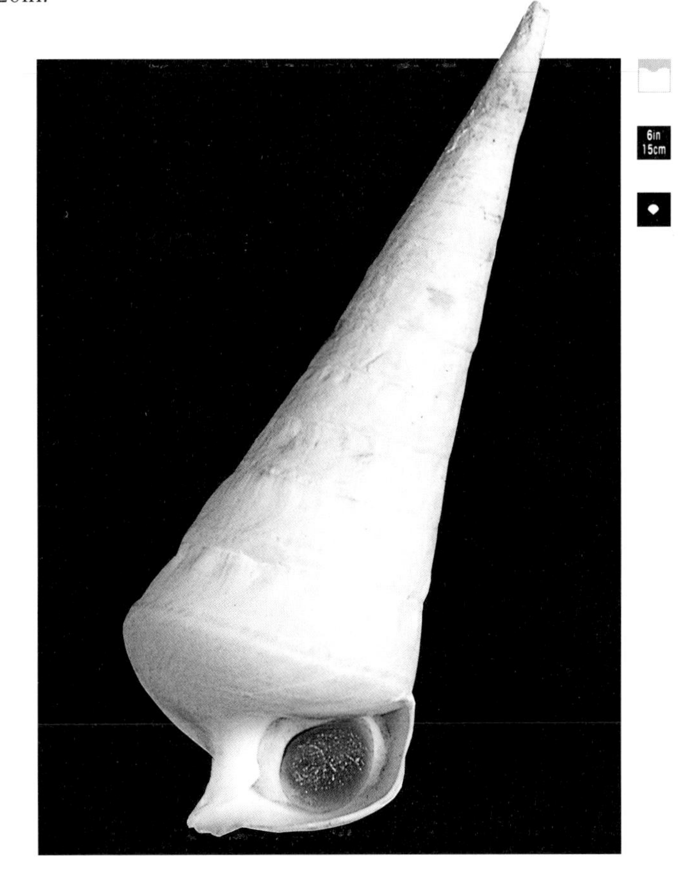

6in
15cm

GENERAL DESCRIPTION The bell clapper has an operculum, and its chalky-white shell has a fossil-like look. The whorls are devoid of patterning, but they are sculptured by faint spiral grooves. The apex of most specimens tends to be broken off. It is restricted to south-west Australia and is a vegetarian.
OCCURRENCE South-west Australia.

Family POTAMIDIDAE Horn shells

Horn shells, or mud creepers as they are also known, inhabit tropical muddy or brackish water areas, such as mangrove swamps, where they occur in large numbers, feeding on marine detritus and algae. The animal has a thin, horny, many-coiled, circular operculum.

TELESCOPIUM TELESCOPIUM

TELESCOPE SHELL

GENERAL DESCRIPTION The telescope shell is found in mangrove mud flats throughout the Indo-Pacific area. It is a popular shell with collectors, its tall, straight-sided outline giving it a top-like appearance. The whorls are spirally grooved, and the base of the columella is twisted like a corkscrew. These comparatively heavy shells are usually a uniform dark brown, with a contrasting ridge of light brown, gray or white.
OCCURRENCE Indo-Pacific.

Family TURRITELLIDAE Screw shells

There are more than 100 species of screw shells distributed throughout the world. They inhabit sandy and muddy offshore waters, where they feed upon marine detritus and algae. The animal has a chitinous operculum and no siphonal canal, and the shells are remarkable for their shape rather than their color.

TURRITELLA TEREBRA

COMMON SCREW SHELL

GENERAL DESCRIPTION The common screw shell, or tower screw shell, as it is sometimes known, occurs in the sandy, subtidal muds of the Indo-Pacific area. They may be up to 30 whorls, which are ornamented with a series of fine, rounded spiral ribs. The shell is normally pale to dark brown in color. The aperture is round, and the horny operculum is thin, circular and multispiral, with a central nucleus.
OCCURRENCE Indo-Pacific.

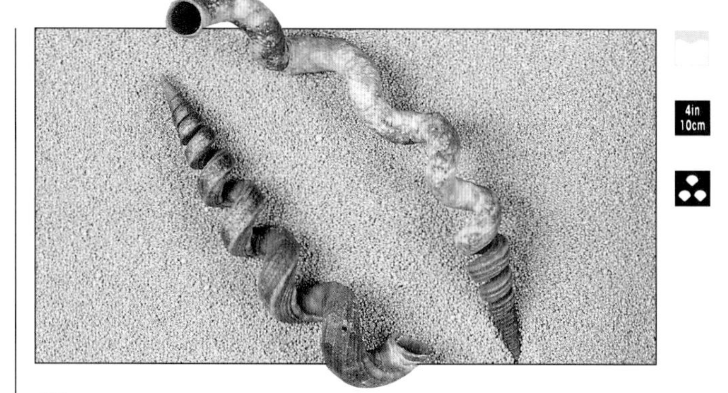

VERMICULARIA SPIRATA

CARIBBEAN WORM SHELL

GENERAL DESCRIPTION The Caribbean or West Indian worm shell derives its name from that fact that its normal coiled turritellid shell, which is very similar to a screw shell, becomes open and irregular after about six whorls, the resulting shell resembling certain marine worms. It occurs in south-east Florida, the West Indies and Bermuda, where it lives among shallow-water sponges.
OCCURRENCE South Florida; West Indies; Bermuda.

Superfamily STROMBOIDEA

Family APORRHAIDAE Pelican's foot shells

Pelican's foot shells occur in sandy mud in the deeper, cooler waters of the north Atlantic and Mediterranean. There are six living species, but many fossil forms are known. The name derives from the appearance of the flattened lip of the aperture of mature specimens. The operculum is small in all the species, but the number and shape of the extensions may vary widely, even within species.

APORRHAIS PESPELICANI

COMMON PELICAN'S FOOT

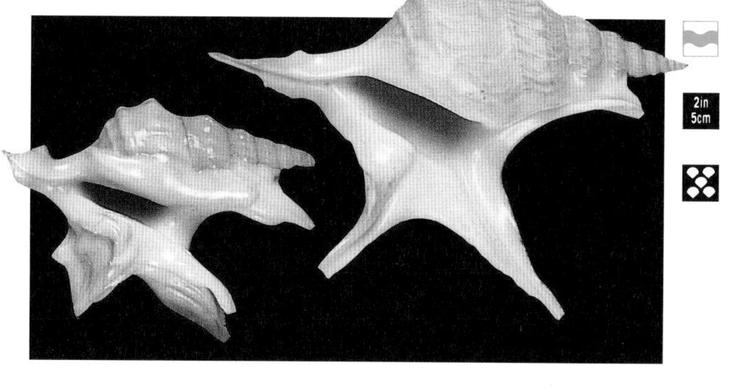

GENERAL DESCRIPTION The aperture of the common pelican's foot is extended to produce four finger-like outgrowths, resembling a bird's foot, hence its common name. The whorls are angular and nodulose. The shells are usually cream-colored or off-white, although some may be darker brown. The species is widely distributed, inhabiting deeper muddy offshore areas down to depths in excess of 450ft.

OCCURRENCE Mediterranean; north-west Europe.

Family STROMBIDAE Conch shells

Strombs (conches) and spider shells possess medium to large, thick shells, which are distinguished by the presence of the stromboid notch, a furrow towards the front end of the outer lip, through which the animal extends its stalked left eye. The shell may be smooth or ridged. Spider shells are so named because of the finger-like extensions of the aperture. Strombids inhabit intertidal and subtidal areas among sand, coral or mud, where they feed on algae and detritus. They possess a long, claw-like operculum, which is used to assist with locomotion.

LAMBIS LAMBIS

COMMON SPIDER CONCH

GENERAL DESCRIPTION This is one of the best known and most widely distributed species, with its finger-like extensions to the outer lip of the wide aperture. The shell of the female has longer spines and tends to be bigger; immature shells lack spines altogether. The larger of the shells illustrated is the rarer, orange form from west Australia. Usually, the shells are a creamy-white with orange-brown markings.

OCCURRENCE Indo-Pacific.

LAMBIS SCORPIUS SCORPIUS

SCORPION SPIDER CONCH

GENERAL DESCRIPTION This species, which is found on coral reefs, is popular with collectors, its irregular shape and striking coloration giving it a spectacular appearance. The nodular exterior is coarsely ribbed and is colored in various shades of brown, while the deep purple inner lip is also strongly ribbed. The spines, which are slender and crimped, are closed and flat.

OCCURRENCE Western Pacific.

Lambis chiragra chiragra

CHIRAGRA SPIDER CONCH

General description This familiar species has a large, thick, heavy shell. There are five characteristic slightly curved, finger-like projections, and the siphonal canal extends from the base of the columella, giving rise to a "sixth", straight spine. The white body whorl has irregular, lumpy, spiral ridges and is spotted with brown. The aperture may be pink, yellow, red or brown. It occurs in shallow sandy areas and on coral reefs.
Occurrence Indo-Pacific.

6in
15cm

Strombus gigas

QUEEN CONCH

General description This large, solid shell, reaches up to 9in. in length and with a wide, flaring lip. The aperture is colored in the most delicate shades of pink, while the cream-colored exterior is normally covered by a brownish periostracum. Immature shells do not have the flaring lip. It occurs in shallow water on sandy substrates. The species sometimes produces pink pearls.
Occurrence South Florida; Caribbean.

9in
23cm

Strombus lentiginosus

SILVER CONCH

General description The silver conch has a solid shell with a short, pointed spire and a body whorl bearing blunt nodules. The outer expanded lip, which is thickened and reflexed, is patterned by approximately eight broad, greyish-brown bands. The upper surface is a creamy white, mottled with orange-brown streaks and blotches. It occurs on coral sand and down to about 12ft.
Occurrence Indo-Pacific.

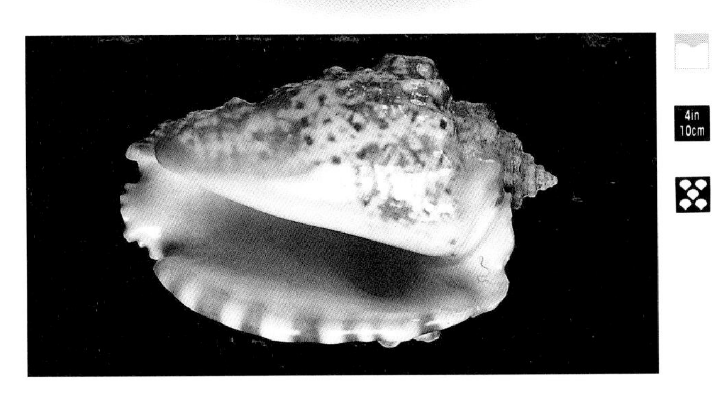

4in
10cm

Strombus mutabilis

MUTABLE CONCH

General description This is, as its name implies, a highly variable species. It has a large angular body whorl and a short spire. Both the aperture and the columella are ridged. Colour variations abound, but the aperture is normally orange to pink, with fine striations. It occurs in sandy, coral areas down to about 60ft.
Occurrence Tropical Indo-Pacific.

1in
2.5cm

STROMBUS VOMER

VOMER CONCH

GENERAL DESCRIPTION This slender shell, with its angular, coronated whorls and anterior finger-like extension to the aperture lip, is an uncommon species, much sought after by collectors. The upper surface is a pale cream mottled with reddish-brown, while the interior of the aperture is orange. It occurs on sand in shallow water.
OCCURRENCE South-west Pacific.

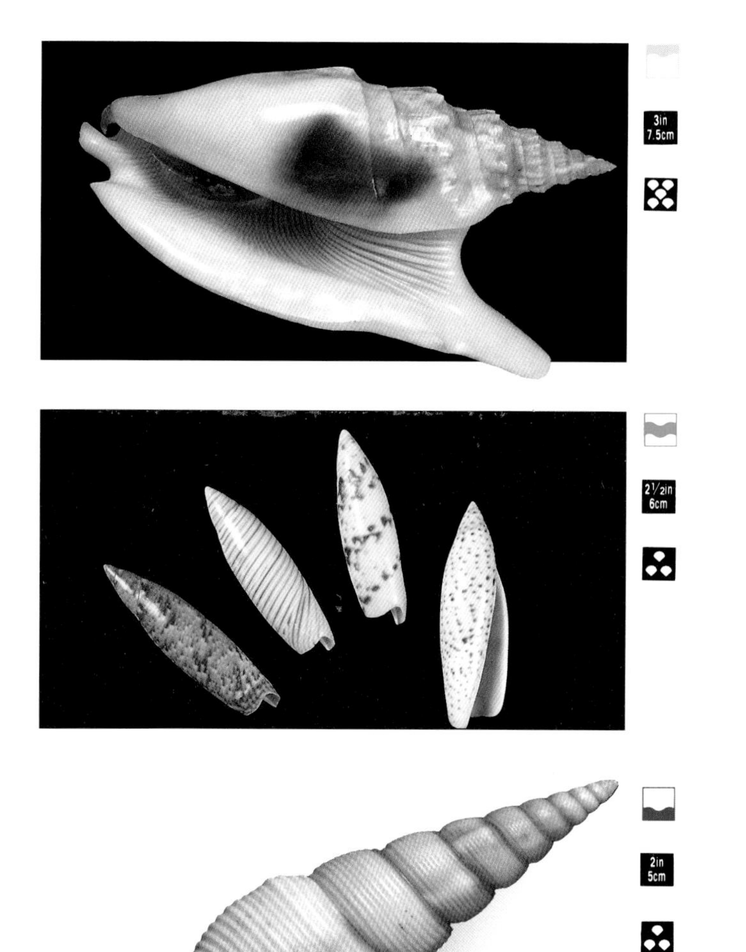

TEREBELLUM TEREBELLUM

LITTLE AUGER SHELL

GENERAL DESCRIPTION These slim, highly glossy shells are readily identified by their bullet-like appearance. Although it is a monotypic genus, the color and pattern variations within the species differ considerably, as can be seen from the examples illustrated. All the shells have an enlarged body whorl and short, straight-sided spire. The aperture is narrow. They inhabit shallow-water, sandy bays.
OCCURRENCE Indo-Pacific.

TIBIA POWISI

POWIS'S TIBIA

GENERAL DESCRIPTION The beautifully smooth apical whorls of Powis's tibia contrast strongly with the spirally ribbed later whorls. The spire is high, and the aperture is small, its white outer lip projecting to form five spine-like processes. The siphonal canal is extended to form a hollow spine. The shells range in color from pale beige to pale brown. This is a relatively scarce species, inhabiting moderately deep water.
OCCURRENCE South-west Pacific to Australia.

Superfamily CREPIDULOIDEA

Family CREPIDULIDAE Slipper, cup-and-saucer shells

The slipper shells and cup-and-saucer limpets have a worldwide distribution. They have no operculum but possess either a shelf-like process or small internal cup to protect the animal's soft organs.. They live on rocks or on the backs of other shelled creatures, where they filter-feed on vegetable matter.

CREPIDULA FORNICATA

COMMON ATLANTIC SLIPPER

GENERAL DESCRIPTION The common Atlantic slipper inhabits the eastern United States and north-east Atlantic coasts, having been introduced to UK waters with oysters. The light brown, or pinkish-beige mottled shell is a flattened boat shape, and it has an extremely large body whorl. It may be either smooth or ridged. The aperture is partially closed by a white, shelf-like partition. It is a subtidal, rock-dwelling species, which lives in chain-like colonies.
OCCURRENCE Eastern United States; north-west Europe.

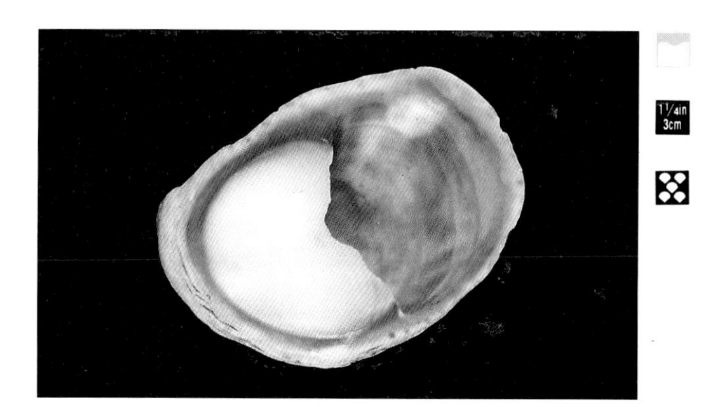

Superfamily XENOPHOROIDEA

Family XENOPHORIDAE Carrier shells

Carrier shells of the genus *Xenophora* are among the most fascinating of all molluscs and may, perhaps, be regarded as the true "original shell collectors" because most species cement sea-floor debris such as coral or shells to their own shells. It is not known if this bizarre behaviour is to provide a means of camouflage, to provide strength and rigidity, or simply to prevent the creatures from sinking into a muddy substrate. They possess a corneous operculum and inhabit tropical and warm seas.

STELLARIA SOLARIS

SUNBURST CARRIER SHELL

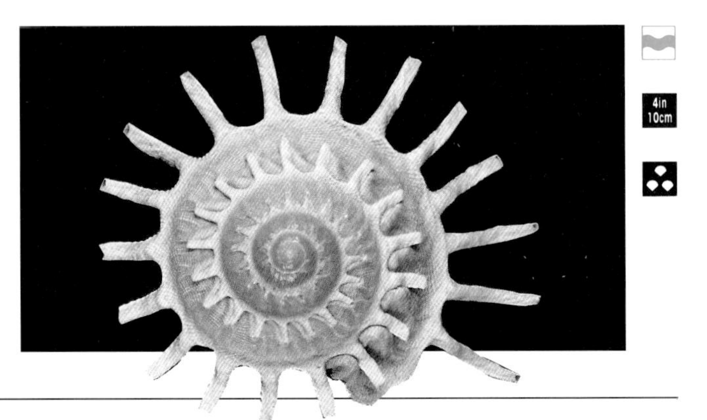

4in 10cm

GENERAL DESCRIPTION The cream-coloured sunburst carrier shell is atypical since it does not usually ornament itself by cementing coral or shell material to its shell, although the apical whorls are covered with debris. It makes up for this by producing the radiating hollow spines that give it its outline. These spines touch but are not attached to the underlying whorl. It occurs offshore to considerable depths.

OCCURRENCE Indo-Pacific.

Superfamily CYPRAEOIDEA

Family CYPRAEIDAE Cowry shells

The Cypraeidae inhabit the tropical waters of the Indo-Pacific. They are among the most collectable and popular of all shells, being brightly coloured, glossy and smooth. The aperture of adult specimens is slit-like and generally "toothed", and it appears to be on the lower surface since the body whorl grows over and encases the shell spire. There are more than 200 different species, all of which are omnivorous, but there are numerous local variations in size and color.

7½in 19cm

CYPRAEA CERVUS

ATLANTIC DEER COWRY

GENERAL DESCRIPTION The largest in the genus, but it has become scarce, through over-collecting, and it is now unusual to find specimens larger than 6in. The shell is surprisingly light. It is a rich brown color, with paler gray spots, which cease at the margins. There is a wide dorsal line. The interior is a pale lavender. The aperture bears prominent, dark brown teeth. It can be found from low-tide level to about 60ft.

OCCURRENCE North Carolina to Cuba; Bermuda.

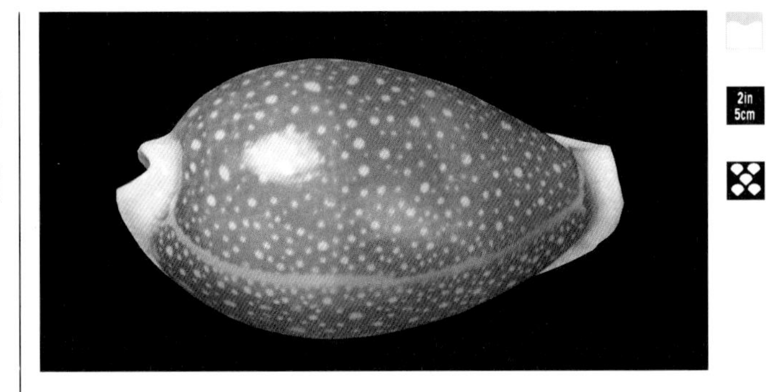

2in 5cm

CYPRAEA MILIARIS

MILLET COWRY

GENERAL DESCRIPTION This shallow-water species, with its slightly humped dorsum, is relatively common throughout the west Pacific as well as off north Australia. The shell, a pale mustard yellow, is covered by small irregular spots. There is a clear dorsal line, and the base and margins are white. The aperture bears coarse teeth. It grows up to 2in. but average specimens measure just over 1in.

OCCURRENCE West Pacific; north Australia.

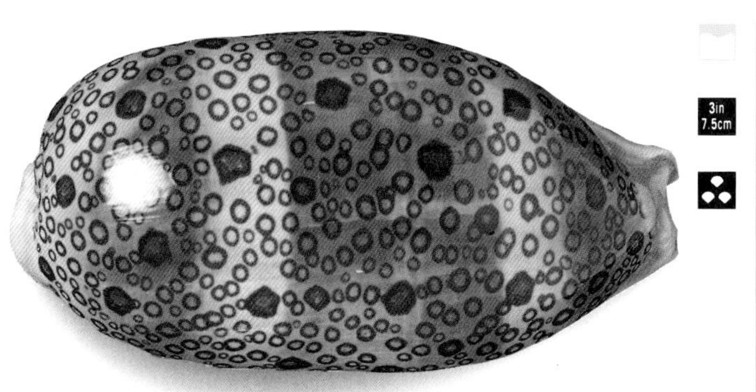

CYPRAEA ARGUS

EYED COWRY

GENERAL DESCRIPTION This is an unmistakable species. The upper surface of the parallel-sided shell is covered with irregular rings or "eyes" and dark brown blotches on a beige ground. The aperture, which is wider at the front than at the rear, is fringed with moderately coarse teeth. The base is pale brown with two distinctive dark bands. It inhabits coral reefs in the Indian Ocean and south-west Pacific, including Australia, but is uncommon.
OCCURRENCE Indian Ocean; south-west Pacific.

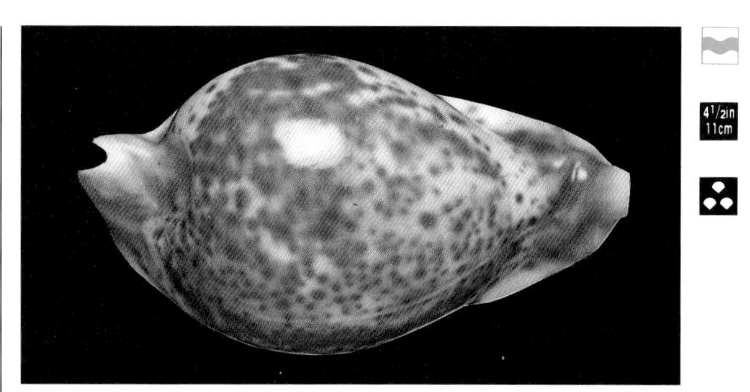

CYPRAEA HESITATA

UMBILICATE COWRY

GENERAL DESCRIPTION This strikingly shaped cowry, with its humped dorsum and extended anterior and posterior canals, is found in several forms, and its taxonomic status is, therefore, uncertain. The shell is basically off-white, covered in light brown blotches. The teeth are short and quite fine. It occurs offshore in south-east Australia and was once considered rare; it is now trawled in fairly reasonable numbers, however.
OCCURRENCE South-east Australia.

Family OVULIDAE Egg shells

The false or egg cowries are similar in shape to their close relations, the true cowries, but they tend to have few or no apertural teeth. They inhabit tropical seas, most being found in Indo-Pacific waters, where they live among colonial sponges, soft corals, sea fans and gorgonian corals.

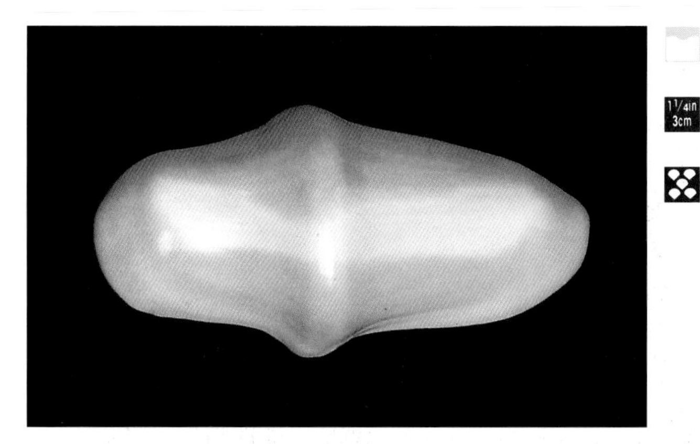

CYPHOMA GIBBOSUM

FLAMINGO TONGUE

GENERAL DESCRIPTION The flamingo tongue occurs in shallow waters on sea whip and gorgonian corals from the south-east United States to Brazil as well as Bermuda. It is a relatively common species, which has a thick, rather solid shell with a central raised ridge. The shell is a pale apricot color, and the aperture and base are creamy white. The aperture is devoid of teeth.
OCCURRENCE South-eastern United States to Brazil; Bermuda.

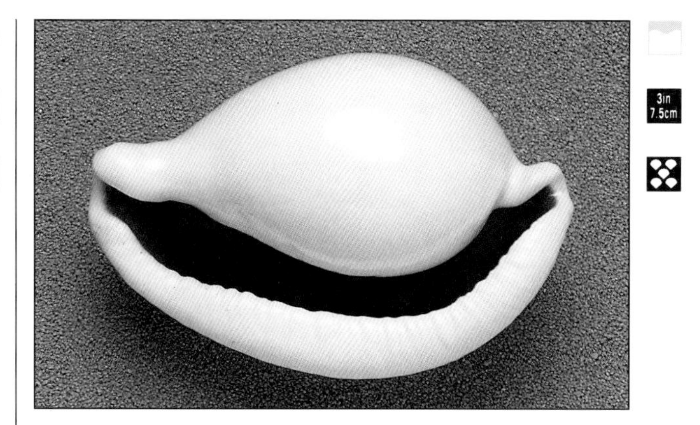

OVULA OVUM

COMMON EGG SHELL

GENERAL DESCRIPTION This well-known shell, with its attractive, glossy white dorsum and orange-brown interior, occurs throughout the Indo-Pacific, including Australia, where it lives in shallow-water reefs among black sponges. The aperture curves smoothly over its entire length, and the lip is coarsely ridged on the underside. It is often used to decorate native canoes as well as being used for fish and octopus lures.
OCCURRENCE Indo-Pacific.

Family TRIVIIDAE Allied cowries

Members of the Triviidae family resemble small cowries, but their shells are less glossy and are traversed by radial ridges. The animal has no operculum. The majority occur in the tropics and can be found beneath stones and rocks at low tide feeding on ascidians and sponges.

TRIVIA MONACHA

EUROPEAN COWRY

GENERAL DESCRIPTION The European cowry, which is also known as the bean cowry, has a small, solid shell, which is distinctly ribbed. The dorsal surface is pale beige or gray and bears three darker spots. The base is white. It inhabits the north-east Atlantic and Mediterranean where it is to be found feeding on encrusting sponge under rocks exposed at extreme low tide. The shells illustrated are from Portugal.
OCCURRENCE North-east Atlantic; Mediterranean.

1/2in 1cm

Superfamily NATICOIDEA

Family NATICIDAE Moon or necklace shells

Moon or necklace shells are found throughout the world. The species are all carnivorous, feeding mainly on other molluscs and crustacea by rasping a circular hole in the shell of their prey by means of a file-like radula. The glossy shells range in size from small to medium, and they have short spires and large body whorls with large, semicircular apertures. The animal has an operculum and lives in sand or mud from the intertidal zone to deep water.

4in 10cm

EUSPIRA LEWISI

LEWIS'S MOON

GENERAL DESCRIPTION This is the largest species in the family, and specimens can grow to 4in. in length. It has a thick, heavy, chalky white shell, but the interior and lip are pale brown. There is an open umbilicus. It lives in sandy areas and can be found in the intertidal zone and subtidal waters. The specimen shown here was collected in Puget Sound, Washington.
OCCURRENCE British Columbia to Baja California.

1in 2.5cm

NATICA ALAPAPILIONIS

BUTTERFLY MOON

GENERAL DESCRIPTION The butterfly moon has a tiny spire and a large, globose body whorl, which is decorated by four distinct spiral rows of brown dashes on a pale beige background. The aperture and surrounding area are white. The shell illustrated was obtained from off Thailand.
OCCURRENCE Indo-Pacific.

NATICA VIOLACEA

VIOLET MOON

GENERAL DESCRIPTION The distinctive violet and tan coloration has made this shell extremely popular with collectors. It has a globose body whorl, a rounded spire and a small umbilicus. The aperture is white. It may be found in shallow water down to about 70ft. and the shells shown here were collected from Kwajalein Atoll in the Marshall Islands in the western Pacific Ocean.

OCCURRENCE Indo-Pacific.

Superfamily TONNOIDEA

Family TONNIDAE Tun shells

Tuns or cask shells comprise a small family, but the shells are medium to large. The thin, globose shells have short spires and inflated body whorls, which are spirally corded and covered by a thin periostracum. The aperture is expanded and normally has a crenulate outer lip. The umbilicus is deep and there is no operculum. They are mainly tropical creatures, inhabiting deep water where they feed carnivorously on fish, sea urchins, sea cucumbers and crustacea.

TONNA PERDIX

PARTRIDGE TUN

GENERAL DESCRIPTION The high, pointed spire readily distinguishes this species from other tuns. The body whorl bears flattened spiral ribbing and is cream with a series of brown squares and dashes. The outer lip is thickened but not crenulate. The name is said to derive from the resemblance of the shell's coloration to the plumage of the European partridge. The shell, although large, is comparatively fragile. It is found offshore in sandy areas throughout Indo-Pacific waters.

OCCURRENCE Indo-Pacific.

TONNA SULCOSA

BANDED TUN

GENERAL DESCRIPTION The brown banding on the cream background has given this species its common name. The apex is a darker, purple colour. The lower edge of the aperture is dentate, and there is a deep siphonal canal. Live examples are covered with a dark brown periostracum. The specimen shown here was obtained in the central Philippines.

OCCURRENCE Indo-Pacific.

Family FICIDAE Fig shells

These shells get their name from their characteristic shape, reminiscent of figs, with a short spire enveloped in the large, inflated body whorl. The thin outer lip is curved, and there is an elongated siphonal canal. The shell surface is crossed by a series of raised vertical and spiral ridges to form a reticulate decoration. There is no operculum. They inhabit tropical seas, occurring in sand or rubble from shallow to deep water, where they feed on sea urchins and other echinoderms.

FICUS SUBINTERMEDIA

UNDERLINED FIG

GENERAL DESCRIPTION This is one of the more rubust members of the group. The coarse reticulate decoration, in medium to dark brown, contrasts with the four or five cream spiral bands, which enclose darker spots. The aperture runs almost the whole length of the body whorl. The interior is usually a pale mauve, although it is sometimes grayish-brown. It occurs in shallow water with sand or mud bottoms.

OCCURRENCE Indo-Pacific.

4in
10cm

Family CASSIDAE Helmet or bonnet shells

This is a large family, containing some 80 living species. Helmet or bonnet shells are medium to large in size, solid and often heavy. They have a short spire and an inflated body whorl, which may be sculptured by a series of nodular ribs. The aperture is long and often has a thickened, toothed outer lip, which may be expanded. The operculum is thin, semicircular and horny. Helmet shells prefer warmer seas, where they burrow into sand from the intertidal zone to deep water. They feed on echinoderms.

CASSIS FLAMMEA

FLAME HELMET

GENERAL DESCRIPTION This shallow-water dweller has a low spire and a nodulose body whorl, especially on the shoulders. The cream-colored aperture has a triangular outline, and the outer lip has a series of dark blotches. The main body whorl is cream colored, mottled with light and dark brown. The siphonal canal is twisted and upturned.

OCCURRENCE Bermuda; Florida; Caribbean.

5in
13cm

CYPRAECASSIS RUFA

BULLMOUTH HELMET

GENERAL DESCRIPTION This thick, solid, heavy, reddish-brown shell is often known as the cameo shell. Large quantities are exported from Africa to Italy to be used in the manufacture of cameos, which are produced by selective carving of the different shell layers. The present industry began about 150 years ago. The spire is low, and the aperture large. The shell has rounded dorsal nodules, and the lip is thick and dentate. It is found near coral reefs.

OCCURRENCE Indo-Pacific.

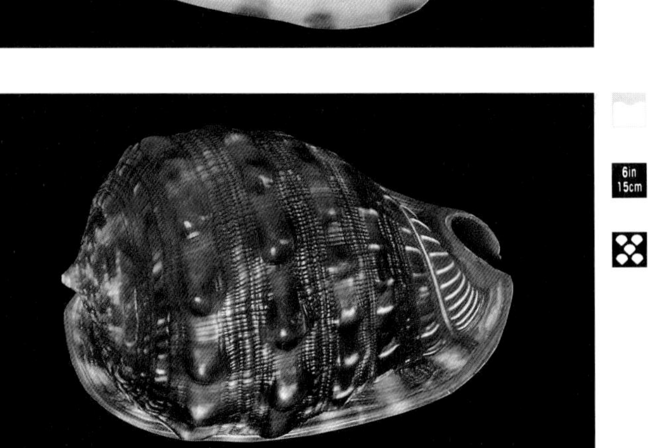

6in
15cm

PHALIUM AREOLA

CHEQUERED BONNET

GENERAL DESCRIPTION This attractive ovate shell has a smooth, glossy surface, which is decorated with a series of rich orange-brown squares. The spire is medium sized and has several raised varices. The apertural lip is thin and folded, and there are about 20 sharp teeth on the outer edge. It occurs in sandy mud in intertidal and offshore waters.
OCCURRENCE West Indo-Pacific.

3in 7.5cm

Family **RANELLIDAE Tritons**

Tritons have small to large, solid shells with strong varices, spiral cords and nodular sculpture. Living specimens are covered in a thick, often hairy, periostracum. The outer lip is thickened and is often toothed or crenulate. The columella is plicate, while the operculum is thick and horny. Tritons have a wide distribution, possibly because some species produce free-swimming veliger larvae, which can survive for over three months. They occur on coral and rocky reefs from intertidal to deep water.

RANELLA OLEARIUM

WANDERING TRITON

GENERAL DESCRIPTION This is one of the most widely distributed species. Although the shells vary in size, thickness and color, the constant shape, rounded body whorl and tall spire with a pair of oblique varices down each side, make them easy to identify. The aperture is round, with a small canal at the top, and there are approximately 17 teeth on the outer lip.
OCCURRENCE Caribbean; Mediterranean; Africa; Australia; New Zealand.

7in 18cm

CHARONIA TRITONIS

TRUMPET TRITON

GENERAL DESCRIPTION This is the largest and best known species in the family, with its tall, elegant spire, rounded whorls and distinctive coloration. The aperture is a deep orange, and the large lip has white channels between the teeth on the outer edge. As its common name suggests, it has often been used as a trumpet by drilling a hole near the apex into which a mouthpiece is then inserted. It occurs on coral reefs in shallow water.
OCCURRENCE Indo-Pacific.

16in 40cm

CYMATIUM PARTHENOPEUM

NEAPOLITAN TRITON

GENERAL DESCRIPTION Another widely dispersed species, the Neapolitan triton has a solidly built shell with heavily corded whorls and a medium spire. The wide aperture has six teeth on its thickened outer lip and a ridged columella wall. It occurs offshore down to a depth of over 200ft. Live examples have a densely bristled periostracum, which masks the pale brown shell with its darker brown varices and aperture.
OCCURRENCE Worldwide in tropical and warm seas.

4in 10cm

Family BURSIDAE Frog shells

Frog shells are superficially very like tritons, but they may be distinguished by the short, distinct groove at the upper corner of the aperture. The shell is thick and heavy, with angular whorls sculptured by nodules and varices. The outer lip is thick and crenulate. The operculum is thick and horny and has a marginal nucleus. They live in sand or mud or on coral or rocky reefs in shallow water, feeding on marine worms.

BURSA THOMAE

ST THOMAS FROG SHELL

GENERAL DESCRIPTION This is a small species. There are a few nodular whorls, and the varices are aligned. The lips are crenulate, and the pale lavender color of the aperture contrasts with the overall pale beige of the shell body. A fairly common shell, it lives on or under rocks down to about 250ft.
OCCURRENCE South Carolina to Brazil; Cape Verde Islands.

1in 2.5cm

Superfamily EPITONIOIDEA

Family EPITONIIDAE Wentletraps

Wentletraps are found throughout the world, and there are about 200 living species of these exquisitely ornamented shells. The small to medium-sized shells are often loosely coiled and decorated by prominent axial varices or cancellate sculpture, and the common name derives from the Dutch word for a spiral staircase. The circular aperture has a thickened lip, and the operculum is horny. Wentletraps occur in shallow to deep water, feeding on corals and sea anemones.

1¼in 3cm

EPITONIUM CLATHRUM

COMMON EUROPEAN WENTLETRAP

GENERAL DESCRIPTION Dead shells are often found in shell debris among rocks on the southern coasts of the UK. It is a small, narrow but robust shell, with many suture-joined varices, which hold together the rounded whorls. The colors vary from white to tan, traversed by a series of fine brown spiral bands, particularly evident on the varices.
OCCURRENCE North-east Atlantic; Mediterranean.

2½in 6cm

EPITONIUM SCALARE

PRECIOUS WENTLETRAP

GENERAL DESCRIPTION Once considered rare and greatly coveted, this species has recently been obtained in relatively large numbers by dredging off Taiwan and the Philippines. The large, openly coiled shell is white or cream in color. The loose, rounded whorls are separated by strong, blade-like varices, which are connected to each other at the open suture. The wide umbilicus is open. It occurs from extreme low water downwards to about 100ft. Tradition has it that this species was so rare that the Chinese produced replicas of it in rice paste in the 18th century.
OCCURRENCE Japan to south-west Pacific.

Family **JANTHINIDAE Purple sea snails**

The distinctive violet coloration of members of this family gives them their common name, and also makes them popular with collectors. The small to medium-sized shells are thin and fragile. The inflated body whorl, expanded aperture and absence of an operculum are suited to the pelagic existence of these sea snails, which float upside down on the ocean surface by means of a "raft", composed of mucus-enveloped air bubbles, feeding on pelagic jellyfish and mollusc larvae.

JANTHINA JANTHINA

COMMON JANTHINA

1½in 4cm

GENERAL DESCRIPTION This, the largest member of the family, exhibits considerable variation in shell shape, but because it is so difficult to observe these animals, the reason for this variation is unclear. Some shells have a low, rounded spire, while others have a medium spire with almost flat-sided whorls. The body whorl, however, is always large and inflated. After severe storms shells periodically get washed up on shores worldwide. The examples illustrated are from northern Queensland.
OCCURRENCE Worldwide in tropical seas.

Superfamily MURICOIDEA

Family **MURICIDAE Rock shells**

There are more than 1000 species of rock shell distributed worldwide, and they range in size from small to large. They have high, pointed spires, and the siphonal canal may be extended as a long spiny process. The oval aperture may have dentate lips. There is a thick, horny operculum. The whorls may be smooth, nodular or spiny, or they may have strong varices. Rock shells occur on rocks, coral, sand or mud from intertidal to deep subtidal, where they feed on molluscs, barnacles, corals and marine worms.

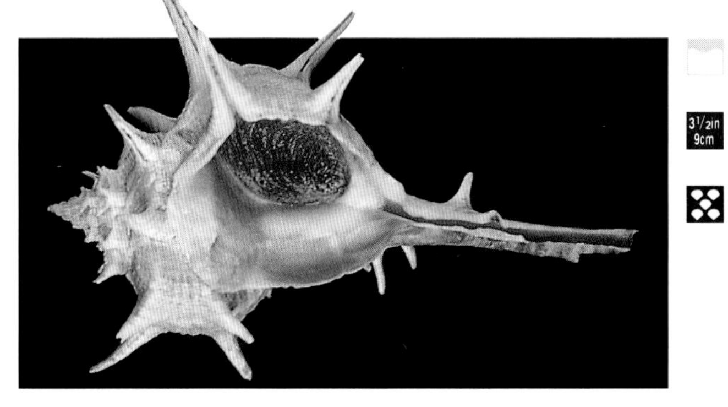

3½in 9cm

BOLINUS BRANDARIS

PURPLE DYE MUREX

GENERAL DESCRIPTION This well-known Mediterranean species is one of the two shellfish used in Roman times in the production of the purple dye, Tyrian purple. The club-shaped shell varies in sculpture, and there may or may not be spines. It is generally pale brown with a richer brown interior. It occurs in sandy areas in shallow subtidal waters.
OCCURRENCE Mediterranean, north-west Africa.

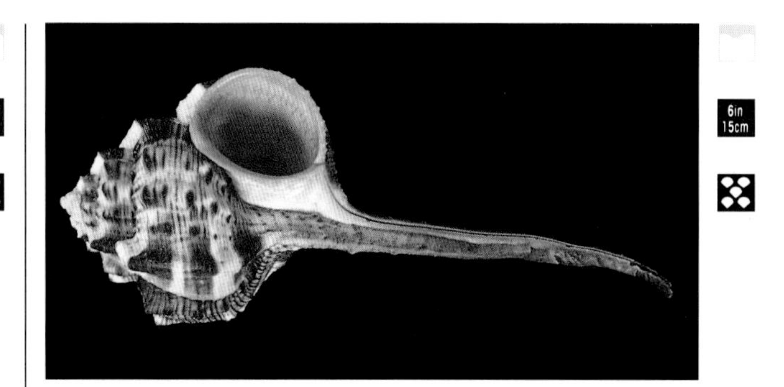

6in 15cm

HAUSTELLUM HAUSTELLUM

SNIPE'S BILL MUREX

GENERAL DESCRIPTION The distinctive shape gives this species its common name – the side view is thought to resemble a bird's head. It is the largest in its genus, and is a low-spired, solid shell. There is a bulbous, enlarged body whorl, with a long, straight siphonal canal, which may be recurved at the anterior. The whorls are decorated with fine spiral cords and low, rounded nodules. The shell is colored in shades of brown, which contrast with the pink aperture. It can be found in shallow water.
OCCURRENCE Indo-Pacific.

3in 7.5cm

Hexaplex trunculus

TRUNCULUS MUREX

General description This species, sometimes known as the trunk murex, is confined to the Mediterranean and is the other species used in the production of Tyrian purple. The two specimens shown here illustrate the variations in shape that can occur, but the color of the banded shades of brown is fairly constant. The body whorl is large, and the spire is pointed. It is readily distinguished from *Bolinus brandaris* by its short, broad siphonal canal.
Occurrence Mediterranean.

6in 15cm

Murex pecten

VENUS COMB MUREX

General description This is one of the most attractive of the spiny murexes. Its long, often curved spines look so fragile that it is amazing that these exquisite shells can survive intact. The whorls are rounded and bulbous and bear many spiral cords. The shell is pale beige to mid-brown, but the aperture is white. It occurs in sandy offshore areas. The shell illustrated came from the central Philippines.
Occurrence Indo-Pacific.

2in 5cm

Ocinebra erinaceus

STING WINKLE

General description The oyster drill or common sting winkle is a very variable shell. It has a pointed apex and large body whorl, with up to nine varices, covered with fluted scales. The color varies through shades of brown, but the aperture is normally white. It occurs in subtidal areas, where it feeds on bivalves, and it is considered a pest in oyster beds.
Occurrence North-west Europe to west Africa.

1¼in 3cm

Drupa morum

PURPLE DRUPE

General description This species is easily recognized by its flat spire, large, nodular body whorl and purple aperture, which is strongly dentate. The outer lip of the aperture extends to form spines. It is whitish-gray with black nodules. This is a relatively common shell, which can be found on most tropical, intertidal coral reefs, feeding on small invertebrates.
Occurrence Indo-Pacific.

PURPURA PATULA

WIDE-MOUTHED PURPURA

GENERAL DESCRIPTION This well-known shell has a large body whorl and a relatively small spire. The aperture is large, and the outer lip is slightly toothed. The exterior is sculptured with rows of blunt nodules and fine cords. The dull gray-brown exterior contrasts with the rich orange columella and grayish-white interior. It occurs on intertidal rocky cliffs. This species is still used by Central American Indians as a source of dye.
OCCURRENCE South-east Florida; West Indies.

NUCELLA LAPILLUS

ATLANTIC DOG WHELK

GENERAL DESCRIPTION The sturdy shell of this species is highly suitable for life on the wave-swept rocky shores of the Atlantic coasts. The shell may be smooth or covered by regularly placed, distinct, frill-like ribs. It feeds on barnacles and other molluscs, and the considerable variation in color and banding seen in these specimens from Cornwall, UK, may be caused by differences in its prey.
OCCURRENCE North-east United States; west Europe.

Family CORALLIOPHILIDAE Latiaxis shells

Latiaxis shells, with their exquisite shapes and delicate coloration, are greatly prized by collectors. The shells vary in size and shape, with short or long siphonal canals. The whorls may be smooth or covered with spines, but a brown, horny operculum is normally present. They differ from rock shells in shallow to deep water, feeding on corals and sea anemones.

BABELOMUREX SPINOSUS

SPINED LATIAXIS

GENERAL DESCRIPTION The spined latiaxis well deserves its common name, as can be seen from the specimen illustrated here, which was collected off south-west Taiwan. These delicate shells are off-white, cream or pale brown. They have a tall spire, angular whorls and a short, narrow, recurved canal. They are found in subtidal, offshore waters.
OCCURRENCE Japan to Philippines; Australia.

BABELOMUREX LISCHKEANUS

LISCHKE'S LATIAXIS

GENERAL DESCRIPTION This widespread species, with its pagoda-like outline, may vary from place to place, but the true beauty of its highly spinose spiral ridges and large, triangular shoulder spines cannot be fully appreciated until they are seen under a hand lens. The shells inhabit relatively deep water; the specimen illustrated was fished off Taiwan.
OCCURRENCE Japan; Philippines; Australia; New Zealand.

1½in 3.5cm

CORALLIOPHILA VIOLACEA

VIOLET CORAL SNAIL

GENERAL DESCRIPTION This globuse shell, with its large body whorl and low spire, is normally heavily encrusted, which makes it difficult to see as it shelters under coral. Fine spinal cords are visible on exposed parts. The deep purple aperture with its delicate spiral ridges is characteristic. This example was obtained from the central Philippines.
OCCURRENCE Indo-Pacific.

3in 7.5cm

RAPA RAPA

BUBBLE TURNIP

GENERAL DESCRIPTION This whelk is the largest of the turnips. It has a thin, fragile but large and globose shell with a short spire and a pointed apex that is almost lost in the body whorl. It lives embedded in the soft corals on which it feeds. It is normally a uniform white, but occasional orange forms occur. The aperture is always white. The whorls are decorated by spiral shell ribbing. The animal's thin, horny operculum is too small to be an effective closure for the aperture.
OCCURRENCE South-west Pacific.

Family BUCCINIDAE Whelks

Members of the whelk family have small to large globose shells with tapered spires. The aperture is expanded and smooth and often has a thickened outer lip. The whorls are smooth or sculptured with radial ribs and spiral cords. The siphonal canal varies from short to long, and a thin, horny, brown operculum is present. They occur among rocks, coral or in sand from the intertidal area to deep cold water, feeding on bivalves, worms and carrion.

3in 7.5cm

BUCCINUM UNDATUM

EDIBLE EUROPEAN WHELK

GENERAL DESCRIPTION This well-known species, sometimes known as the common northern whelk, has been used for food for centuries. It lives at various depths, from shallow to deep water. It is variable in shape, but is normally gray-brown in colour. Live shells are covered by a greenish-brown periostracum. It feeds chiefly on carrion and often comes up in crab-pots. Left-handed examples occasionally occur.
OCCURRENCE North-east United States; west Europe.

4in 10cm

NEPTUNEA TABULATA

TABLED NEPTUNE

GENERAL DESCRIPTION The distinctive, shelf-like, shouldered whorls readily identify this deep-water species, which lives at depths around 1300ft. It is a uniform yellowish-white in color. The spire is high, and the body whorl is long. The elongated aperture has a sharp-edged outer lip.
OCCURRENCE West Canada to California.

Phos senticosus

PHOS WHELK

General description This attractive little species, which is also sometimes known as the thorny thos, can be found in tropical tidal sand and mud flats down to about 30ft. The strong axial ribs are spinose where they are crossed by spiral cords. The siphonal canal is short, and there are up to four indistinct ridges at the base of the columella. Specimens vary in color from cream to brown, and they may be banded. The aperture may be white or lavender.

Occurrence Indo-Pacific.

1½in
4cm

Family COLUMBELLIDAE Dove shells

This large family of mainly small, smooth, solid and brightly colored shells occurs in intertidal to deep waters of warm and tropical seas. The shell aperture is long and thickened with a denticulate outer lip. The whorls are smooth or have axial and spiral ribbing. A long, horny operculum is normally present. They can be found beneath rocks or on sand, mud or seaweeds, scavenging on animal matter. The family contains over 400 species.

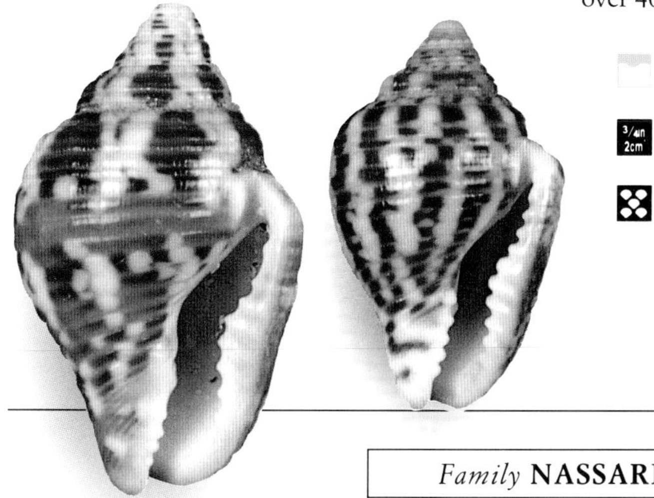

3/4in
2cm

Columbella mercatoria

COMMON DOVE SHELL

General description The apex of this small, solid species is often missing. The spire is fairly short, and the body whorl, which is large, is sculptured by a series of fine spiral cords. The aperture has a dentate outer lip and a ridged columella. The shell is white, mottled by variable orange or brown patches. It occurs under rocks in shallow water, the shells illustrated being from Yucatan, Mexico.

Occurrence Florida to Brazil; Bermuda.

Family NASSARIIDAE Dog whelks

The large family of dog whelks or nassa mud snails consists of small, solid and ovate shells, which are often strongly nodular. The rounded aperture is notched at its base. The columella has a marked callus deposit, and the small, horny operculum has a serrated edge. The shells commonly occur on intertidal sands and mud flats, although some species live on sand or coral in subtidal waters. They are active scavengers, feeding on dead molluscs and other carrion.

1in
2.5cm

Nassarius pullus

BLACK NASSA

General description The whorls of this small shell, with its cream-colored parietal callus, are sculptured by a series of fine axial ribs, which are crossed by several radial cords. It is pale gray to brown in color and often has brown spiral bands. The glazed parietal area and columella are a rich cream color. It inhabits mud flats.

Occurrence Indo-Pacific.

Family MELONGENIDAE Crown and swamp conches

This family includes the giant whelks, and, as this common name implies, includes medium to very large, solid shells of variable shape. The body whorl is inflated and often nodular or spinose at the shoulder. The expanded aperture has a smooth columella. The operculum is thick and horny. Giant whelks are commonly found on sand and mud flats or in subtidal waters, where they feed on bivalves and carrion.

BUSYCON CONTRARIUM

LIGHTNING OR LEFT-HANDED WHELK

GENERAL DESCRIPTION This shell may be easily recognized by its naturally sinistral or left-handed coiling, although right-handed examples sometimes occur. It has a low spire and an enlarged body whorl, and the whorls are often spinose at the shoulder. Young shells are usually more distinctly coloured, with dark streaks traversing the surface. These streaks, which are reputed to represent lightning, are ill-defined in the more uniform beige color of very large shells. It is common subtidally down to 100ft. in sand.
OCCURRENCE South-east United States.

12in
30cm

MELONGENA CORONA

FLORIDA CROWN CONCH

GENERAL DESCRIPTION This exhibits considerable variation in form and color which may be because the young develop directly in the egg capsule to emerge as miniature adults capable of crawling only short distances. As a result, populations become isolated and develop their own local characteristics. The basic color is cream with spiral bands of grey, brown or orange. There are fine axial striations and coarse, strong growth lines. A single broken spiral ridge appears on the lower part of the body whorl.
OCCURRENCE Florida to north-eastern Mexico.

4in
10cm

SYRINX ARUANUS

AUSTRALIAN TRUMPET

GENERAL DESCRIPTION This is probably the largest living marine gastropod, which may achieve lengths of 30in. Its rich orange-brown color is hidden in live examples by the thick, coarse, brown periostracum. The damaged apex of adult shells results from the breaking off of the large embryonic shell or protoconch. The body whorl is large, and all the whorls bear weak spiral ribs of varying widths. It occurs from low tide down to 30ft. This species has been over-collected in recent years and is now protected by Australian law.
OCCURRENCE North Australia.

30in
80cm

Family **FASCIOLARIIDAE Tulip shells**

This large group, also known as spindle shells, contains medium to large, high-spired shells, which are often sculptured by nodules and spiral cords. The aperture is oval, and the columella is often ridged. The live shell is covered by a brown periostracum, and there is an oval, horny operculum. Tulip shells occur on sand or coral reefs from intertidal to deep water, and they feed on worms, bivalve molluscs or carrion.

FASCIOLARIA LILIUM HUNTERIA

BANDED TULIP

GENERAL DESCRIPTION The distinctive brown spiral banding, the rounded apex and smooth whorls make this an easily identified species. The shell is dull gray with yellowish streaks, or a yellowish-beige. There is no ridging or beading of the suture. It has an ovate, horny operculum, as can be seen in the illustration of a specimen from Florida. It occurs from the intertidal area down to depths of around 40ft.
OCCURRENCE North Carolina to Texas.

3½in 9cm

FUSINUS NICOBARICUS

NICOBAR SPINDLE

GENERAL DESCRIPTION This relatively small, stocky spindle has coarsely sculptured whorls with nodular shoulders and strong spiral ribbing. The body whorl has a secondary spiral rib. It is generally off-white, decorated with irregular brown patches. The aperture is white, and there are teeth inside the outer lip. The illustrated example was obtained off south-east India.
OCCURRENCE Indo-Pacific.

2in 5cm

FUSINUS AUSTRALIS

AUSTRALIAN SPINDLE

GENERAL DESCRIPTION The angular whorls of this attractive uniform orange-brown species are sculpted by strong spiral cords. The shoulders are covered with fine tubercule-like projections. It has a horny operculum, and the aperture is white. It occurs in shallow water.
OCCURRENCE Southern and western Australia.

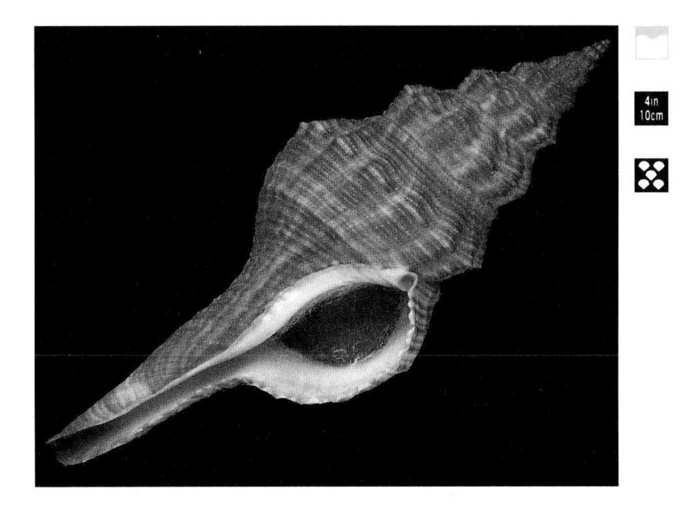

4in 10cm

Family VOLUTIDAE The volutes

The volutes are a large and highly collectable family of medium to large shells. Most species are colored and patterned, and they have a narrow or expanded aperture, a ridged columella and generally smooth sculpture. Some species possess an operculum. They chiefly occur around the coasts of Australia, in shallow subtidal waters, buried in sand, mud or rubble, and they feed carnivorously on bivalves, gastropods or crustacea.

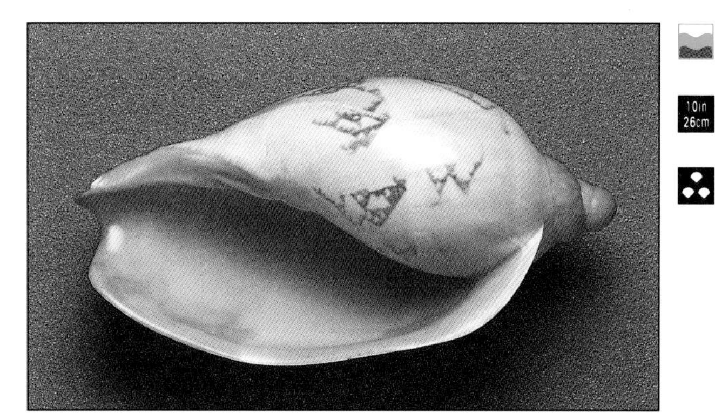

10in 26cm

LIVONIA MAMMILLA

MAMMAL VOLUTE

GENERAL DESCRIPTION Also known as the false melon volute. The shell is generally pale orange or cream marked by irregular brown squiggles, and the penultimate whorl is a darker brown. The aperture is wide, and the lip is expanded and flaring to reveal the rich orange interior. This species is native to south-eastern Australia, where it occurs in deep water at depths around 650ft.
OCCURRENCE South-eastern Australia.

12in 30cm

MELO AMPHORA

AUSTRALIAN BALER

GENERAL DESCRIPTION This is the largest species in the family and may reach sizes up to 38cm (15in). The common name derives from its having been used for baling out canoes by Aborigines and islanders of the Torres Straits. In recent years numerous examples have been caught by Taiwanese fishermen, and it is now often easier to obtain specimens from Taiwan than from their native Australia.
OCCURRENCE Tropical Australia; Papua-New Guinea.

4in 10cm

VOLUTOCONUS BEDNALLI

BEDNALL'S VOLUTE

GENERAL DESCRIPTION The distinctive dark brown, lattice-like markings over a cream-colored base make this one of the most striking of all volutes, and this handsome species still commands high prices among collectors. The extended body whorl accounts for more than half the length, and the aperture is long, revealing the pale pink interior. The shell is native to the Northern Territory, where it prefers sandy areas at depths of 30 to 300ft.
OCCURRENCE North-west Australia.

3½in 9cm

AMORIA ELLIOTI

ELLIOT'S VOLUTE

GENERAL DESCRIPTION Elliot's volute is another handsome volute that is native to north-western Australia. Its smooth, glossy appearance has made it a collector's favourite since its initial description well over 100 years ago. The spire is low, and the large body whorl tapers slightly at the anterior. This overall shape, combined with the distinctive, undulating dark brown markings on a cream background, contrasting with the rich brown interior, make it an easy species to identify.
OCCURRENCE North-west Australia.

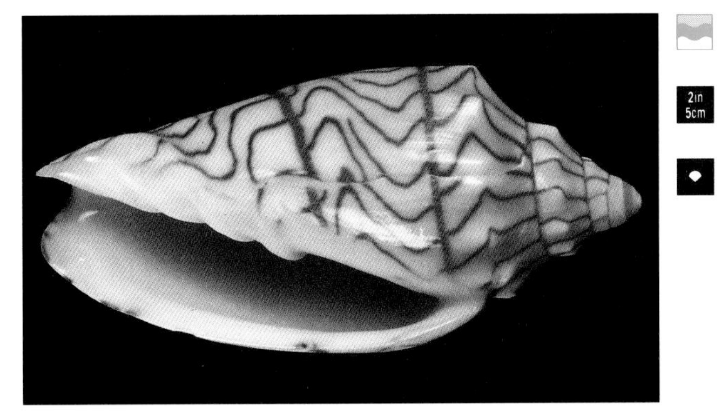

2in 5cm

PARAMORIA GUNTHERI

GUNTHER'S VOLUTE

GENERAL DESCRIPTION To own a Gunther's volute is a collector's dream – its beautiful chocolate brown undulating lines, crossed by two spiral bands of the same color on a background of pinkish-cream present an exquisite picture. The margins of the aperture are cream, as is the columella. The interior is pale peach. The species is restricted to southern Australia, and the fortunate collector who found this example on a granite reef at a depth of just over 50ft. off Memory Cove, Thorny Passage, must have been elated, since it normally occurs at depths of 130–260ft.
OCCURRENCE Southern Australia.

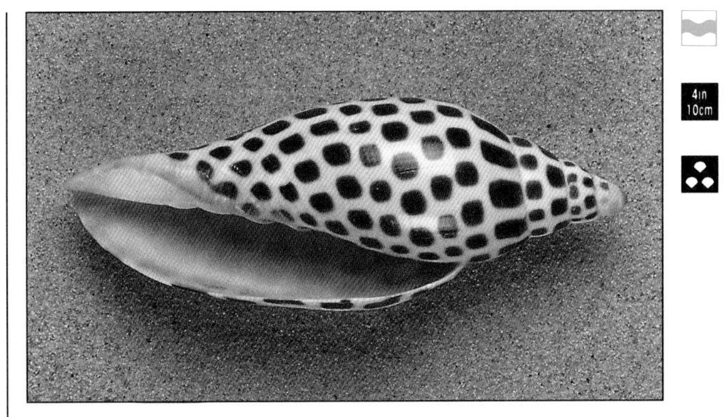

4in 10cm

SCAPHELLA JUNONIA

JUNO'S VOLUTE

GENERAL DESCRIPTION This species, also sometimes known as the junonia, is also greatly prized by collectors. The almost straight-sided body whorl is patterned by striking dark brown squares on a white background. Its overall shape is fusiform, with a long, tapering body whorl and a moderate spire. The long aperture reveals a creamy-pink interior, on which the brown blotches of the exterior may be seen. It is a rare species, since it is rarely cast ashore, although it is fairly plentiful at depths of between 50 and 250ft. offshore.
OCCURRENCE South-eastern United States.

Family HARPIDAE Harp shells

Harp shells are carnivores with a worldwide distribution. Most of the species inhabit shallow waters, but some are found at depths of over 600ft. There are 14 living species. They chiefly feed on crustacea, which they entrap in a film of mucus and sand before devouring. The shell has strong axial ribs, a wide aperture and smooth columella. There is no operculum.

HARPA HARPA

TRUE HARP

GENERAL DESCRIPTION The true harp or noble harp is common on sandy mud in deep water throughout Indo-Pacific waters and extending to the Great Barrier Reef of Australia. This species is variable in color, but the low spire and the ribs, which can be broad or narrow, with the characteristic black lines, are typical. The shoulders bear sharp spines. The harp shells get their name from the smooth ribs, which are regularly spaced around the shell whorls, supposedly resembling the strings of a harp.
OCCURRENCE Indo-Pacific.

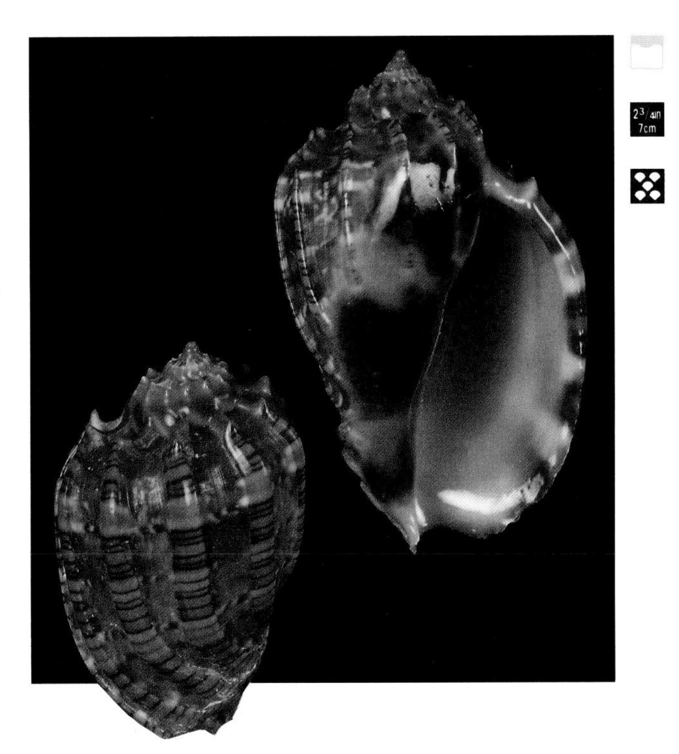

2¾in 7cm

Family VASIDAE Vase shells

Vase or chank shells belong to a small family with about 25 living species, which inhabit tropical coral reefs. The heavy, rather thick shells have from three to five strong spiral ridges on the columella, and they may be ornamented with short or long spines. They are carnivorous, feeding on worms and small bivalves, and possess a chitinous operculum.

ALTIVASUM FLINDERSI

FLINDER'S VASE

GENERAL DESCRIPTION Flinder's vase or chank shell comes from deep, offshore waters of southern and western Australia, and is possibly the largest species of vase, growing to over 6in. The spire is tall, and the body whorl is about the same length. The color is variable, ranging from white, through peach to a deep orange. The aperture is small, and the thin outer lip has a wavy edge. The larger of the shells illustrated is from west Australia; the smaller one is from Coffin's Bay, south Australia.
OCCURRENCE South and west Australia.

6in
15cm

Family VASIDAE Pagoda shells

Pagoda shells are considered here as a subfamily of the Vasidae. Some authorities regard them as a distinct family, Columbariidae. There are about 30 of these deep-water species, and they occur in tropical waters throughout the world. These small shells are characterized by the long siphonal canal and spines on the whorl shoulders. The animal has a chitinous operculum.

COLUMBARIUM SPINICINCTUM

SPINY PAGODA SHELL

GENERAL DESCRIPTION The delicate, lightweight spiny pagoda shell is uncommon. It is found in east Australia, being most commonly dredged at depths of around 300ft. off Queensland. The shells are beige, and are decorated with fine brown lines. The whorls are angular and are adorned with a central row of sharp, spiral, triangular spines. The long, narrow canal is also weakly spinose.
OCCURRENCE Eastern Australia.

2in
5cm

Family OLIVIDAE Olive shells

These small to medium-sized cylindrical shells have a distinct posterior siphonal notch. The columella is often callused and sometimes has definite plicate ridges. The genus *Oliva* does not have an operculum, although some members of the family have a thin, horny operculum. They occur in intertidal to deep water, burrowing through sand and mud in search of the small bivalves and crustacea on which they feed.

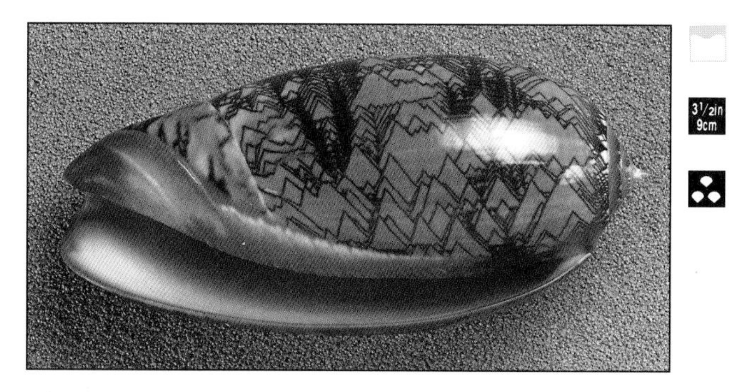

3½in 9cm

OLIVA PORPHYRIA

TENT OLIVE

GENERAL DESCRIPTION This handsome shell is the largest member of the genus. It has a low spire with a sharp apical whorl and the large body whorl is rather long and swollen. The columella has definite plications. The background pale pinkish-violet color is overlaid with the rich brown markings, said to resemble tents, from which the shell's common name is derived. In common with other members of the family, this species tends to remain hidden by burrowing in the sand during daylight, emerging only at night in search of food. It occurs in sand from the intertidal zone down to over 20m (60ft).
OCCURRENCE Gulf of California to Panama.

¾in 2cm

OLIVA CARNEOLA

CARNELIAN OLIVE

GENERAL DESCRIPTION This is an extremely variable species that is, nevertheless, easily recognized. The distinctive little white shell is marked with two bands of varying color. It is common on sand in shallow water, and was often used by islanders to produce necklaces or other ornamental decorations.
OCCURRENCE Tropical Indo-Pacific.

1¼in 3cm

OLIVA OLIVA

COMMON OLIVE

GENERAL DESCRIPTION This species, which is the true type of the genus, exhibits an enormous range in colour and pattern, and this variety has resulted in a large number of names being given to it in the past. However, the characteristic elongated shape with a short spire and the constant dark gray color of the interior should readily distinguish this from other species. It occurs in sandy areas in shallow water.

A pure black form occurs, known as *O. o. orieola*.
OCCURRENCE Tropical Indo-Pacific.

1¼in 3cm

OLIVA AUSTRALIS

AUSTRALIAN OLIVE

GENERAL DESCRIPTION This shallow-water species is one of the few olives to vary little in color and shape, although shells may be bleached white by being placed in hot ashes. The creamy white background is overlaid with light brown lines and squiggles. The spire is high, and the shell has a slender, fusiform shape.
OCCURRENCE Australia; New Guinea.

ANCILLA CINGULATA

HONEY-BANDED ANCILLA

3½in 9cm

GENERAL DESCRIPTION This beautiful, thin, fragile shell, with its rounded glossy whorls and high spire, is restricted in distribution to Australian waters, where it is found on sand flats in shallow water. The apex and shoulder of the body whorl are white, which contrasts with the honey or amber color of the early whorls. The body whorl is a delicate pink. Iredale gave it the name *Ancillista velesiana* in 1936, and it is sometimes described under that synonym.

OCCURRENCE East and South-east Australia.

Family MARGINELLIDAE Margin shells

This is a large family of usually small, highly polished shells with over 600 species, the majority of which are found in shallow sandy areas, especially the tropical seas around West Africa. The name derives from the thickened outer lip of the aperture, and the columella has several distinct ridges or plications. The classification of this group is highly complex and is based chiefly on anatomical features.

PRUNUM LABIATA

ROYAL MARGINELLA

1in 2.5cm

GENERAL DESCRIPTION This solid, medium-sized, shallow-water sand dweller has a flat, heavily callused spire and a slightly inflated posterior. It is a rich cream color, which contrasts markedly with the thickened yellow lip, which shows evidence of small denticles.

OCCURRENCE Lower Caribbean to Brazil.

Family MITRIDAE Mitre shells

These small to large, smooth or spirally sculptured shells possess tall, pointed spires and narrow, elongated apertures, with plicate columellas. The shells tend to be brightly colored, but they are often covered by encrusting algae. There is no operculum. The animal is found in sand or mud, under rocks or coral as well as among algal beds, where it feeds on sipunculid worms. The family contains several hundred carnivorous species, which are distributed throughout warm seas worldwide.

MITRA MITRA

EPISCOPAL MITRE

4in 10cm

GENERAL DESCRIPTION This well-known and attractive shell is probably the largest in the family, and it is a shallow-water sand dweller. The rather heavy, elongate shell is colored by rich, red squares and blotches on a white background. The tall spire is longer than the body whorl, which has almost straight sides. The aperture is a creamy yellow, the lips are dentate, and the columella bears strong plaits.

OCCURRENCE Indo-Pacific.

Family COSTELLARIIDAE Mitre shells

Members of this family closely resemble shells of the Mitridae family, and they were at one time classed with them. They live in a variety of habitats in intertidal to deep water, feeding on gastropods and other small invertebrates.

VEXILLUM VULPECULA

LITTLE FOX MITRE

GENERAL DESCRIPTION This is a well-known, popular and highly variable species, as can be seen from the three specimens illustrated, all of which were collected in the central Philippines. The body whorl is longer than the spire, and the apex is usually broken off. The aperture is long and narrow, and there is a swelling at the top of the aperture. Colors can range from cream to brown, with red, black or orange spiral bands. They inhabit shallow sandy areas.
OCCURRENCE Indo-Pacific.

2in 5cm

Superfamily CANCELLARIOIDEA

Family CANCELLARIIDAE Nutmeg shells

These small to medium-sized, strongly reticulated shells occur throughout the world, most in warm or tropical seas. They have elevated spires and expanded apertures, which often have thickened, crenulated outer lips. The columella is usually strongly ridged, and there is no operculum. Nutmegs are vegetable feeders, living in moderate to deep water on sand or rubble. The animal has a distinctive radula and is believed to feed on small protozoa.

CANCELLARIA RETICULATA

COMMON NUTMEG

GENERAL DESCRIPTION This is perhaps the best known member of the family. Its relatively large, solid shell is decorated by a series of low, spiral cords, which are, in turn, crossed by axial ridges to produce a reticulate pattern. The background color is cream or off-white, and the bands are dark brown. It occurs subtidally down to about 60ft.
OCCURRENCE South-eastern United States to Brazil.

1½in 3cm

Superfamily CONOIDEA

Family CONIDAE Cone shells

The shell is often covered by a periostracum. There is an elongate aperture and smooth columella. The operculum is small and elongate; it may even be absent. Cones live from intertidal to deep water, and may be found under rocks and coral or buried in sand. They are carnivorous, and highly developed poison glands and the modified, harpoon-like radular teeth are used to capture their prey. It has been reported that some species, notably *Conus geographus,* have caused human deaths. There are over 300 species.

4in 10cm

CONUS GEOGRAPHUS

GEOGRAPHY CONE

GENERAL DESCRIPTION This large but surprisingly light, shallow-water species can eat fish as large as itself, and its poisoned venom is known to have killed at least one human, the shell concerned now being in the British Museum (Natural History). The aperture of this species is especially large, and the body whorl is inflated. The base of the body whorl is encircled by several ridges. The background color varies from bluish-white to cream, and the markings are various shades of brown. The two shells illustrated originated from the Philippines.
OCCURRENCE Indo-Pacific.

1½in 4cm

CONUS SCULLETTI

SCULLETT'S CONE

GENERAL DESCRIPTION This species has been only relatively recently described, and the shell illustrated was obtained at a depth of some 480ft. off Cape Moreton, Queensland. It is a slender, fairly light shell, with a low spire. The body whorl may be straight sided or slightly concave. The background color is off-white or cream, with light brown patterning.
OCCURRENCE South Queensland and north New South Wales.

2in 5cm

CONUS TESSULATUS

TESSELLATED CONE

GENERAL DESCRIPTION The tessellated (or tessellate) cone, with its low spire, violet-fringed columella base, rounded body whorl and its pattern of red or orange markings on a white background is a pretty sight, which would grace any collection. The early whorls and slightly blunt apex are raised, and spiral ridges usually occur on the whorls. In old specimens, the base of the columella may be white, rather than violet.
OCCURRENCE Indo-Pacific.

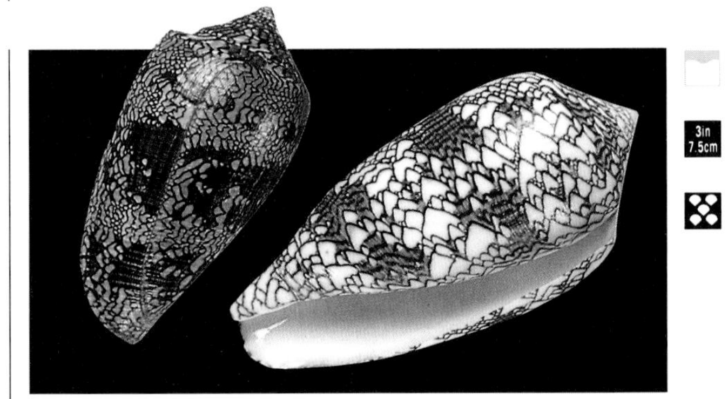

3in 7.5cm

CONUS TEXTILE

TEXTILE CONE

GENERAL DESCRIPTION The textile or cloth of gold cone is one of the best known and more attractive species. It is, however, one of the most venomous. The short spire has straight or slightly concave sides, while the body whorl may have more markedly convex sides. The long aperture reveals a glossy white interior. The smaller, blue form is known as *Conus euetrios*; this specimen is from Mozambique.
OCCURRENCE Indo-Pacific.

Family TURRIDAE Turrid shells

Although these small to medium-sized shells often resemble other groups in shape, they are readily distinguished by the apertural notch on the shoulder of the body whorl. The siphonal canal is frequently lengthened to produce a spindle-like appearance. A leaf-shaped operculum is small and horny, but may be absent. Turrids, which number over 1000 named species, inhabit intertidal to very deep water, sheltering under rocks or coral in sand or muddy areas. They are carnivorous, feeding on marine worms and other small invertebrates. Some possess harpoon-like teeth.

GEMMULA KIENERI

KIENER'S TURRID

2in 5cm

GENERAL DESCRIPTION This beautiful species, with its sculpture of brown spiral beads and the extended siphonal canal, would grace any collection. The spire is tall, and the body whorl is inflated at the centre, before tapering to the canal. The off-white or cream background is patterned in brown and reddish-brown, and there are fine brown dashes on the lower part of the body whorl. It has a wide distribution, from Japan, the China Sea and the Philippines, although the specimen shown here comes from Cape Moreton, Queensland.
OCCURRENCE West Pacific; Australia.

Family TEREBRIDAE Auger shells

These small to large, elongate shells have a sharply pointed spire and a small aperture with a thin outer lip. The shell lacks a periostracum, but the surface may be sculptured or smooth and is often brightly colored. The animal, which has a small, horny operculum, lives in sand or sandy muds in both intertidal and subtidal warm and temperate waters, where it feeds on marine worms. The family contains about 300 species.

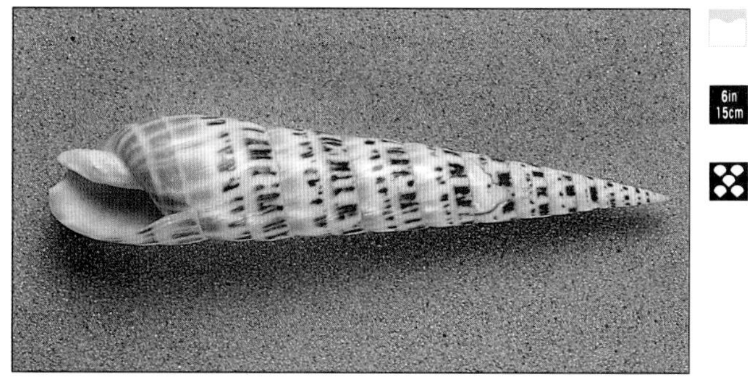

6in 15cm

TEREBRA MACULATA

MARLINSPIKE AUGER

GENERAL DESCRIPTION The shell is extremely thick and heavy, and it is the largest species in the family, the present world record size being over 10in. in length. The shell has a very tall spire, and there are about 15 slightly convex-sided whorls. The body whorl is narrow and rounded, with an elongate aperture. The background color is cream or light fawn, and the spiral patterning is brown or grayish-blue. It occurs in shallow water in sand.
OCCURRENCE Indo-Pacific.

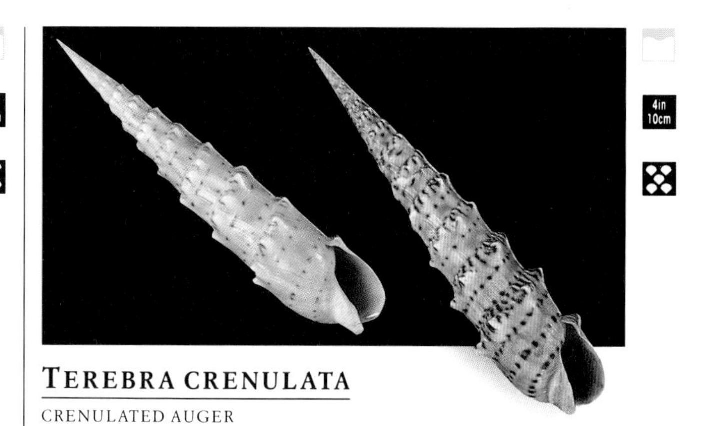

4in 10cm

TEREBRA CRENULATA

CRENULATED AUGER

GENERAL DESCRIPTION The crenulated or notched auger has a rather stocky shell. It is a medium-sized species, with variable sculpturing and color pattern, as shown by the two examples illustrated here. The darker of the two shells comes from the Solomon Islands, while the lighter specimen is from Tahiti. Some specimens have almost smooth, straight-sided whorls; others have prominent nodules below the suture. The species occurs in sandy areas in shallow water.
OCCURRENCE Indo-Pacific.

5in 13cm

TEREBRA SUBULATA

SUBULATE AUGER

GENERAL DESCRIPTION This strikingly colored shell is probably one of the best known of the family. It has over 20 sharply elongated, slightly convex-sided whorls. The body whorl, as in all augers, narrows to form a short canal. The background of cream or beige is patterned with two distinct spiral rows of squarish, dark brown blotches. The species is also known as the chocolate spotted auger because of its bright coloration. It occurs in sandy areas in shallow water.
OCCURRENCE Indo-Pacific.

2in 5cm

DUPLICARIA DUPLICATA

DUPLICATE AUGER

GENERAL DESCRIPTION This medium-sized, highly glossy shell is sculptured by a spiral groove on each whorl, crossed by numerous grooves running parallel to the axis. It is highly variable in color, as can be seen from the three shells illustrated. It occurs in sandy areas in shallow water.
OCCURRENCE Indian Ocean; west Pacific.

Superfamily ARCHITECTONICOIDEA

Family ARCHITECTONICIDAE Sundial shells

This is a small family of flat, disc-like shells in which the relatively large and open umbilicus produces a staircase appearance, which results in these shells being known as staircase shells. The animal has a horny operculum, which normally has a tooth-like process on its inner surface. They generally occur in warm water, where they live in sandy areas and feed on corals and sea anemones.

1¼in 3cm

ARCHITECTONICA PERDIX

PARTRIDGE SUNDIAL

GENERAL DESCRIPTION This small, sand-dwelling shell has the characteristic spiral and beaded umbilicus, which create the staircase effect. The color varies from off-white to cream with darker brown spiral bands and blotches, the sculpture consisting of weak, closely spaced striae. The shell illustrated comes from Keppel Bay, Queensland. It is unusual to find specimens with undamaged apertures.
OCCURRENCE West Pacific; Indian Ocean.

¾in 2cm

PHILIPPIA RADIATA

RADIAL SUNDIAL

GENERAL DESCRIPTION This small species has a rather humped spire and a small, open umbilicus, with the base tending to be convex. The shell's surface is smooth and moderately glossy. It is cream in color with a distinct spiral orange band and axial streaks. It was described by Iredale in 1931 under the name *Philippia stipator*. It occurs in sandy areas in shallow water.
OCCURRENCE West Pacific; Indian Ocean.

Superfamily PHILINOIDEA

This superfamily contains a group of molluscs that are generally devoid of shells. It includes the nudibranchs or sea slugs and sea hares. A few members of this superfamily do, however, possess shells that are of interest to the collector, and these are known generally as bubble shells.

Family HYDATINIDAE Bubble shells

The shells within this family are small to medium and thin. They have a depressed spire and, often, colored banding. The animal, which does not have an operculum, may be found in sandy pools or beneath rocks in the intertidal zone. They are mostly carnivores, feeding chiefly on marine worms, although some feed on algae.

HYDATINA PHYSIS

PAPER BUBBLE SHELL

GENERAL DESCRIPTION This is probably the best known of the bubble shells. It is a thin, rather fragile shell, with a depressed spire and an enlarged, bulbous body whorl. The flared aperture reveals a white interior, while the exterior is cream or yellowish, with pretty olive green to dark brown banding. It occurs in sandy mud, on banked-up weed growths such as eel-grass or even on coral reefs.
OCCURRENCE Indo-Pacific.

1½in 4cm

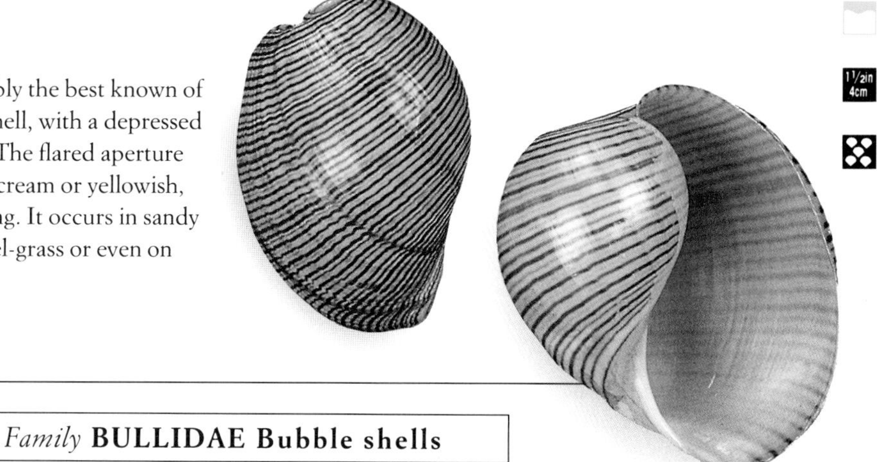

Family BULLIDAE Bubble shells

Medium-sized shells with an inflated body whorl and sunken spire. The aperture is expanded and differs from the hydatinids by the presence of a callus deposit on the columella. Bullids occur in sand or on coral in intertidal and shallow water. The animal feeds on green algae.

BULLA STRIATA

COMMON ATLANTIC BUBBLE

GENERAL DESCRIPTION This pretty but sturdy shell is usually ovate, and the spire is depressed. The body whorl is compressed at the anterior. The shells are extremely variable in pattern, having brown, white or gray blotches. The aperture is white. The two examples illustrated, which indicate the range of colors, were collected off Yucatan, Mexico.
OCCURRENCE Florida to Brazil; Mediterranean.

1¼in 3cm

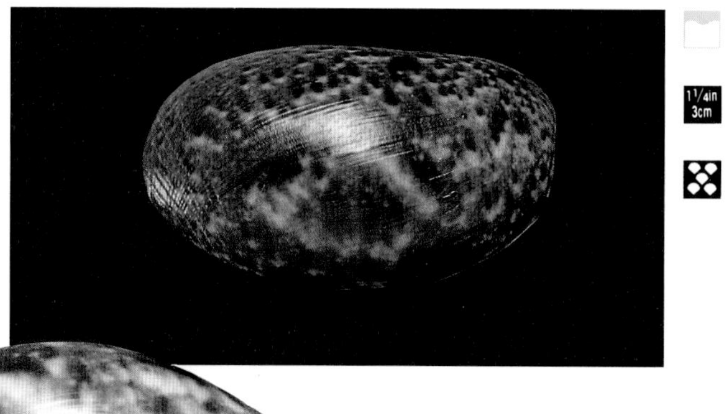

Family HAMINEIDAE Bubble shells

These small, thin shells are usually white or yellow. They may be smooth or be covered with fine spiral grooves. The animals, which live in sand or sandy mud from intertidal to deep water, are all herbivores.

ATYS NAUCUM

WHITE PACIFIC ATYS

1½in 4cm

GENERAL DESCRIPTION This fine, lightweight shell is white in colour and is decorated with a series of fine spiral striations. It is globose – living up to the name bubble shell – and the posterior lip extends upwards, almost over the depressed, virtually absent spire. As can be seen in the photograph, the columella has a small fold or plication. The shell illustrated comes from the central Philippines, and the species can be found on sand or sandy mud from the intertidal zone down to deep water throughout the Indo-Pacific area.

OCCURRENCE Indo-Pacific.

Class BIVALVIA

Superfamily LIMOPSOIDEA

Family GLYCIMERIDIDAE Bittersweet clams

Bittersweet clams have thick, rounded, heavy and porcellaneous shells, covered by a thick skin or periostracum. The hinge plate bears many fine, radiating, interlocking hinge teeth. There are more than 100 species (some authorities say as many as 150), which are distributed mainly in the Indo-Pacific in sandy, shallow waters. Many are used for food.

GLYCYMERUS GIGANTEA

GIANT BITTERSWEET

4in 10cm

GENERAL DESCRIPTION This species grows to 4in. and is locally common offshore in the Gulf of California at depths of 20–40ft. The attractive shells are often washed ashore following storms. The symmetrical valves are thick and very heavy. The white interior shows brown or purple staining, while the off-white or cream exterior is decorated with reddish-brown zigzag marks.

OCCURRENCE Gulf of California.

Superfamily MYTILOIDEA

Family MYTILIDAE Mussel shells

The Mytilidae or true mussels are found throughout the world in shallow intertidal waters. The shells are relatively thin but strong, elongated and are covered by a thick periostracum. The interior is often pearly and has weakly developed hinge teeth. Most species live in colonies attached to rocks, stones and so forth by a byssus (group of filaments). Some species, however, burrow into rock or coral.

MYTILUS EDULIS

COMMON BLUE MUSSEL

GENERAL DESCRIPTION The common blue or edible mussel has been well known to man as a source of food since prehistoric times, being plentiful on rocky shorelines throughout the world. The triangular blue shell with its pearly interior is generally found on rocky shores from the intertidal area down to 30ft. The valves are joined by a long, thin ligament. In recent years it has provided a new industry, being farmed in many areas in beds or offshore on raftings.
OCCURRENCE Worldwide.

PERNA CANALICULUS

CHANNEL MUSSEL

GENERAL DESCRIPTION This is a large, attractive species, with a green periostracum and radial rows of black lines. The umbones are rounded, although somewhat pointed, and there is a rudimentary tooth structure. A long ligament joins the valves. It can grow to 6in., although smaller specimens are more common, and it is found on rocks exposed at low tide around the coasts of New Zealand. The shell illustrated comes from the Hauraki Gulf region of North Island.
OCCURRENCE New Zealand.

Superfamily PTERIOIDEA

Family PTERIIDAE Wing and pearl oysters

The Pteriidae family includes the wing oysters, which are characterized by well-developed, wing-like extensions of the hinge-line and by a byssus, by which they attach themselves to coral rubble, rocks and sea fans. The family also contains pearl oysters, which are rounder. Their highly developed pearly interior is used to produce articles for the curio trade, and many species are used in the production of pearls, both natural and cultured. They mainly occur in tropical seas.

PTERIA PENGUIN

PENGUIN WING OYSTER

GENERAL DESCRIPTION The penguin wing oyster has a fragile, ovate shell with asymmetric valves, the right, or upper, valve being inflated. The interior is pearly. It inhabits shallow waters and normally grows to 6in. but sometimes reaches 10in. The illustrated example, which is from the central Philippines, clearly exhibits the characteristic extension of the hinge-line from which the common name derives.
OCCURRENCE Indo-Pacific.

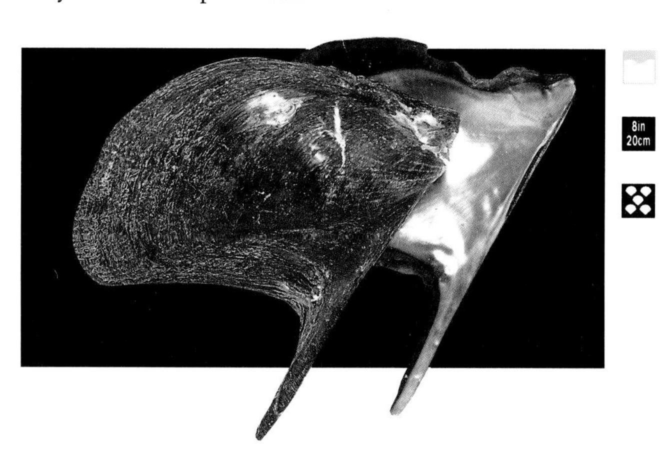

Family MALLEIDAE Hammer oysters

The hammer oysters comprise a small group. They have a semi-nacreous interior, while the hinge-line combines with an elongation of the shell body to give a hammer-like appearance. The ligament is accommodated in a small depression in the centre of the top edge of the hinge. Most species live in tropical seas among flattened coral reefs or in rock crevices.

MALLEUS ALBUS

WHITE HAMMER OYSTER

GENERAL DESCRIPTION The white hammer oyster occurs in shallow sandy areas on grass and rock flats throughout the Indo-Pacific, including Australia. The extended hinge-line and elongate body shape of the beige-colored shell gave rise to its common name. It was greatly sought after by collectors at the beginning of the nineteenth century, and is still popular with collectors who specialize in bivalves.
OCCURRENCE Indo-Pacific.

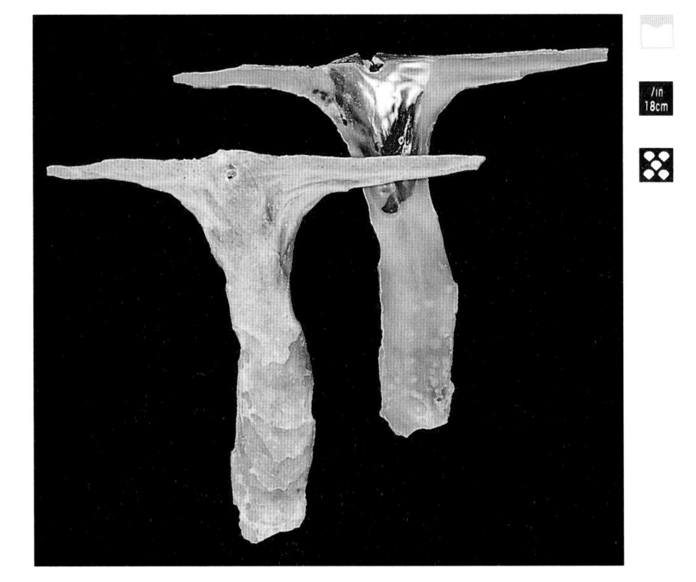

7in
18cm

Superfamily PINNOIDEA

Family PINNIDAE Pen shells

The members of this small family of large, thin, fan-shaped shells, are attached to the substrate by means of a fine, silky byssus. In the past this was used as a form of natural silk and formed the basis of a small industry in the area around Taranto in southern Italy. The small amount of byssal silk produced by each mussel together with the introduction of artificial silk have long since made this industry obsolete.

PINNA RUDIS

RUDE PEN SHELL

GENERAL DESCRIPTION The fan-shaped exterior of the rude (or rough) pen shell is decorated by a series of low radial ridges, from which arise a series of upturned, hollow spines. The thin, translucent shell is orange-brown or olive brown. The interior is smooth but uneven, and there is a pearly layer towards the narrower end. It occurs locally offshore in sandy areas.
OCCURRENCE Mediterranean to north and west Africa.

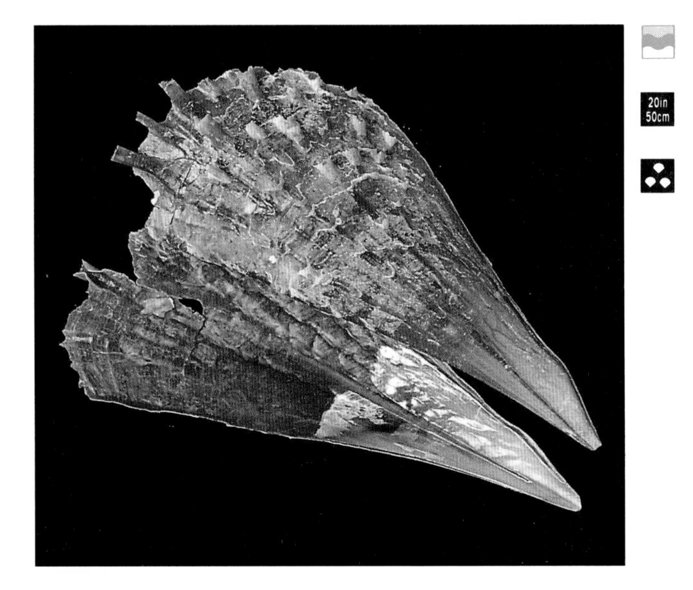

20in
50cm

Superfamily OSTREOIDEA

Family OSTREIDAE True oysters

Members of the oyster family have been used as a source of food since prehistoric times, and they are now cultivated in oyster beds all over the world. The shells are normally irregular in outline and are cemented to rocks or to each other by the lower, left valve.

OSTREA EDULIS

COMMON EUROPEAN OYSTER

GENERAL DESCRIPTION This is the edible oyster of culinary fame, which has been farmed commercially in the UK and elsewhere for centuries. It is roughly circular in outline, with a virtually flat lower valve and a slightly inflated upper valve. It has a greyish-white interior, unlike the Portuguese oyster *Crassostrea angulata,* which tends to be irregularly elongate and have a white interior. The example illustrated is from Langstone Bridge, Hampshire, UK.
OCCURRENCE Western Europe; Mediterranean.

3in 7.5cm

Superfamily PECTINOIDEA

Family PECTINIDAE Scallop shells

Pectens or scallops are among the best known of the bivalves, and they are extremely popular with collectors because of their attractive colours, rounded outline and varied surface sculpture. There are several hundred species, distributed throughout the world, occurring in both deep and shallow habitats. The right valve has an anterior byssal notch, and the hinge-line is produced to form two "ears", one on each side of the umbones. Many scallops swim by rapidly opening and closing their valves. Several species are fished commercially as food.

ARGOPECTEN CIRCULARIS

CIRCULAR SCALLOP

GENERAL DESCRIPTION The circular scallop has, as the name suggests, a rounded shell with inflated, equal valves and ears. The valves are traversed by about 18 raised, rounded ribs. The shells show considerable variation in color and pattern, as may be seen from those illustrated. The circular scallop lives in subtidal waters, down to depths of over 300ft., and is fished commercially for food.
OCCURRENCE Western Mexico to Peru.

4in 10cm

Chlamys tigerina

TIGER SCALLOP

General description This small, rounded shell, which tapers sharply at the umbones, has unequal ears. The symmetrical valves have a smooth but dull surface. It is relatively common in deeper waters around northern Europe but tends to be scarce in collections since it is not thought commercially viable by North Sea fishermen. The shells illustrated, which exhibit some of the diverse color forms, were dredged at about 500ft. off southern Iceland.

Occurrence West Europe; Iceland; Norway to Spain.

Mesopeplum tasmanicum

TASMAN SCALLOP

General description The Tasman scallop has rounded equal valves, but unequal ears. The upper valve is normally pink to reddish-purple, while the lower valve is white or pink. Both valves are traversed by five strong radial ridges, with numerous smaller, finer ones between them. It is relatively uncommon, occurring at depths of 60–250ft. The shell seen here came from Port Lincoln.

Occurrence Tasmania; South Australia.

Lyropecten nodosa

LION'S PAW

General description This shell, with its fan-shaped, equal valves, is greatly sought after by collectors. Each valve has seven or eight rounded radial ribs, which normally bear large rounded nodules. The ears are not equal, the anterior being slightly larger. The color is generally brown or red but occasionally very desirable yellow or orange forms also occur. The interior is purplish-brown. It is found offshore down to about 100ft.

Occurrence South-east United States to Brazil.

Patinopecten caurinus

GIANT PACIFIC SCALLOP

General description The Pacific scallop is possibly the largest of the scallop species, achieving up to 8in. across. It has rounded, equal and slightly convex valves, with strongly developed, low and rounded, radial ribs. The upper, left valve is beige or pale brown in color, while the lower, right valve tends to be pale cream. The anterior ear is slightly larger than the posterior ear. This species has proved to be ideal for commercial fishing.

Occurrence Alaska to California.

Family SPONDYLIDAE Thorny oysters

These close relations to scallops live permanently attached to corals or rocks. The marine growths on their elongated spines act as camouflage for the oyster. They vary greatly in shape, size and color, but all have a characteristic ball-and-socket hinge structure which is not dissimilar to the human elbow. Their attractive shapes, long spines and varied colors make perfect examples of this group highly prized.

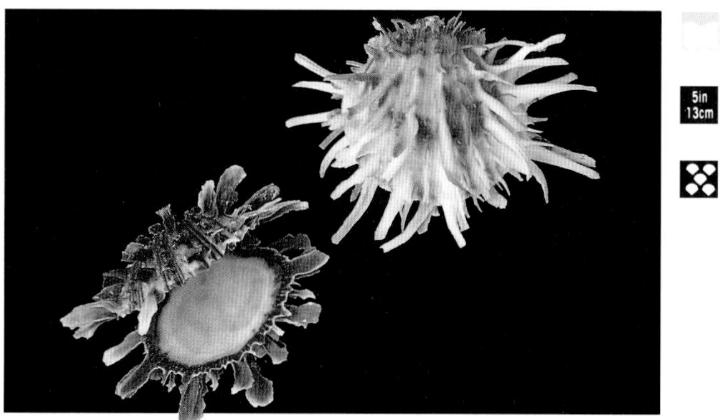

5in 13cm

SPONDYLUS PRINCEPS

PACIFIC THORNY OYSTER

GENERAL DESCRIPTION The heavy shell of this extremely variable species bears long, thick but blunt spines. Both valves are inflated and equal, and the ears are small. The valves are usually red or pink, while the spines are generally white, which combine to give a highly attractive appearance. Perfect examples are greatly sought after. They occur offshore attached to coral or rocks.

OCCURRENCE Gulf of California to Panama.

3in 7.5cm

SPONDYLUS WRIGHTIANUS

WRIGHT'S THORNY OYSTER

GENERAL DESCRIPTION Wright's thorny oyster is perhaps one of the most outstanding species in this remarkable group. Its long spines are often twice the overall size of the shell, and they are interspersed by several finer spines. The small, rounded valves are not equal, the lower one being flat, while the upper valve is inflated. The colour varies from off-white to pink or lavender, and the largest spines often remain white. It is native to west Australia, where it occurs offshore down to about 150ft.

OCCURRENCE West Australia.

Superfamily TRIGONIIDEA

Family TRIGONIDAE Brooch clams

Often referred to as living fossils, the few Australian species of brooch clam are all that remain of a group that was dominant in Jurassic seas some 200 million years ago. The triangular shells have three hinge teeth in one valve and two in the other. The interior is pearly and highly iridescent, the shells often being collected and used to make jewelry.

NEOTRIGONIA BEDNALLI

BEDNALL'S BROOCH CLAM

GENERAL DESCRIPTION This small, rather solid, triangular shell may be readily recognized. It has a rich lavender or pale orange iridescent interior, and the exterior bears strongly granulate radial ribbing. There is a complex, V-shaped hinge. It is common around south-east Australia on mud in offshore waters down to about 150ft.

OCCURRENCE South-east Australia.

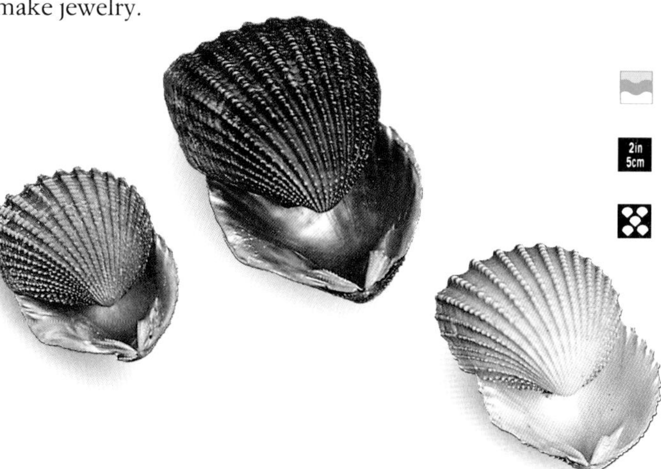

2in 5cm

Superfamily LUCINOIDEA

Family LUCINIDAE Lucina clams

The lucina clams are a large family. The shells are thick, white and circular to oval, with a very small lunule and a long ligament, which may be external or internal. The anterior muscle scar is relatively narrow and elongate and, unlike the similar venus shells, there is no pallial sinus. They inhabit both shallow and deep water worldwide but prefer warmer waters, where they burrow into mud or sand.

CODAKIA TIGERINA

PACIFIC TIGER LUCINA

GENERAL DESCRIPTION This attractive shell has a distinctive, reticulated, chalky white exterior, which contrasts with the interior of pale yellow bordered by pinkish-red. The hinge area and ligament are large; the teeth are small. The species occurs throughout the Indo-Pacific from extreme low water to depths of over 60ft.

OCCURRENCE Indo-Pacific.

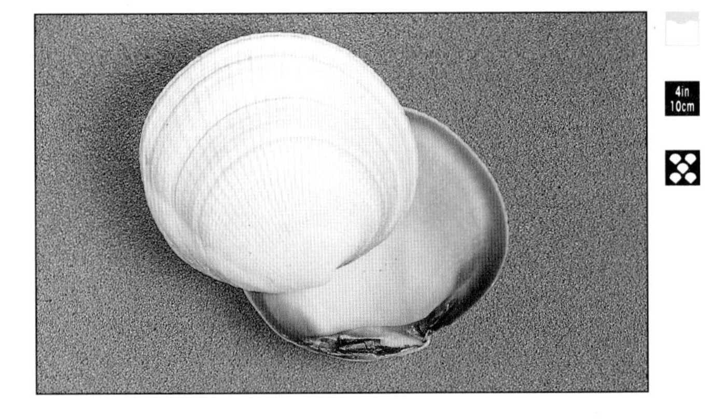

4in 10cm

Superfamily CARDITOIDEA

Family CARDITIDAE Cardita clams

The distinctive cardita clams, with their strongly ribbed, boat-shaped shells, anteriorly placed beaks, external ligament and crenulate internal margins, have a worldwide distribution. There is no pallial sinus, and some species have a byssus. Most species in this group retain their young inside the mantle cavity.

2in 5cm

CARDITA CRASSICOSTA

LEAFY CARDITA

GENERAL DESCRIPTION The leafy cardita, which is also known as the Australian cardita, has a distinctive shell with four or five large radial ribs, which are normally covered by strongly fluted scales. It is common from low-tide level down to depths of over 300ft. There is considerable variation in color, as can be seen in the shells shown here, which came from the Sulu Sea, between the Philippines and Borneo.

OCCURRENCE West and south Australia; Philippines.

1½in 4cm

CARDITA LATICOSTATA

WIDE-RIBBED CARDITA

GENERAL DESCRIPTION This thick and solid shell has about 15 ribs, which radiate from the umbones and which often bear small scales. There is a strong hinge and two large cardinal teeth. It is normally off-white with bands or flecks of various shades of brown. The interior is white. It is common and can be found intertidally down to about 170ft.

OCCURRENCE Gulf of California to north Peru.

Superfamily CHAMOIDEA

Family CHAMIDAE Jewel boxes

These attractive, thick and heavy-shelled bivalves bear a strong resemblance to the thorny oysters, but they may easily be distinguished by their rudimentary hinge structure. Most species within the family are cemented to rocks, to coral or to each other. They possess foliated spines and scales and live in shallow tropical waters.

ARCINELLA ARCINELLA

TRUE SPINY JEWEL BOX

GENERAL DESCRIPTION The triangular shell is solid and strong. It is normally white and has between 16 and 35 radial ribs, bearing both long and short spines. The interior may be stained pink, yellow or purple. It is normally cemented to a firm surface but may occasionally be free. It occurs from low water to depths of over 250ft.

OCCURRENCE West Indies to Brazil.

Superfamily CARDIOIDEA

Family CARDIIDAE Cockle shells

This large, well-known family has a worldwide distribution and includes numerous edible species. The shells vary in size from small to very large, and most exhibit a radial sculpture of ribbing. They have a rounded, oval outline and large, inflated, centrally placed umbones. There are two equal adductor scars and no pallial sinus. The animal has a large foot and is capable of leaping several inches through the water when disturbed. There are over 200 species in the family.

ACANTHOCARDIA ECHINATA

EUROPEAN PRICKLY COCKLE

GENERAL DESCRIPTION The inflated round or oval shell has 18–22 radiating ribs bearing a central row of sharp spines. The broad umbones rise above the hinge-line of the equal valves. It is of a pale yellow or brown color, occasionally mottled, and the inner edge of the valves is crenulate. It lives in sandy areas from just offshore to considerable depths.

OCCURRENCE West Europe; north-west Africa.

PLAGIOCARDIUM SETOSUM

HAIRY COCKLE

GENERAL DESCRIPTION The hairy cockle has a typical oval cockle shape with numerous ribs radiating from the umbonal area. These ribs bear small, blunt nodules. The large, inflated valves are equal. The shells are beige or light brown and normally patterned by intermittent darker bands. The interior is white, and the shell margins are crenulate.

OCCURRENCE South-west Pacific; north Australia.

CERASTODERMA EDULE

COMMON EUROPEAN COCKLE

GENERAL DESCRIPTION This well-known species is widely used for food and is often farmed commercially. The medium-sized, oval shell has 22–28 radial ribs, each of which bears scale-like spines. The color varies from dirty white through pale yellow to various shades of brown. The interior is white, and the posterior muscle scar is frequently stained brown. It is widely distributed and often abundant in intertidal sands and mud flats.
OCCURRENCE Norway to north-west Africa.

2in 5cm

Superfamily TRIDACNOIDEA

Family TRIDACNIDAE Giant clams

The members of this group have thick, heavy shells with strong radial ribs, which normally bear scales. The shell edges are strongly scalloped and interlock. They possess a byssus and lie with their hinge area on the sea-floor so that the gaping valves face upward towards the surface to allow sunlight to reach the symbiotic algae in the large, fleshy mantle lobes with which the animal feeds. There are about a dozen species inhabiting tropical Indo-Pacific waters.

HIPPOPUS HIPPOPUS

BEAR'S CLAW CLAM

GENERAL DESCRIPTION The triangular shape, white interior and strongly fluted off-white exterior mottled with orange, yellow or crimson made the bear's claw clam popular with Victorians for its decorative potential. This popularity has continued to the present day and has resulted in so much over-fishing that trade in this species is now prohibited. It is, indeed, a striking shell, with its deep, inflated valves. These are strongly sculptured and bear about seven large and numerous small ribs. The long hinge-line runs about half the length of the shell. It occurs on coral reefs in shallow water.
OCCURRENCE South-west Pacific.

8in 20cm

Superfamily MACTROIDEA

Family MACTRIDAE Mactra clams

Members of this family, sometimes called trough shells, have a worldwide distribution in shallow waters, and there are about 100 species. They have no byssus, and the shells may be smooth or possess concentric sculpturing. The triangular shape, centrally placed umbones, deep pallial sinus and two equal muscle scars plus internal ligament readily distinguish this group. The animal burrows in sand, and many species are edible.

MACTRA CORALLINA

RAYED MACTRA

GENERAL DESCRIPTION This smooth, glossy and light triangular shell is a pale reddish-brown, and a series of lighter cream-colored, broad and narrow radial rays is often present. The interior is a pale violet. The ligament is external. It lives in clean sand in shallow water, and specimens are often cast ashore after storms. The shell illustrated is from Camber Sands, on the south coast of England.
OCCURRENCE UK to the Mediterranean.

1½in 4cm

Superfamily SOLENOIDEA

Family SOLENIDAE Razor shells

Solens or razor shells are thin and elongate, and they have parallel dorsal and ventral margins, which make them ideally suited for burrowing into sand or mud. The ligament is external. The hinge has a single cardinal tooth in each valve. There are no lateral teeth. They occur throughout the world, and many species are fished commercially.

SOLENS MARGINATUS

EUROPEAN RAZOR CLAM

GENERAL DESCRIPTION The long, straight-sided valves, with their truncated ends and single cardinal tooth, may be readily distinguished from the jackknife clams. The shells are beige or a dirty-looking yellow, with a mid-brown periostracum. The species is characterized by a groove that runs just behind and parallel to the anterior margin.
OCCURRENCE West Europe; Mediterranean; west Africa.

5in 12cm

Superfamily SOLENOIDEA

Family CULTELLIDAE Jackknife clams

Known as jackknife clams, these appear remarkably similar to the true razor shells, but they may be readily distinguished by the cardinal and lateral teeth – razor shells have no laterals. Most species have the elongate razor shape, but some are squarer and boat-shaped. They inhabit shallow sandy areas and have a worldwide distribution.

ENSIS ENSIS

NARROW JACKKNIFE CLAM

GENERAL DESCRIPTION The fragile, elongated, slightly curved shell, with its external ligament, is covered by a pale olive green periostracum, which is ornamented by concentric growth lines. The right valve has one small cardinal tooth and one lateral tooth; the left valve has two cardinal and two lateral teeth. It occurs from low-water mark down to 250ft.
OCCURRENCE Norway to Mediterranean.

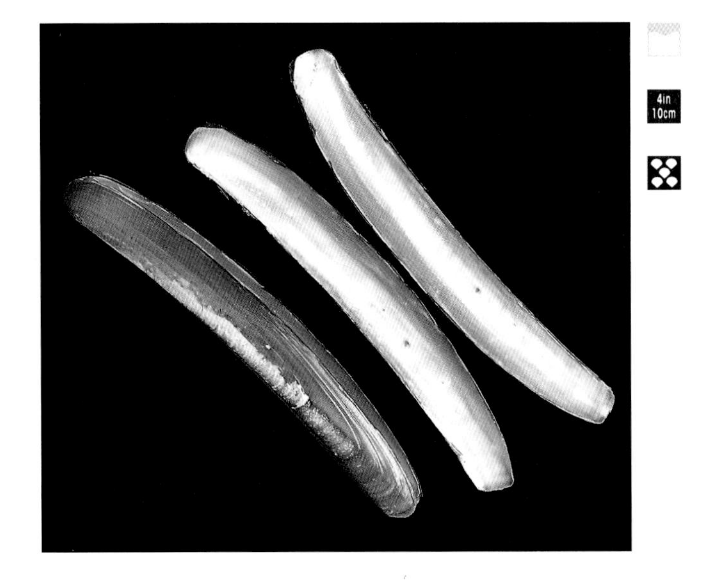

4in 10cm

Superfamily TELLINOIDEA

Family TELLINIDAE Tellins

Tellins have small to medium-sized shells, which tend to be flattened, thin and rounded in front and angular behind. The ligament is external and the hinge has two small cardinal teeth in each valve. There is a well-defined pallial sinus. They are also known as butterfly shells, and there are over 200 species worldwide, occurring in shallow water where they burrow into sand or mud.

TELLINA ALBINELLA

LITTLE WHITE TELLIN

GENERAL DESCRIPTION The little white tellin is something of a misnomer since, although white shells do occur, it is more commonly pink or pale orange with delicate white concentric lines. The thin, shiny shell is sculptured by a series of fine, crowded concentric striations. The posterior beak-like part of the shell tends to be compressed.
OCCURRENCE South coasts of Australia.

2½in 6cm

Superfamily GLOSSOIDEA

Family GLOSSIDAE Heart clams

Although few species exist today in cool and tropical seas, the family is well represented in fossil records. The thick, inflated shells have prominent beaks or umbones which are turned in on themselves, producing a distinctive ram's horn effect. The ligament is external, and the shell surface may be smooth or ribbed.

GLOSSUS HUMANUS

OX-HEART CLAM

GENERAL DESCRIPTION The common name for this species is derived from its characteristic shape, the shell being covered by a fine, glossy brown skin or periostracum. The hinge bears three cardinal teeth in each valve, and there is no pallial sinus. The shell is yellow-brown in colour and bears numerous growth lines. It lives in sand or mud at depths ranging from 26 to 1000ft.
OCCURRENCE Norway to Mediterranean.

3½in 9cm

Superfamily VENEROIDEA

Family VENERIDAE Venus clams

The Veneridae family contains over 400 species, which are distributed worldwide. The solid-walled shells exhibit a variety of shapes, textures and colors, but all possess a pallial sinus. Most inhabit shallow water, although some prefer ocean depths. Many species are used for food.

2½in 6cm

VENUS VERRUCOSA

WARTY VENUS

GENERAL DESCRIPTION This solid and heavy medium-sized species has equal, rather inflated valves, which are sculptured with strong, concentric ridges. These tend to become nodular towards the anterior and posterior edges. The warty venus, which is an edible species, occurs from extreme low-tide zone down to 40ft.; the shell illustrated is from shallow water off Cadiz, Spain.
OCCURRENCE North-east Atlantic to the Mediterranean.

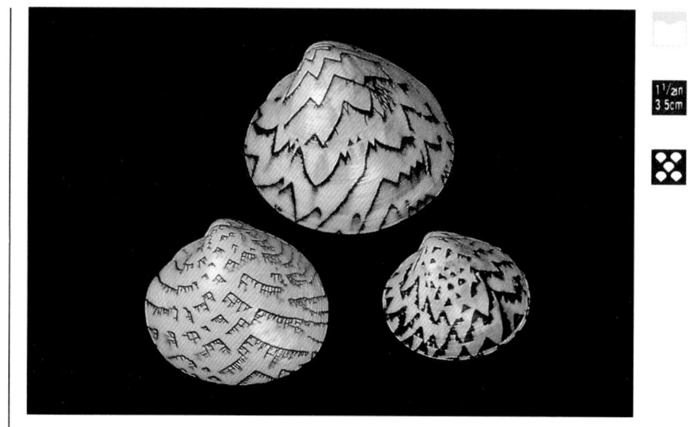

1½in 3.5cm

LIOCONCHA CASTRENSIS

CHOCOLATE-FLAMED VENUS

GENERAL DESCRIPTION The chocolate-flamed or Camp Pitar venus is widely distributed throughout the Indo-Pacific, including Australia, and it is common in shallow sandy bays. The cream surface of the round or oval shells is overlain by vivid dark brown zigzag lines, which vary considerably, and no two shells appear identical. The rounded umbones are prominent. There is a large escutcheon, an internal ligament and a shallow pallial sinus. The three shells illustrated are from the central Philippines.
OCCURRENCE Indo-Pacific.

Superfamily PHOLADOIDEA

Family PHOLADIDAE Piddocks and angel wings

This family, which contains the piddocks and angel wings, has a worldwide distribution. The thin but strong elongated shells gape at both ends, the ribbed valves possessing accessory plates as well as shelly projections (apophyses) beneath the umbones. They burrow or bore into rock, clay, soft limestones, coral and wood.

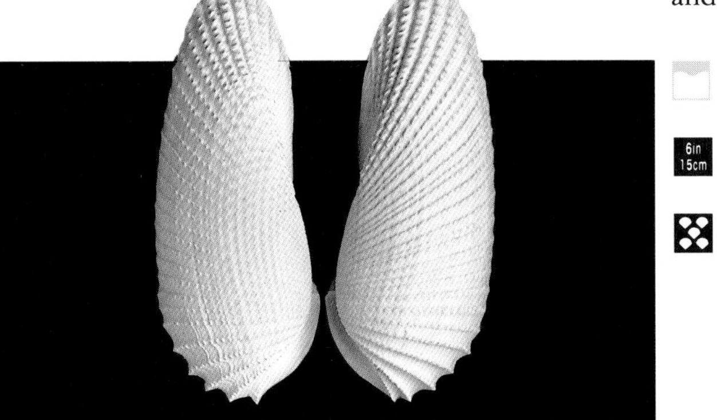

6in 15cm

CYRTOPLEURA COSTATA

ANGEL WING

GENERAL DESCRIPTION The angel wing occurs from the south-east United States to Brazil and may burrow as deep as 3ft. into the mud substrate. It has a beautiful thin, elongated, delicate white shell. The radially ridged valves resemble a pair of wings when they are opened out on the sand. The species can grow to 7½in., although recently caught specimens rarely exceed 6in.
OCCURRENCE East United States to Brazil.

4in 10cm

PHOLAS DACTYLUS

EUROPEAN PIDDOCK

GENERAL DESCRIPTION This species has a thin, brittle off-white shell, the valves being sculpted by a series of about 20 circular ridges crossed by about 40 ribs, which radiate from the umbones. It bores into muds, shales, chalk and sandstones and is widely distributed throughout the north-east Atlantic and the Mediterranean. The animal has the remarkable property of producing phosphorescent substances, which cause it to glow in the dark with a greenish-blue light.
OCCURRENCE North-east Atlantic; Mediterranean.

Class POLYPLACOPHORA

1in 2.5cm

LEPIDOCHITONA CINEREUS

GREY CHITON

GENERAL DESCRIPTION This species occurs from just below high-tide level down into the subtidal zone. The underside of its shell plates is a pale bluish-green. The upper surface is beige to grayish-brown but is normally heavily encrusted.
OCCURRENCE Scandinavia; west Europe; west Mediterranean.

2½in 6cm

CHITON MAMORATUS

MARBLED CHITON

GENERAL DESCRIPTION This species is relatively common in intertidal areas on most rocky shores throughout its range. The smooth upper surface is beige to greyish brown with paler blotches or streaks whilst the girdle has alternating bands of gray or green.
OCCURRENCE South-east Florida to West Indies.

Class CEPHALOPODA

Family NAUTILIDAE Chambered nautilus shells

The four or five living species of chambered nautilus are the last remnants of a group that dates from the beginning of fossil records. The external shell is divided into chambers, and the animal, which has about 90 tentacles, lives in the last or "body" chamber. The other, earlier chambers are filled with gas, which provides a buoyancy mechanism that permits the nautilus to rise or fall in the ocean depths. The flame-like radial markings on the outer shell surface camouflage by breaking up its outline when it is viewed from below.

NAUTILUS POMPILUS

COMMON CHAMBERED NAUTILUS

GENERAL DESCRIPTION The common nautilus differs from other living species because it has no umbilicus, the body whorl completely covering the earlier whorls. The white or creamy shell is thin and light. It lives in colonies around the Philippines and Palau Islands in the Pacific Ocean, but dead shells are often washed ashore throughout the west Pacific, including Australia. The pearly shell is often used to produce souvenirs such as the half-section illustrated, which shows the internal shell chambers.
OCCURRENCE South-west Pacific.

8in 20cm

Family SPIRULIDAE Spirulas

Squid-like cephalopods, possessing an internal, loosely coiled, chambered shell, which is completely embedded within the living animal. There is only one species.

SPIRULA SPIRULA

COMMON SPIRULA

GENERAL DESCRIPTION Shells of this species are often washed onto beaches after storms. They may be readily recognized by the loosely coiled and chambered shell, which, in life, is embedded within the tissues of this deep-water squid. The thin, fragile shell chambers are filled with gas, which presumably acts as a means of providing buoyancy. When the animal dies and its body rots away, the shell floats to the surface. The species lives at depths of 3000ft.
OCCURRENCE Worldwide.

1in 2.5cm

Family ARGONAUTIDAE Argonauts

ARGONAUTA ARGO

COMMON PAPER NAUTILUS

GENERAL DESCRIPTION The argonaut or paper nautilus is a free-swimming, octopus-like animal, which inhabits warm, open seas throughout the world. The beautiful shell-like structures are not true shells. They are secreted by two specialized arms of the female for use as a receptacle for the animal's eggs. Once the eggs hatch the female dies, releasing the "shell". Numerous low, wavy ridges extend from the tightly coiled spire to the margin. The structure is off-white to cream, the early part of the keel and spines being faintly gray. The male has no shell. The common paper nautilus is often washed ashore after storms.

OCCURRENCE Worldwide.

Class SCAPHOPODA

Family DENTALIIDAE Tusk shells

Over 1000 species of tusk shell occur throughout the world in a variety of habitats. They live in sand or mud from shallow water to considerable depths. The shell consists of a simple tube which is open at both ends. They have little use to man, although one North American species was once used for currency, as the shells could easily be strung together.

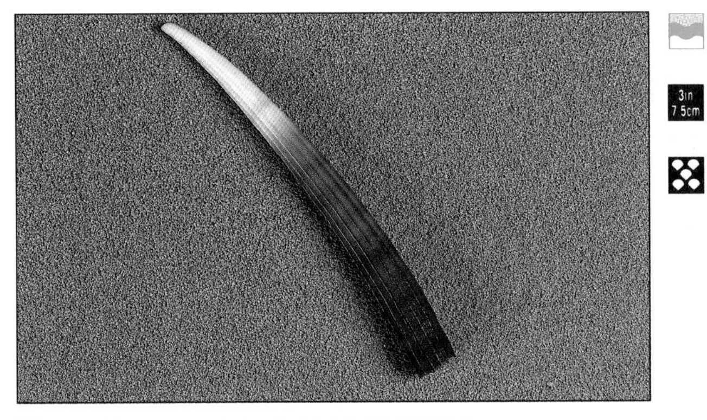

DENTALIUM ELEPHANTINUM

ELEPHANT'S TUSK

GENERAL DESCRIPTION The popularity of the elephant's tusk shell among collectors is due no doubt to its large size. Approximately 10 strong, rounded ribs run the whole length of the shell. It occurs throughout its range at depths from 6 to 150ft. It burrows down into the substrate of sand or mud, with the smaller end protruding above the surface. In common with all tusk shells, it is carnivorous, feeding on foraminifera and other microorganisms.

OCCURRENCE South Philippines; Japan; north Australia.

ANTALIS DENTALIS

EUROPEAN TUSK SHELL

GENERAL DESCRIPTION This shell is slightly curved and often traversed by strong longitudinal ridges. The shell is normally white but may be pale brown or pink. The animal, which is white in colour, normally occurs in colonies buried in sandy substrates at depths below 20ft. The shells are often washed ashore after storms.

OCCURRENCE Mediterranean; Adriatic.

Part IV FOSSILS

We commonly talk about something old as being a "fossil", but the process requires a lot more than simple age. There must be precisely the right combination of conditions, or else the dead animal or plant will simply decompose into nothing. Under normal circumstances, a dead animal or plant is attacked almost from the time of death by decomposers, ranging from scavenging vertebrates to microbes. Fleshy tissue disappears first, leaving bones, shells and other hard parts. Given time, these, too, vanish.

ABOVE *Still wickedly sharp after nearly 100 million years, this tooth was shed by a sand shark of the genus* Odontaspis. *Teeth fossilize exceptionally well and in many cases are the only body parts to survive.*

Very occasionally, however, an organism settles in a place where oxygen levels are so low that decomposers cannot function. It may be buried in a thick layer of fine mud in a lake delta, swallowed by a landslide or shifting sand dune, or covered by the constant rain of sediment falling on the ocean floor. Here, although the soft parts of the organism will soon disappear, any bones, teeth, shell or wood, which are made up of more durable substances such as calcium carbonate, chitin or cellulose, can take many years to go. This gives the opportunity for chemical changes to occur either to preserve the organism in stone or to use the space it occupied as a mould.

The way in which a fossil formed depends on the original chemical composition of the organism, its surrounding matrix and the length of time it has been fossillized.

Petrified wood is a good example: the original cellulose has been replaced by silica, which infiltrated the wood in solution. Sometimes the mineralization only extends to the empty spaces between the wood fibres (**permineralization**), while in other specimens the wood itself dissolves, to be replaced completely by minerals (**replacement**). If the wood dissolves, leaving a gap in the harder matrix, and later fills with another mineral, the result is known as a **pseudomorph** or natural cast.

These processes can occur not just with wood but with a wide range of fossils. While it is not unusual to find unaltered gastropod shells that are 150 million years old, many more undergo replacement with such minerals as pyrite or quartz. Plant material (and, more unusually, soft-bodied animals) may undergo carbonization, in which the tissues are converted to a thin carbon film. The beautiful Carboniferous fossils of ferns, horsetails and clubmosses are usually examples of carbonization.

Not everything that appears to be a fossilized organism really is one. **Trace fossils** are the result of biological activity, but are not the organisms themselves. This category includes faeces (coprolites), burrows, borings, worm tubes, trails and footprints of living things.

PERMINERALIZATION

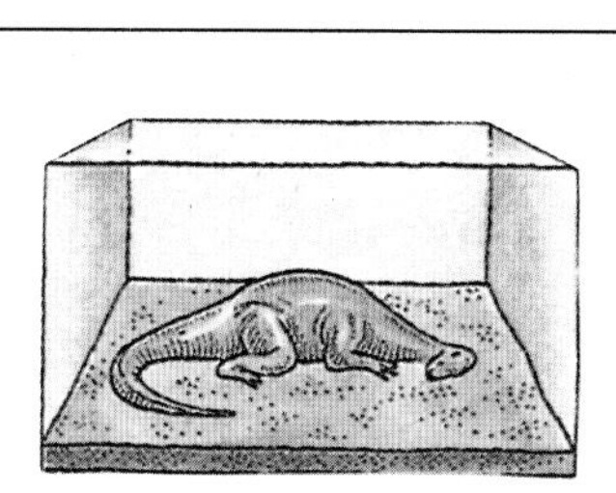

1 The animal dies and falls to the sea or lake bed. The soft parts are decomposed by bacteria, but the hard parts remain.

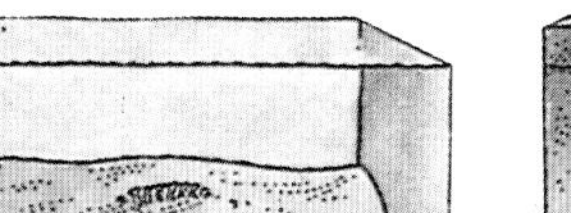

2 Sediments continually rain down from the water above and settle on and around the skeleton.

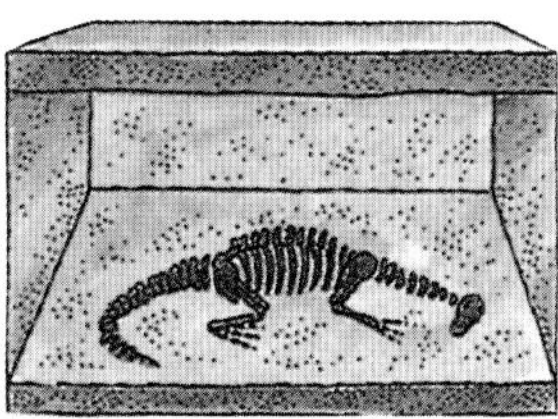

3 The sediments compact into rock, and percolating water slowly replaces the chemicals in the bones with hard minerals.

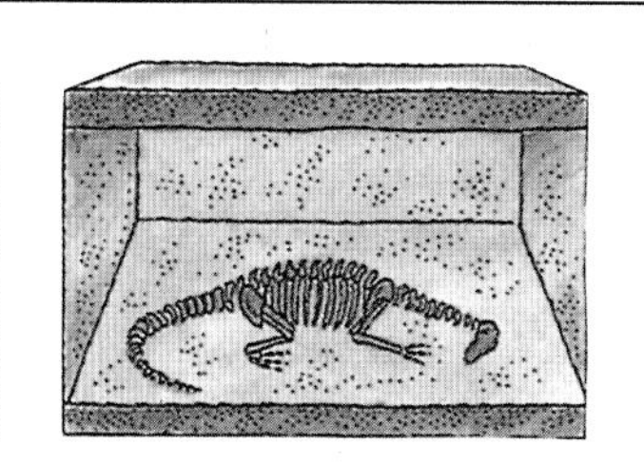

4 Percolating water may dissolve the bones, leaving a mold fossil, or fill the mold with minerals, forming a cast fossil.

THE GEOLOGICAL CALENDAR

To break geological time into manageable pieces, palaeontologists use eons, eras, periods and epochs, each unit encompassing shorter stretches of time than the one before. At the moment we are in the Cenozoic Era, Quaternary Period and Holocene Epoch. Units of geological time are not of standard length; the Triassic Period lasted about 35 million years, while the Jurassic Period lasted 69 million years.

CENOZOIC ERA

63–65 million years BP – present

QUATERNARY PERIOD

HOLOCENE EPOCH

11 000 years BP – present

PLEISTOCENE EPOCH

1.8–2 million years BP – 11 000 years BP

Climate cooling continues, ice sheets advance; Ice Age megafauna evolve. Mass extinction of megafauna ends epoch. *Homo erectus* appears in early Pleistocene, followed by *Homo sapiens* in late Pleistocene.

TERTIARY PERIOD

PLIOCENE EPOCH

5–7 million years BP – 1.8–2 million years BP

Climate cools, grasslands dominate. First hominids appear early in epoch.

MIOCENE EPOCH

24–26 million years BP – 5–7 million years BP

Mammalian diversity reaches peak. Old World monkeys and apes appear. *Carcharodon*, a huge shark, appears.

OLIGOCENE EPOCH

37 million years BP – 24–26 million years BP

Grasses, toothed whales, New World monkeys appear. *Mesohippus* evolves.

EOCENE EPOCH

54 million years BP – 37 million years BP

First horses *(Eohippus)*, elephants, whales, anthropoids.

PALEOCENE EPOCH

65 million years BP – 54 million years BP

Beginning of the Age of Mammals; first prosimians appear. *Diatryma* and other flightless, predatory birds appear.

MESOZOIC ERA

225 million years BP – 65 million years BP

CRETACEOUS PERIOD

144 million years BP – 65 million years BP

Flowering plants dominate gymnosperms; dinosaurs include *Tyrannosaurus* and *Triceratops*. Birds, mammals diversifying. Period ends with mass extinction of dinosaurs and ammonoids.

JURASSIC PERIOD

213 million years BP – 144 million years BP

Dinosaurs dominate, including stegosaurs and brontosaurs; *Archaeopteryx*, frogs, salamanders appear. Gondwanaland splits and continents begin to shift towards modern positions.

TRIASSIC PERIOD

248 million years BP – 213 million years BP

Dinosaurs rise to prominence. Ammonoids common in seas; turtles, lizards appear. Pangea splits.

PALEOZOIC ERA

565 million years BP – 248 million years BP

PERMIAN PERIOD

286 million years BP – 248 million years BP

Reptiles diversify; protomammals and protodinosaurs appear late in period. Mass extinction eliminates trilobites.

CARBONIFEROUS PERIOD

345 million years BP – 286 million years BP

(Including Mississippian and Pennsylvanian periods, also known as Lower and Upper Carboniferous respectively) Warm, wet climate fosters development of coal-swamp forests. Amphibians dominate on land; ammonoids and brachiopods in sea. Conifers appear.

DEVONIAN PERIOD

395 million years BP – 345 million years BP

Jawless fishes dominate oceans, with trilobites, brachiopods and crinoids. Ammonoids, amphibians, bony fishes appear; first forests.

SILURIAN PERIOD

430 million years BP – 395 million years BP

Fishes diversify; first primitive land plants appear.

ORDOVICIAN PERIOD

500 million years BP – 430 million years BP

Jawless fish appear; wide variety of gastropods, bivalves, brachiopods and other shellfish.

CAMBRIAN PERIOD

565 million years BP – 500 million years BP

Trilobites, shelled invertebrates appear.
Nautiloids arise on threshold of Ordovician.

COLLECTING FOSSILS

HOW TO FIND FOSSIL DEPOSITS

Fossils are not distributed randomly through the world's rock strata. Certain kinds of rocks yield abundant fossils, while others are utterly barren, so a basic knowledge of geology will obviously help immensely with your hunting.

Rocks come in three basic varieties – igneous, metamorphic and sedimentary. Igneous rocks are formed from crystallized lava or magma. Metamorphic rocks are so named because they have undergone fundamental changes due to pressure and heat. For obvious reasons, metamorphic and igneous rocks are poor hunting grounds for fossils. Instead, you must search for sedimentary rock, which is created when dust, mud, sand or other soil particles collect in layers, then are solidified (through compaction and other processes) into rock. The same cloudburst that washes a thick new layer of silt into a lake may also carry down the remains of dead animals and plants, which are buried – potential fossils in the making.

Limestone provides one of the best hunting grounds for fossils, since it was often created from thick deposits of invertebrate shells in the first place. Nummulitic limestone, for example, comes from deposits of foraminiferan tests, while ancient corals were also major contributors to many limestones.

Digging in rocky soil may turn up an occasional lucky find, but for more consistent results you must look for places where the sedimentary bedrock has been exposed, either naturally or, more often, through human activity. They include quarries, road and railway cuts, mines, tunnels and construction sites, as well as natural sites such as outcroppings, fault lines, river banks and coastal or mountain cliffs.

Sometimes, the fossil hunter's work is done by animals. Anthills are the most productive spots to find conodonts, the minute, toothlike fossils from soft-bodied invertebrates, which are carried to the surface by ants in the course of their digging. An examination of anthills may also turn up shark's teeth, bone fragments and tiny mammal teeth.

The best sources of information for the fossil hunter are geological survey departments, which can supply lists of well-known fossil sites open to the public, geological and topographical maps and pertinent regulations. The geology department of a local college or university is another excellent starting place for locating nearby fossil sites, and the faculty may be able to direct you to organizations offering collecting trips. Some departments may even offer enrichment courses for the public that include fossil study.

ABOVE *Having long ago fallen into the ocean, this tree trunk was encased in limestone and eventually dissolved. The mold it left behind was filled with minerals, creating a natural cast or pseudomorph.*

FIELD TECHNIQUES

Anyone can collect fossils with their bare hands, but the good finds aren't always lying on the surface, weathered free in a handy size. For the more serious hunter, a few pieces of equipment are essential. Start with the right clothing: sturdy pants, a long-sleeved shirt to prevent sunburn, work gloves, a brimmed hat and heavy boots. Whenever you are working in a quarry, along a high road

ABOVE *Sea cliffs provide an excellent place to prospect for fossils. This cliff of shale in northern Iceland shows thick beds of several different varieties of fossil bivalves.*

cut or below cliffs, wear a hard hat, and always wear safety goggles when splitting or hammering rock.

A good knapsack, or shoulder bag, should contain a geologist's rock hammer, an assortment of chisels, a good quality hand lens, a small and medium brush (shaving brushes are terrific), a trowel and a sieve; depending on the site and the kinds of fossils you're expecting, a coarse sieve and one with finer mesh may be needed.

Your most important pieces of equipment are a notebook and pencil. Good fossil hunters are obsessive note-takers, recording data and making small, detailed sketches of the site, the fossils and their positions in the strata. If you are a reasonably competent photographer, supplement your field notes with clear photographs, but remember not to fall into the trap of believing that a picture can take the place of field notes. A camera does not discriminate, and cannot sort out the important details from the trivial the way the human eye and mind can.

At a minimum, your field notes should record the general and specific location, overall appearance and layout of the exposed bed, with particular attention to the bedding planes (the surface of old sediment deposits) and their position if they have been inclined through folding. Note the angle of incline (dip) and the strike, which runs at a 90-degree angle to the dip. On your topographical map or a hand-drawn sketch, note compass bearings to several distant points so you can triangulate to find the bed again. The notes should also include descriptions of the rock types and fossils present, both by group and relative abundance, and specific information about the beds and individual positions of the fossils you collect.

Only when the preliminary note-taking is finished should you begin removing fossils. Work with the rock, rather than against it, using the hammer as a last resort rather than an initial attack. Many shales will split apart along bedding planes with hand pressure or a prying twist from an awl or an old knife, for instance, but will fracture from the smack of a hammer.

Loose specimens rattling around inside your bag will be chipped and scratched, so wrap each individually in paper, including a temporary label which may be numbered for reference to your field notes.

CLEANING

Many of the specimens will be greatly improved by some judicious cleaning and preparation at home. Because the matrix and the fossil are often of different composition – and thus different hardness – it is usually possible to remove the softer matrix without damaging the fossil. This may be as simple as washing with water and a brush, or may require the use of power tools. Most of the time the effort falls somewhere between these extremes, with the collector patiently removing the matrix with hand tools and perhaps trimming the edges to a more presentable appearance with a rock saw. Sometimes the fossil can be removed from a limestone matrix by soaking the specimen in vinegar, which contains acetic acid.

Always experiment on a worthless specimen from the same site first, just in case something goes wrong, and, when working on the piece containing the fossil, develop the habit of always starting with a hidden surface where unexpected damage won't be disastrous.

STORING AND MAINTAINING A COLLECTION

Most collections start out stored in old cigar boxes, but as you develop as a fossil hunter, you will want to be more professional when storing your collection.

There are three basic criteria: the collection must be organized logically; everything must be clearly labeled; and the storage method must not endanger the specimens. The exact style of storage case is immaterial, but it should protect the fossils from direct sunlight and dust, and should have adjustable partitions in each drawer to make it easy to store specimens of different sizes and shapes. As a final touch, consider installing a glass top above the uppermost drawer, and putting in lighting to illuminate your best finds.

Each fossil in your collection needs a pedigree, the paper trail that leads from the field to the display case, without which the specimen is a mere curiosity. Label each specimen by dabbing a spot of white paint on a hidden surface, then writing in the catalog number in ink. The number corresponds to an entry in your catalog – traditionally kept in a ledger or a card index, but maintained much more easily today on a home computer. The catalog entry should include identification, age, location and collection date as a bare minimum.

Being a Responsible Fossil Hunter

Always seek permission before collecting on private land, and be scrupulous in obeying any requests or rules that the landowner might lay down. Be considerate of the landowner's property by closing any gates behind you, and staying away from machinery and out of fields.

Be aware of those who will come after you. Be restrained in your collecting, taking only what you need; while the vast majority of fossils will never be seen by human beings, those few that are exposed in accessible beds are a finite resource, and should be treated with great respect.

Finally, know your limitations. Amateurs have made many important discoveries in the field of paleontology, but reckless or sloppy extraction may ruin any value the find would otherwise have. If you stumble upon a true rarity, record as much as you can *in situ* and then seek professional help.

Above *Much of a fossil's value lies in its relation to the surrounding strata, and the hallmark of a professional dig is meticulous attention to such detail. This sauropod skeleton is being removed very carefully, with each step noted and the position of the bones scrupulously recorded.*

Above *Home computers make labeling your collection much easier. The specimen number at the upper left refers to a catalog entry, which includes all pertinent information about the fossils.*

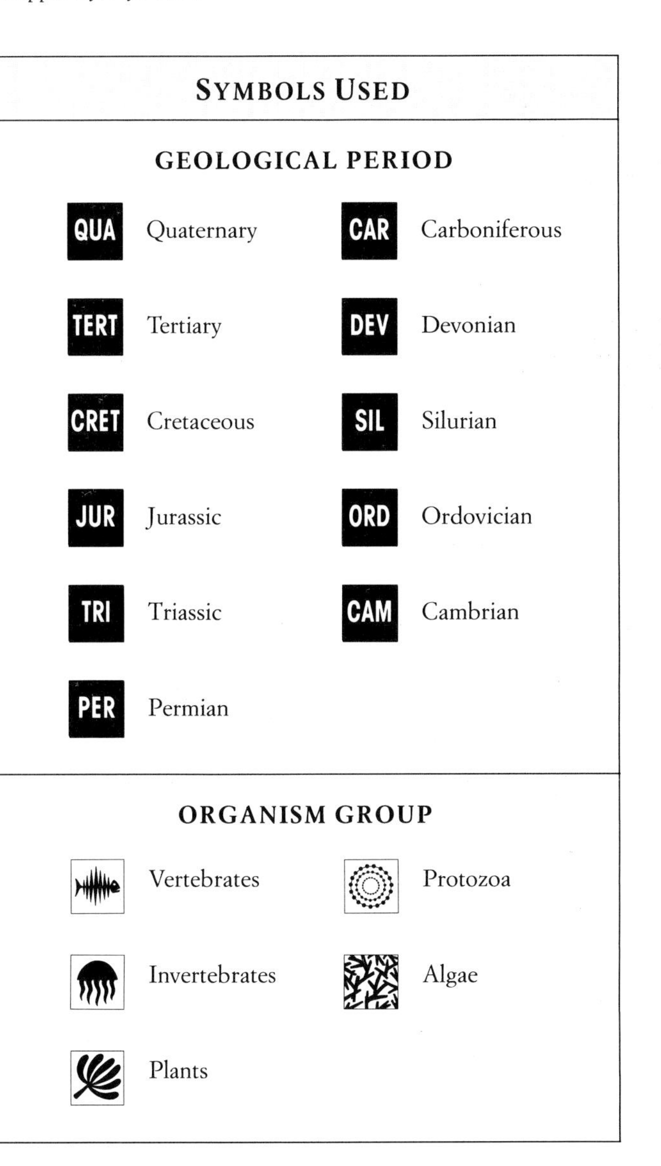

Symbols Used

GEOLOGICAL PERIOD

Symbol	Period	Symbol	Period
QUA	Quaternary	CAR	Carboniferous
TERT	Tertiary	DEV	Devonian
CRET	Cretaceous	SIL	Silurian
JUR	Jurassic	ORD	Ordovician
TRI	Triassic	CAM	Cambrian
PER	Permian		

ORGANISM GROUP

Vertebrates
Protozoa
Invertebrates
Algae
Plants

CYANOPHYTES

Also known as blue-greens, or blue-green algae, cyanophytes are among the most primitive of organisms, scarcely higher on the evolutionary scale than bacteria. They contain chlorophyl and can photosynthesize like true green plants. Cyanophyte colonies are known as stromatolites, and their distinctive shapes have been found, by microscopic examination, in rocks as old as 3000 million years. In some tropical lagoons, where evaporating seawater raises the salinity and temperature beyond that which most living things can stand, cyanophytes still make stromatolites, secreting lime to form squat, wide-topped pillars that echo the fossil stromatolites perfectly.

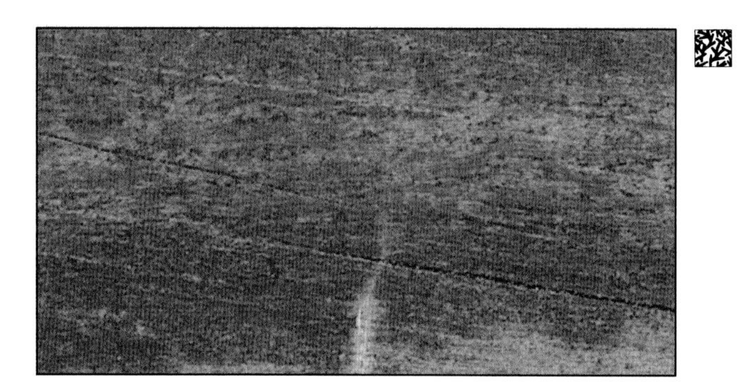

FORAMINIFERANS

Important out of all proportion to their size, these often microscopic protozoans were and are staggeringly plentiful in the oceans, beginning in the Ordovician and continuing through to the present. Their limey tests, falling to the sea floor in thick layers, are a major contributor to the formation of limestone, and are so common that they serve as valuable indicator fossils for paleontologists, recording past climates.

CAMERINA SPP.

GENERAL DESCRIPTION One of the larger forams (as this group is commonly called), *Camerina* has a lenticular test that ranges from 0.5cm to 7.5cm (¼–3in) in diameter. The test consists of a tightly coiled whorl with thick, calcareous walls and small septae, or chambers. Large and small forms are sometimes divided specifically.

OCCURRENCE *Camerina* occurred from the Jurassic to the Miocene, but is found in extraordinary large numbers in deposits from the Eocene, indicating a warm, shallow oceanic environment; beds of *Camerina* limestone have been important since the days of the Ancient Egyptians. It is found in southern Europe, parts of Asia and the South Pacific, and around the Gulf of Mexico.

RANGE Jurassic–Miocene.

JUR

NON-FLOWERING PLANTS

Mosses and liverworts were the first land plants but, lacking true roots and a rigid cell structure, they were restricted to extremely moist environments, and grew to only a few centimetres in height. Later, horsetails, clubmosses and ferns arose with roots and rigid stems, allowing them greater access to the land (although they still required fairly moist soil in which to grow). These are among the most common of fossilized plants, particularly in Carboniferous rocks.

Non-flowering plants reproduce by several methods. Mosses alternate between sterile generations and sexual generations that produce spores; spores are also used by ferns and their relatives. In the more advanced seedferns (now extinct), cycads, gingkos and conifers, wind-blown pollen fertilized the cone, which contained eggs and later produced unprotected seeds. Collectively these plants are known as gymnosperms, and while their reproductive system is an improvement on earlier methods, wind-borne pollution is still quite chancy.

CAR

CALAMITES

GENERAL DESCRIPTION Horsetails were an important part of the Carboniferous forests; this type, one of the more common fossils from this period, reached heights of 60ft. The fossils represent stems, which were longitudinally ridged and in jointed segments of varying lengths, depending on the specimen.

Only recently was it discovered that *Calamites* is the stem of the same plant whose leaves were known as *Annularia*. The names have been retained here to avoid confusion.

Horsetails remain common wetland plants in many parts of the world, but the surviving species are small, usually no more than waist-high.

OCCURRENCE Worldwide.

RANGE Upper Carboniferous.

CAR

ANNULARIA

GENERAL DESCRIPTION The whorled, slightly spatulate leaves of *Annularia* are common in Pennsylvanian (Upper Carboniferous) deposits; they are the leaves of the same sphenophyte horsetail whose stems were once mistakenly assigned to the genus *Calamites*. In the specimen shown, the leaf clusters have been dislodged and have fossilized individually, but they are frequently found still attached to the upper surface of the twig, which apparently grew out of the joint-nodès of the *Calamites* stem.

OCCURRENCE Worldwide.

RANGE Upper Carboniferous.

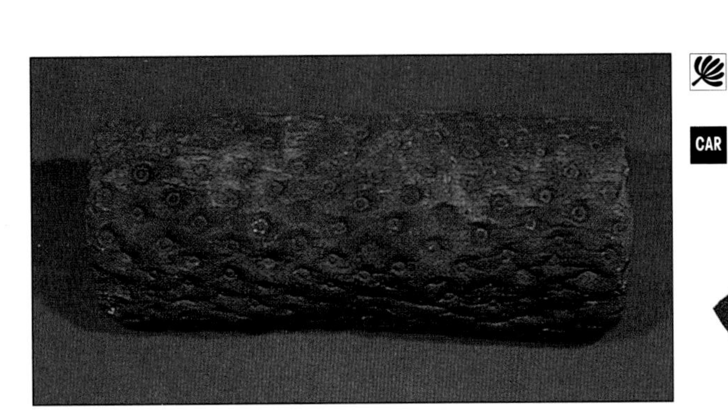

CAR

STIGMARIA FICOIDES

GENERAL DESCRIPTION Not a true genus unto itself, *Stigmaria* are the fossilized roots of tree clubmosses, *Lepidodendron*. While not a strictly correct usage, *Stigmaria* has been retained here for simplicity's sake. Tree clubmosses such as *Lepidodendron* are common fossils from the Carboniferous, and apparently formed a significant portion of the coal-swamp forests. While most surviving clubmosses are small, this genus attained heights of more than 150ft., with a heavily scaled trunk and wide-spreading root system. The genus is extinct, but at its peak numbered more than 100 species, judging from the fossil record.

Stigmarid roots are usually found as casts, in sediment layers immediately beneath coal seams – layers that once were the soil in which the clubmoss trees grew.

OCCURRENCE Europe.

RANGE Carboniferous.

CAR

PECOPTERIS SPP.

GENERAL DESCRIPTION *Pecopteris* was a true fern, or pteridophyte, although there is a suspicion that some members of the genus had developed into seed-ferns, a trait difficult to determine from carbonized fossils. True ferns represented several "firsts" in evolutionary history, including the first complex leaves and branched stems. These features, coupled with an improved vascular system, allowed the true ferns to evolve quickly into giants nearly 50ft. tall. Ferns today are much smaller, inhabiting the shade of the more advanced angiosperm trees, which now dominate the world's forests.

OCCURRENCE Europe; North America; North Africa; Asia.

RANGE Carboniferous.

CAR

ALETHOPTERIS SPP.

GENERAL DESCRIPTION The coal-swamp forests of the Carboniferous covered a great deal of what is now the Northern Hemisphere, so that many of the distinctive plant fossils of that period can be found in the United States, Europe and Asia. *Alethopteris* is a seed-fern (pteridosperm) that is common in this stratum; it has relatively thin, tapered leaflets that are straighter than many of its close relatives.

Seed-ferns were a big step forward in plant evolution. By enclosing the plant embryo in a tough, resilient cover and supplying it with nourishment, the seeds would not need perfect growing conditions immediately, but could hold out for longer periods of time, germinating when the situation improved.

OCCURRENCE Europe; North America; North Asia.

RANGE Carboniferous.

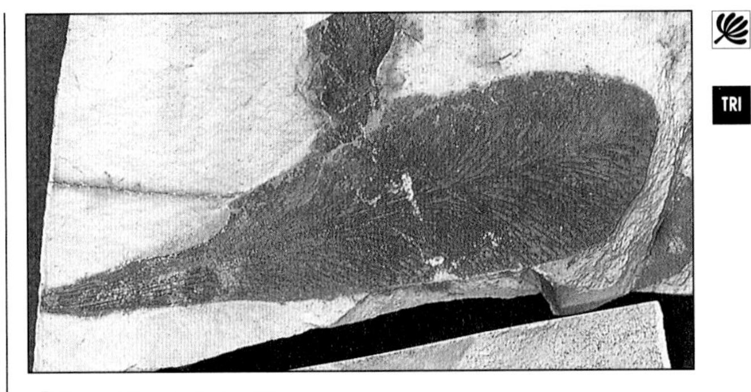

TRI

GLOSSOPTERIS

GENERAL DESCRIPTION *Glossopteris* is a critically important fossil in determining the make-up of the prehistoric supercontinent known as Gondwanaland. It has been found in most of the southern landmasses that once made up Gondwanaland, including Antarctica, which had a subtropical climate at the time. Most fossils are of single leaves, lanceolate or spatulate. *Glossopteris* was a seed-fern that grew into tree form, first appearing during the Permian and remaining common through the Triassic, when this specimen from New South Wales was fossilized.

RANGE Triassic.

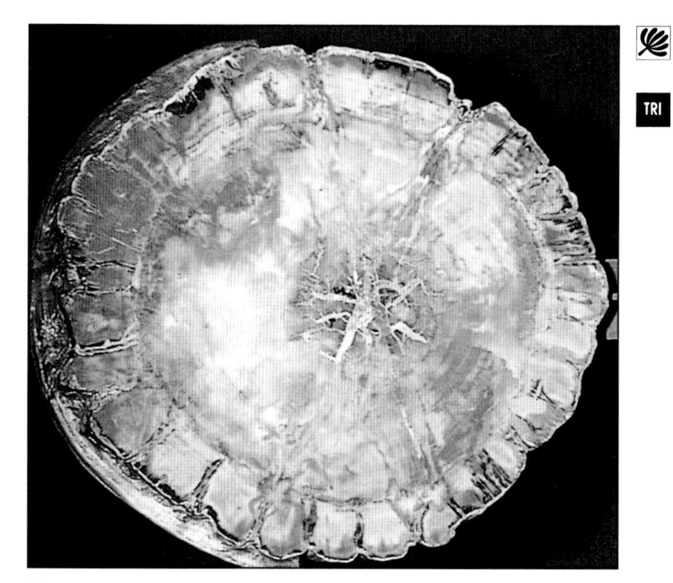

PETRIFIED WOOD

GENERAL DESCRIPTION Petrified wood is an unusual fossil with a wide distribution; there are significant sites in North America and Europe, as well as elsewhere. This specimen comes from the famous Petrified Forest National Park in Arizona, where primitive protopines, *Araucarioxylon*, were buried in saturated sediment and replaced with agate and jasper, creating a kaleidoscope of colors in each example.

While true petrified wood may preserve even the cellular structure, many more trees have been fossilized as molds or pseudomorphs, which record only the external structure of the log or root system, with none of the internal detail.

OCCURRENCE Worldwide.

RANGE Triassic.

AMBER

GENERAL DESCRIPTION Many trees, particularly conifers, secrete a gummy resin when injured. The resin seals the wound against insects, disease and desiccation, and under some conditions it may harden into a honey-coloured globule of amber.

Amber was apparently prized by Palaeolithic man, and by the time of the Ancient Celts it was an important jewelry item, but its value to paleontologists is less esthetic and more practical. Insects and arachnids often become mired in tree resin, and those trapped in amber display an astounding degree of preservation, even though they are actually hollow molds with thin, carbonized layers around the outside. This is especially fortunate because insects rarely fossilize otherwise, so much of our knowledge of prehistoric insects comes from amber specimens.

FLOWERING PLANTS

HYMENAEA SPP.

GENERAL DESCRIPTION First appearing in the fossil record roughly 100 million years BP, flowers represented a major advance in plant reproduction. By attracting insects (as well as other animals such as birds and bats), the plants enjoyed a much higher rate of pollination success, while greatly reducing their biological investment. Instead of dumping vast quantities of pollen into the wind, flowers produce sweet nectar to lure the animal, which is dusted with pollen from the stamens while eating. When the animal visits the next flower of the same species, the pollen is brushed against the female stigmas, and reproduction occurs.

The earliest angiosperms, or flowering plants, were the magnolias, which arose during the Cretaceous. Shown here is a flower from a species of *Hymenaea*, a member of the vast legume family.

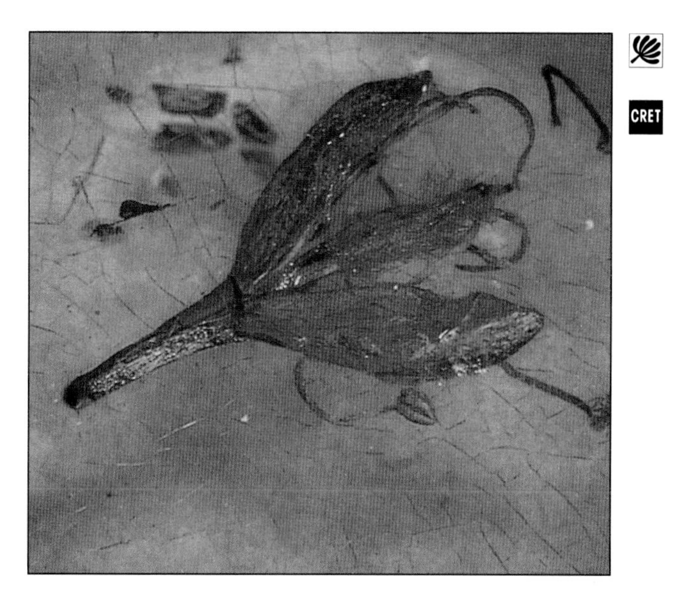

INVERTEBRATES

The term "invertebrates" loosely describes those animals above the protist level that do not possess backbones, including such well-known fossils as brachiopods, molluscs and trilobites. They are by far the most commonly found examples of prehistoric life, and make up the bulk of most fossil collections.

Phylum PORIFERA Sponges

Simplistic in design, sponges are simply aggregations of cells: in fact, there remains uncertainty as to whether sponges are individual animals or colonies of single-celled animals. Form is provided by spicules – minute rods that may fuse to form a skeleton for the sponge – or sponges may exist in unfused form. Some, like *Siphonia*, have siliceous spicules, while others, such as *Raphidonema*, possess calcareous spicules. Still other gain rigidity from a material called spongin, and lack spicules. The fossil record for sponges is patchy, but begins in the Precambrian.

SIPHONIA SPP.

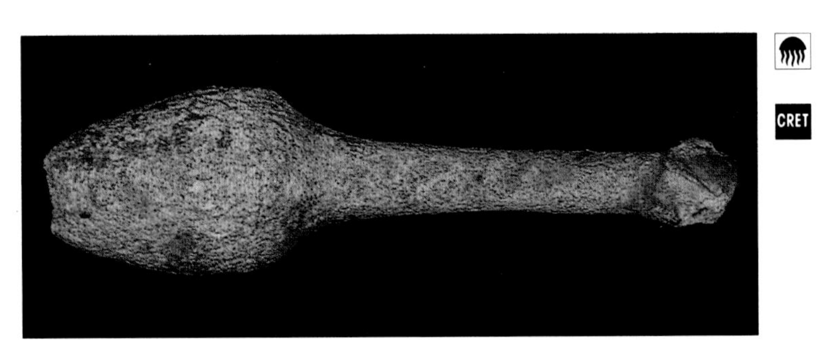

CRET

GENERAL DESCRIPTION Flower-shaped, the stalked sponges of the genus *Siphonia* had siliceous spicules, a large central cavity in the budlike body, and a network of tiny openings that connected to a primitive vascular system. *Siphonia* were "rooted" at the end of the stalk to the sea bed, and like all sponges depended on the ocean currents to bring them food particles.
OCCURRENCE Europe.
RANGE Cretaceous.

VENTRICULITES SPP.

CRET

GENERAL DESCRIPTION Species of the genus *Ventriculites* show a distinctive, vase-shaped body with a fused spicule construction; the body walls are thin and have large pores. This genus belongs to the group of sponges known as lychniskids, which have a unique spicule construction in which diagonal braces buttress the form, creating a pattern that is reminiscent of a Greek lantern, on which the group name is based.

Like *Siphonia, Ventriculites* is a European genus, and while it was common during the Cretaceous, it is rare in today's oceans.
OCCURRENCE Europe.
RANGE Cretaceous.

RAPHIDONEMA SPP.

CRET

GENERAL DESCRIPTION Unlike the preceding two sponge genera, the sponges of the genus *Raphidonema* have calcareous spicules, rather than siliceous; the spicules have three limbs, and are fused into a rigid skeleton. The overall appearance of the sponge is that of an open, widely flared vase, often heavily folded and covered with large pores and lumps. The length is usually 2in. or less. The species shown is *R. parcatum*.
OCCURRENCE Europe.
RANGE Cretaceous.

Phylum CNIDARIA Corals, Jellyfish and Hydrozoans

This phylum includes aquatic, radially symmetrical animals. Unlike sponges, they have definite tissue layers, but remain very simple organisms, lacking internal organs and a central nervous system. There are two major body plans – the polyp, a sedentary, columnar form often with tentacles around the oral opening, and the medusa, a flattened, free-swimming variation of the polyp. Both are radially symmetrical around an axis that runs through the central oral opening. Anemones, corals and hydra are examples of polyps, while jellyfish are medusae, although in many living genera, generations alternate between the two forms. The class Anthozoa includes many colonial species with hard, calcareous skeletons, which fossilize exceptionally well. The corals belong to this class, which arose during the Ordovician.

HALYSITES SPP.

SIL

GENERAL DESCRIPTION Often known as chain coral, *Halysites* is one of the tabulate corals, a group of colonial cnidarians; the specimen shown, *H. cantenularius*, has been cut in cross-section, revealing the individual corallites with their tabulae, the horizontal sections that give this group its name. In life a *Halysites* colony would have been a series of long, thin, upright tubes, joined along the edges. Adjoining walls in tabulate corals were sometimes pierced by a series of holes called mural pores, but these are not found in *Halysites*.
OCCURRENCE Worldwide.
RANGE Silurian.

FAVOSITES SPP.

SIL

GENERAL DESCRIPTION One of the most common fossil corals of the Middle Paleozoic, *Favosites* is a tabulate coral with irregularly five-sided corallites in cross-section. The walls of the corallite, which was secreted by the coral animal, are thin and pocked with mural pores, while the tabulae are closely packed. The corallum may be large and irregularly shaped. Because of its shape, *Favosites* is often known as honeycomb coral.

Tabulate corals were common reef-builders in the Middle and Upper Paleozoic, providing the foundation of the reef, and the living space for many other species of marine invertebrates. Even more so than other corals, tabulate corals seemed to change growth patterns as environmental conditions altered, making identification difficult at times.
OCCURRENCE Worldwide.
RANGE Silurian–Devonian.

ZAPHRENTIS SPP.

DEV

GENERAL DESCRIPTION One of the rugose, or horn, corals, *Zaphrentis* was a solitary type that secreted a cup-shaped corallite; the inside of the "cup" is lined with ridge-like septae, which are the vertical interior walls of the corallite. The pointed end of the coral would have originally been anchored in mud, with the open end of the cup facing upward so the coral animal could filter food particles from the water.
OCCURRENCE Europe; North America.
RANGE Devonian–Lower Carboniferous.

ACERVULARIA SPP.

GENERAL DESCRIPTION One of the colonial rugose corals, *Acervularia* formed large, usually four-sided corallites with pronounced, finely toothed septae. The species shown here, *A. ananas*, known as the pineapple coral, is common in the Wenlockian sediments of England.

The rugose corals had six major septae, which in life would have provided support for six corresponding menesteries, bands of tissue that divided the coral polyp's body.

OCCURRENCE Europe.

RANGE Silarian–Devonian.

LITHOSTROTION SPP.

GENERAL DESCRIPTION *Lithostrotion* corallites may be pentagonal, round or four-sided, but are always marked by cone-shaped tabulae and a conical lump in the centre of the calice, or cup, ridged by septae; the corallites are often long and sinuous. This genus was a colonial rugose coral, with colonies growing to widths of more than 12in. and forming a significant portion of the fossil reefs of the Carboniferous.

OCCURRENCE Most of the Northern Hemisphere; Africa; Australia.

RANGE Devonian–Lower Carboniferous.

PALAEOSMILIA SPP.

GENERAL DESCRIPTION One of the rugose corals, *Palaeosmilia* is found in both haploid (solitary) and compound (colonial) forms. The hallmark of this genus is the tightly packed septae; in *Palaeosmilia* the septae are radially symmetrical, rather than bilaterally symmetrical, as in most other rugose corals.

OCCURRENCE Worldwide.

RANGE Carboniferous.

SCLERACTINID CORALS

GENERAL DESCRIPTION The scleractinids include the sea anemones and the stony corals, the latter being far more important to the fossil record than the soft, rarely fossilized anemones. Scleractinids – or hexacorals, as they are sometimes known – may be solitary or colonial, and include all the world's living hard corals. Shown is an unidentified species of scleractinid from the Jurassic.

OCCURRENCE Worldwide.

RANGE Triassic–Recent.

Phylum BRYOZOA Bryozoans

Similar at first glance to corals or plants (leading to the vernacular name "moss animals"), bryozoan colonies are common fossils from the Ordovician onward. Each individual animal is a polyp-like zooecia, which secretes an exoskeleton, often calcareous. Fossil colonies often show a branching form marked with small openings known as zooids.

Bryozoans remain common marine animals. Adults "brood" the young in special compartments, releasing the larvae into the water when their development is complete. The larvae pass through a planktonic phase before settling down to form a new colony. They do so by attaching themselves to a surface, then "degenerating" into a small mass of larval tissue, from which new individuals, known as ancestrulae, grow. Each ancestrula then produces buds, which in turn bud themselves, expanding the colony. As it grows, the shape and function of the colony may change to adapt to changing environmental conditions.

The shapes of fossil bryozoans vary from flattened funnels like *Fenestella*, to crusting coverings, to delicate branches.

FENESTELLA SPP.

GENERAL DESCRIPTION This common lace bryozoan formed colonies that fanned out gracefully, with thin cross-bars linking the branches. Each branch possessed twin rows of zooids, on one side only, so that a pseudomorph of the wrong side of a *Fenestella* colony may not show the zooids. The species shown is *F. plebeia* from the Lower Carboniferous.
OCCURRENCE Europe.
RANGE Ordovician–Permian.

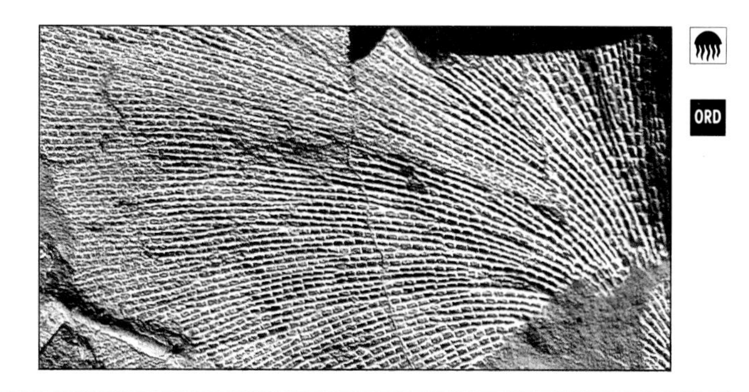

ORD

Phylum BRACHIOPODA Brachiopods

Superficially resembling bivalves, brachiopods are shellfish with valves (shells) of unequal size, and are the largest and most important group of fossil animals. Extremely common in sediments from shallow oceans, brachiopods first appear in the fossil record during the Lower Cambrian, and although a few hundred species survive, they reached their zenith during the Devonian.

There are two classes: the Inarticulata and the Articulata, separated by the lack of a hinge between the two valves in the Inarticulata. Living forms are known as lampshells, because of the resemblance of the lower (or pedicle) valve to a Roman oil lamp. Brachiopods are usually permanently fixed to the substrata by a fleshy stalk that protrudes from a hole in the pedicle valve, known as the pedicle foramen. As a general rule, the larger of the two valves was the ventral valve in life.

Brachiopods, typical of shellfish, are filter-feeders. The feeding organ, known as the lophophore, is covered with fine, hairlike cilia that beat in sequence, creating a current that draws food-bearing water into the shell, where tiny organic particles are strained out before the water is expelled. The branches of the lophophore are known as brachia, and are supported by calcified brachidium, which form complex spirals in some brachiopods.

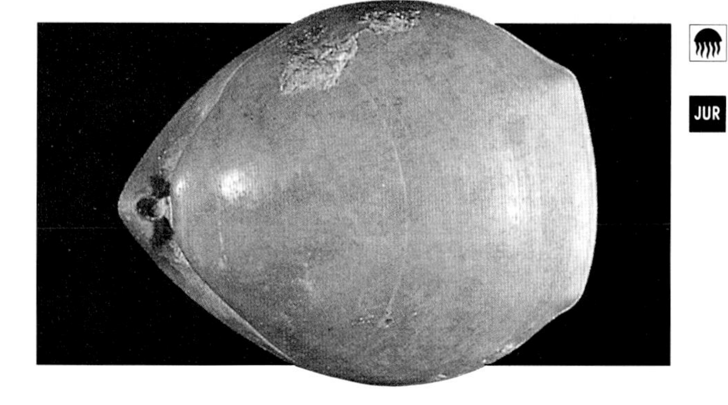

JUR

OBOVOTHYRIS SPP.

GENERAL DESCRIPTION Bulbous in shape, *Obovothyris* is a ribless brachiopod with a small pedicle foramen and a strongly curved umbo, the "point" or beak of the pedicle valve. Length is usually ½in. or less. The species illustrated is *O. magnobovata*.
OCCURRENCE Europe.
RANGE Jurassic.

SPHAEROIDOTHYRIS SPP.

GENERAL DESCRIPTION Similar to *Obovothyris, Sphaeroidothyris* is another bulbous Jurassic brachiopod with poorly defined growth lines on the valves. The species shown is the type, *S. sphaeroidothyris*.
RANGE Jurassic.

RHYNCHONELLA SPP.

GENERAL DESCRIPTION The type genus for the rhynchonellids, *Rhynchonella* has a well-developed pedicle foramen wedged between a pair of deltidial plates on the umbo. Most species have strong, radial ribbing, with a simplistic internal support for the lophophore.

The genus name *Rhynchonella* is sometimes used as an umbrella term for dozens of species of rhynchonellids, which are sometimes so abundant in deposits that they form coquina, a rock made up solely of fossilized shellfish. Surviving rhynchonellids differ little from those fossilized more than 500 million years BP; most lived (and still live) on muddy sea bottoms. The specimen illustrated is *R. capex* from the Silurian, showing the brachial valve.
OCCURRENCE Europe.
RANGE Ordovician–Recent.

LOBOTHYRIS SPP.

GENERAL DESCRIPTION *Lobothyris* is one of the terebratulid brachiopods, which have strongly biconvex shells, well-developed umbones and pedicle foramen; in this genus, the valves are smooth except for distinct, concentric growth marks. *Lobothyris* apparently mastered a difficult environment that other brachiopods could not tolerate, and it is found in great numbers, either by itself or with one other genus, *Tetrarhynchia*, a small, ribbed, triangular brachiopod. In the absence of competition, they dominated their particular niche, which today has been transformed into ironstone deposits. The species shown is *L. punctata*.
RANGE Jurassic.

RUGITELA SPP.

GENERAL DESCRIPTION *Rugitela* has distinct growth lines on its valves, which reach a maximum size of 1½in. in large specimens. The foramen is small and the umbo long and sharply hooked, curving back on the brachial valve.
RANGE Jurassic.

GIBBITHYRIS SPP.

GENERAL DESCRIPTION Globular and smooth, this small brachiopod has biconvex valves and a very small pedicle foramen. Growth lines are obvious and closely spaced on *Gibbithyris*, a common fossil from England. It belongs to a group of brachiopods known as terebratulids, which feature strong umbones and hinge lines less than the width of the valves at their widest point. Most of the surviving brachiopods are terebratulids.
OCCURRENCE England.
RANGE Cretaceous.

PLECTOTHYRIS SPP.

GENERAL DESCRIPTION A small brachiopod, *Plectothyris* has biconvex valves and a well-developed umbo pierced by the pedicle foramen. The valves are ribbed, especially along the anterior edges. The tip of the umbo has been cracked off in this specimen, revealing plain rock – for this, like many fossils, is a natural cast, retaining only the external shape of the animal that made the mold before dissolving away.
RANGE Jurassic.

LEPTAENA SPP.

GENERAL DESCRIPTION This genus of articulate brachiopods has a distinctive shape – the brachial valve is concave, while the pedicle valve is convex, and the anteriors of the valves meet at right angles, forming a squared-off front. It is finely ribbed, with coarse, concentric rings. Paleontologists think that *Leptaena* lived partially buried in the ocean. The specimen shown is *L. rhomboidalis*, from the famous Wenlock limestone deposits in England.
OCCURRENCE Worldwide.
RANGE Ordovician–Silurian.

Phylum MOLLUSCA Molluscs

A diverse phylum, the Mollusca include three broad classes – the gastropods (snails and slugs), bivalves (clams and their relatives) and cephalopods (octopi, squid, nautiloids and ammonoids) – and three smaller classes, the Monoplacophora, Scaphopoda (tusk shells) and the Polyplacophora (chitons). Their shells fossilize readily, making them among the most important of all fossil phyla.

Class GASTROPODA Gastropods

Gastropods are univalves, with single, usually coiled, unchambered shells (although some genera have no shells at all). They are the most common molluscs in the fossil record.

It is not always clear to a neophyte (either fossil hunter or beachcomber) how a gastropod moves, since only the shell is left after death. What is missing from the fossil or wave-tossed shell is the soft animal, with its large, muscular foot that allows the gastropod to glide along the bottom. The foot and head can be withdrawn into the aperture in the event of danger, and the opening sealed with a horny plate known as the operculum.

The shell of a gastropod hides the paired gills, feathery organs in the rear of the body whorl. Water is pumped into the shell, circulated around the gills, then expelled.

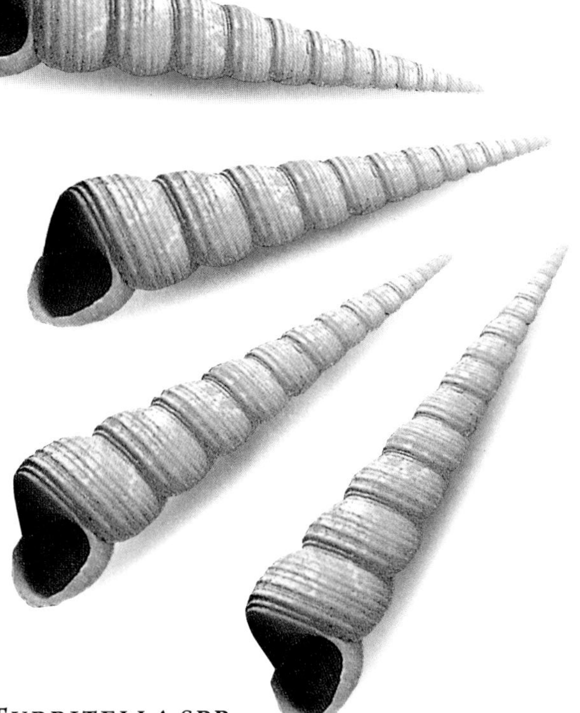

CRET

TURRITELLA SPP.

General description A long, tapered spire with slightly flattened or gently convex whorls distinguishes *Turritella*, a common fossil in strata laid down in shallow oceans. Depending on the species, the shell is usually 2in. or less in length with the whorls ribbed or keeled, and the aperture varying from rounded to square. Known as turret shells, *Turritella* remains a common gastropod in warm oceans, and the fossils are found almost worldwide in appropriate Tertiary deposits, making it an important index species.

Occurrence Worldwide.

Range Cretaceous–Recent.

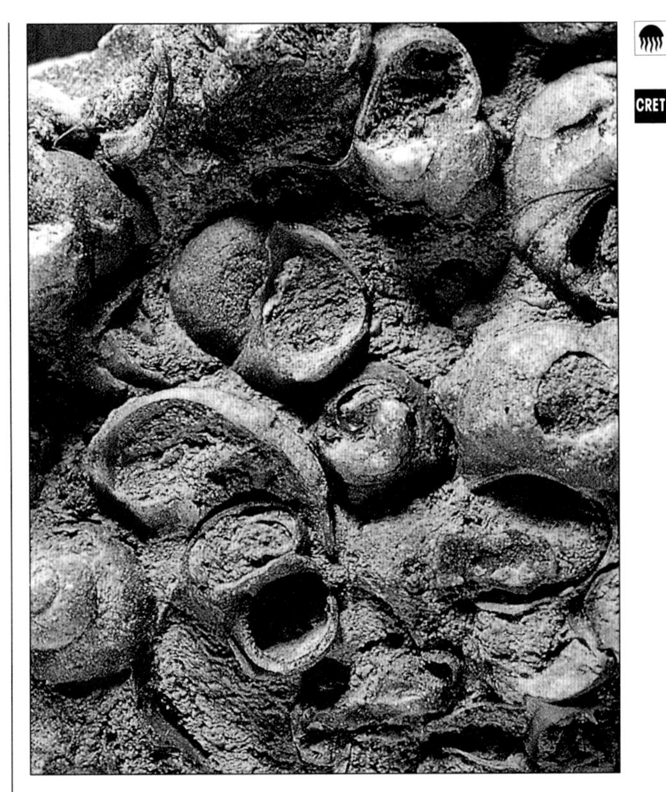

CRET

VIVIPARUS SPP.

General description *Viviparus* snails had smooth, generously rounded whorls and moderate spires, with large, circular apertures. The photograph shows specimens of the species *V. sussexiensis* from Europe. A surviving member of the genus, *V. georgianus*, the Georgia apple snail, is a common freshwater species in the southern United States; it, presumably like its fossilized ancestors, gives birth to live young.

Occurrence Europe.

Range Cretaceous–Recent.

CRET

NEPTUNEA SPP.

GENERAL DESCRIPTION Still an abundant genus in the world's oceans, *Neptunea* whelks first appear in the fossil record in the Cretaceous; the photographs shows *N. contraria* of the Pleistocene (right) alongside its modern equivalent, the smooth whelk. *Neptunea* shells have large, smooth body whorls and moderately tapered spires; the aperture is oval, forming a teardrop where it meets the siphonal canal.
OCCURRENCE Worldwide.
RANGE Cretaceous–Recent.

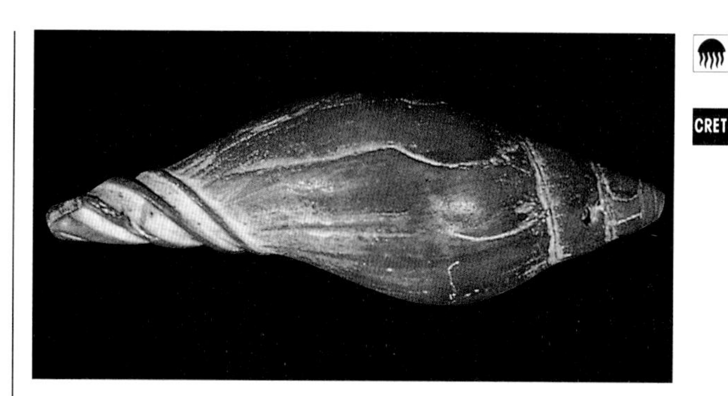

CRET

SCAPHELLA SPP.

GENERAL DESCRIPTION Living *Scaphella*, known as volutes, are colourfully marked shells popular with collectors. Fossils of this genus usually have nodes on the whorls, and four folds on the columella, the central pillar of the shell that surrounds the imaginary axis around which the gastropod coils. The species shown is *S. lamberti* from the Pleistocene.

In most gastropods, the earliest shell growth – the protoconch – is recorded at the very apex of the shell as a tiny, calcareous whorl. In *Scaphella*, however, the first secretions are horny and temporary, dropping off after the calcareous shell is secreted, and leaving a small point as evidence of their presence.
RANGE Cretaceous–Recent.

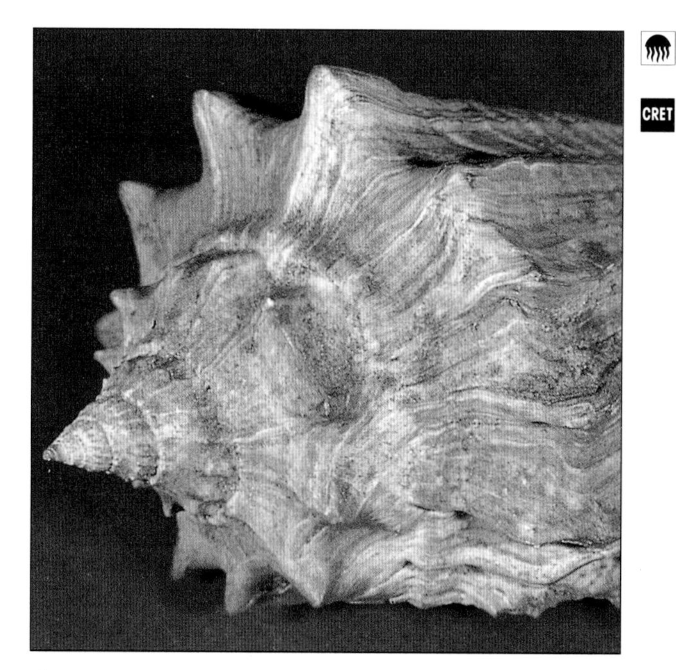

CRET

ATHLETA SPP.

GENERAL DESCRIPTION A robust fossil whelk, *Athleta* (formerly *Voluta*) has weak to strong nodes which may form short spines, and a long, slightly curved siphonal canal. The body whorl is ribbed. This genus includes a wide variety of living species, while fossil forms were especially important during the Cretaceous and Tertiary. The species shown is *A. luctator* from the Eocene.
OCCURRENCE Worldwide.
RANGE Cretaceous–Recent.

QUA

CLAVILITHES SPP.

GENERAL DESCRIPTION This genus features a relatively long to moderate spire, shouldered whorls and faint longitudinal ridging on the whorls. The long siphonal canal is missing from this specimen of *C. macrospira* from the Eocene.

The protoconch on *Clavilithes* is a form known as mammillated, since it takes the shape of two squat, rounded whorls, which are unornamented. In gastropods, the remainder of the shell is called the teleoconch.
OCCURRENCE North America; Europe; Asia.
RANGE Cenozoic.

CONUS SPP.

GENERAL DESCRIPTION So widespread that they serve as index fossils for the Cenozoic, *Conus* shells have flat to short spires with small, tightly wound apicle whorls and a large body whorl with a long, narrow aperture slit at each end. The whorls are usually smooth except for growth lines.

Conus remains one of the most diverse genera of gastropods, with about 350 living species, most found in warm, shallow inshore waters. They are active predators, harpooning other molluscs, worms and fish with a specialized "tooth" and subduing their prey with venom. The venom of some Indo-Pacific species, like the textile cone, has caused human deaths.
OCCURRENCE Worldwide.
RANGE Cretaceous–Recent.

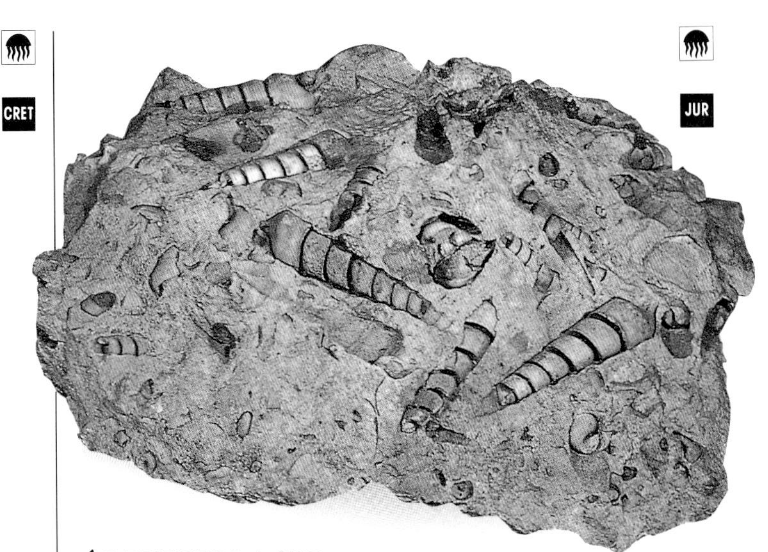

APTYXIELLA SPP.

GENERAL DESCRIPTION One of the most graceful of Jurassic fossils, *Aptyxiella* has a long spire, which in some species becomes extremely tapered, stretching several centimetres in length, with a tiny aperture and slight indentations on the insides of the whorls.

The specimens shown, of *A. portlandica*, are natural casts, formed when sediment entered the shell; the shells later dissolved, leaving a replica of their interiors.
RANGE Jurassic–Cretaceous.

PLEUROTOMARIA SPP.

GENERAL DESCRIPTION The shell of *Pleurotomaria* forms a broad cone, with slight knobbing on the shoulders and growth lines on the whorls that give the appearance of ridging; the aperture is rounded, with a pronounced slit in the outer lip. *Pleurotomaria* is a common gastropod fossil in many Upper Mesozoic deposits worldwide. The specimen shown is *P. bitorquata*.
OCCURRENCE Worldwide.
RANGE Jurassic–Cretaceous.

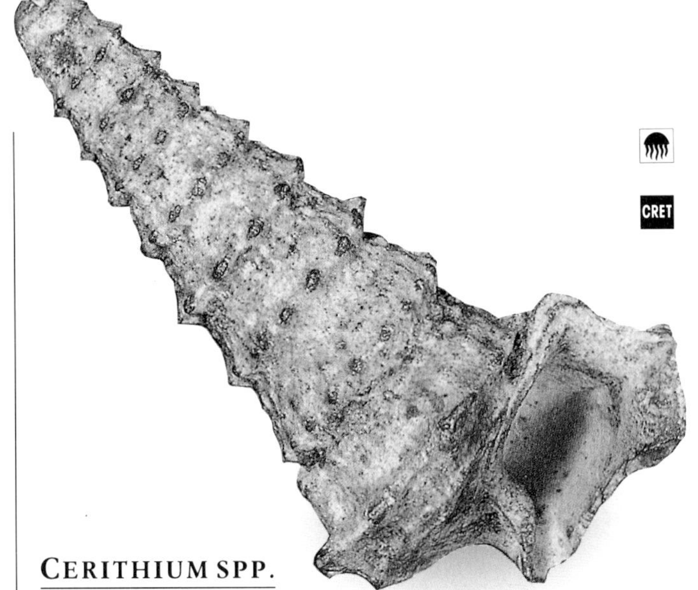

CERITHIUM SPP.

GENERAL DESCRIPTION A small shell, *Cerithium* has a long spire with a sharp apical angle, aperture lips that may flare, and a short, curved siphonal canal; the whorls may be knobbed or ridged with growth lines, or flat and almost unornamented. Modern species, known as ceriths, are highly ornamented and colorful, and inhabit ocean shallows and reefs. Shown is *C. duplex* from Europe.
OCCURRENCE Worldwide.
RANGE Cretaceous–Recent.

Class BIVALVIA Bivalves

Easily confused by beginners with brachiopods, bivalves also have two shells, but the valves are virtual mirror images of each other, since the plane of symmetry is horizontal in bivalves, rather than vertical as in brachiopods. The shapes may be subtriangular, triangular, ovoid or circular.
Many bivalves are adapted for burrowing, using the long, muscular foot to pull themselves through the mud or sand, while others glue themselves permanently to one spot. Still others (like scallops) clap their valves violently and "swim" awkwardly through the water.

ANTHRACOSIA AND CARBONICOLA SPP.

CAR

GENERAL DESCRIPTION Two of the most interesting fossil bivalves, these two small species were strictly freshwater inhabitants, living in the coal-swamp forests and marshes of the Carboniferous – among the first bivalves to make the change from saltwater to fresh. The *Carbonicola* shell is subtriangular, with a curved hinge line and minor growth-line ridging. *Anthracosia* belongs to the same family, and is essentially similar. In some areas, deposits of these two shells (sometimes mixed with a third, *Naiadites*) form "mussel beds" that may be 6ft. or more thick. Shown are the species *A. atra* (left) and *C. communis*.
OCCURRENCE Europe.
RANGE Carboniferous.

CARDIUM SPP.

TRI

GENERAL DESCRIPTION One of the bivalves popularly known as cockles, *Cardium* has valves that appear heart-shaped in profile, with pronounced ribbing (costae) on the external surfaces and distinct muscle scars on the interior. The species illustrated is *C. parkinsoni* from the Pleistocene. *Cardium* species are heterodonts, meaning that they possess lateral teeth on the hinge, in addition to the central radiant, or cardinal, teeth.

The front and rear of a bivalve are the "sides" as the shell is held flat in the palm of the hand; the beak points towards the anterior, or front. *Cardium* species, like many fossil bivalves, retain the roughened patches where the adductor muscles, which hold the shell closed, were attached to the inside of the valve.
OCCURRENCE Worldwide.
RANGE Triassic–Recent.

GRYPHAEA SPP.

TRI

GENERAL DESCRIPTION The odd shell construction of this genus, in which one valve is considerably greater than the other, resulting in a snail-like curl, is known as an inequivalve; the left is by far the larger of the two, with a curved umbo (especially pronounced in the species illustrated, *G. arcuata*), while the right valve is small and flat or concave. Heavy growth lines form concentric ribbing on the valves. The animal was sedentary, living affixed by its left valve to the ocean floor.
OCCURRENCE Worldwide.
RANGE Triassic–Jurassic.

JUR

MYPHORELLA SPP.

GENERAL DESCRIPTION The distinguishing feature of this Upper Mesozoic bivalve is the concentric rows of knobs, sometimes growing out of costae, that cover the triangular to subtriangular valves, with a sharp beak at the dorsal margin. The species shown is *M. hudlestoni*; these bivalves are sometimes assigned to the genus *Trigonia*, and apparently were burrowing shellfish.
OCCURRENCE Worldwide.
RANGE Jurassic–Cretaceous.

TRI

PLEUROMYA SPP.

GENERAL DESCRIPTION By comparing fossil species with living forms (whose lifestyles are known), paleontologists try to deduce how extinct animals lived. Because *Pleuromya* species are desmodont bivalves, with no true hinge teeth, it is believed that they were burrowers, since a buried bivalve has little need for an efficient open-and-close mechanism in the shell. Some heterodonts also burrow, and the fossil record traces the loss of their hinge teeth as well.

Pleuromya species are equivalve bivalves, oval to trapezoidal in shape. External ornamentation may include concentric ribbing, which is more pronounced in some specimens than others.
RANGE Triassic–Cretaceous.

CRET

GLYCYMERIS SPP.

GENERAL DESCRIPTION A common genus in the world's oceans, *Glucymeris* is also abundant in the fossil record from the Cretaceous on. Most species are circular to slightly oval, equivalve, with large umbones; external ornamentation comprises costae, varying in development, and growth lines. Shown is *G. deleta* from the Eocene.
OCCURRENCE Worldwide.
RANGE Cretaceous–Recent.

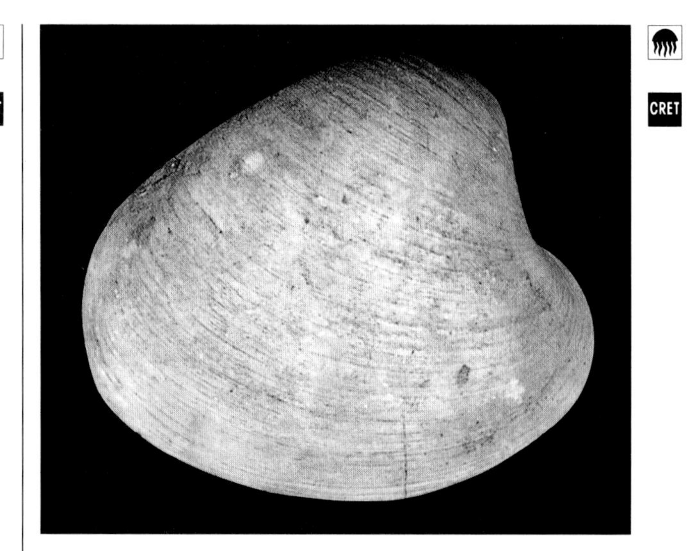

CRET

ARCTICA SPP.

GENERAL DESCRIPTION Clams of the genus *Arctica* showed a preference for cold waters, making them valuable as environmental indicators. The valves are typical of cold-water clams – oval to circular, with curved umbones and no external ornamentation beyond the growth lines. Shown here is a Pliocene specimen of *A. islandica*, a living species, known as the black clam, that appears commonly as a beach shell on North Atlantic shores.
OCCURRENCE North America; Europe.
RANGE Cretaceous–Recent.

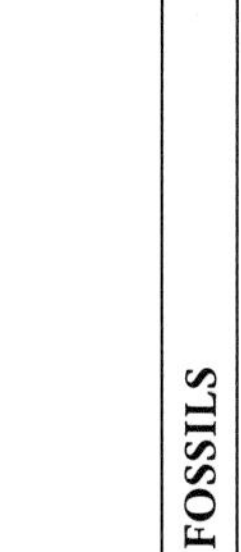

NEITHEA SPP.

GENERAL DESCRIPTION Found abundantly worldwide in Cretaceous deposits, *Neithea* is a lovely inequivalve genus, with its right valve far more convex than the left, which is flattened. The ribbing pattern is distinctive and attractive, with four to six large, roughly equal ribs separated by three or four smaller ribs, creating a scalloped pattern along the anterior margin. The species shown is *N. sexcostata*.
OCCURRENCE Worldwide.
RANGE Cretaceous.

VENERICARDIA SPP.

GENERAL DESCRIPTION Large cockles with heavy, triangular valves, low, flat costae and concentric growth lines, *Venericardia* species have two large, curved, hinge teeth. There are a number of living, cold-water species, found from the lower intertidal zone to several hundred feet of water. The fossil specimens shown are *V. planicosta* from the Eocene. Members of this genus have at times been assigned to *Cardita* and *Cyclocardia*.
OCCURRENCE Europe; Africa; North America.
RANGE Cretaceous/Palaeocene–Eocene.

PLICATULA SPP.

GENERAL DESCRIPTION *Plicatula* species are typical isodonts, bivalves with two identical teeth and two sockets in each valve, placed symmetrically. Illustrated is a Jurassic species, *P. spinosa*. Other specimens from the Jurassic have been found still retaining their natural colour, and are among the few examples of colored shells being found as fossils.

Plicatula species cement themselves in place, thus securing a permanent foothold – a necessity, since this genus prefers shallow waters near the surf line. While such a location provides an abundance of clean water (and thus food, since shellfish are filter-feeders), the wave action requires a bivalve to glue itself in place or else be swept away.
RANGE Jurassic–Recent.

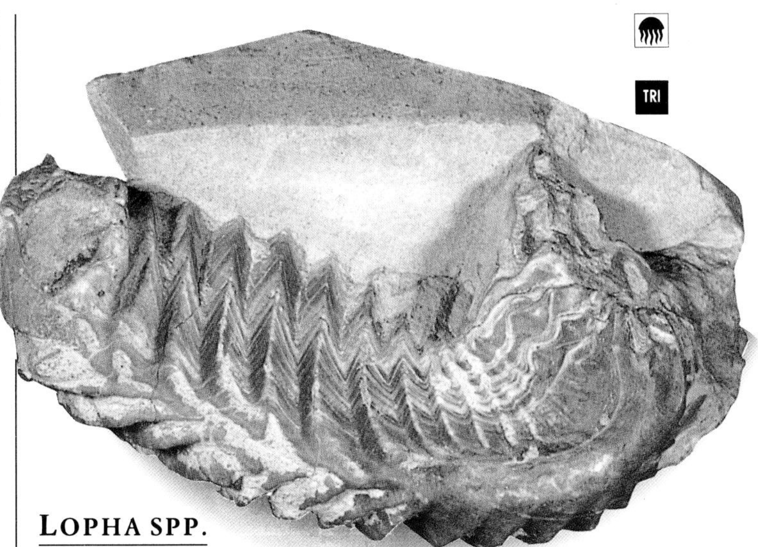

LOPHA SPP.

GENERAL DESCRIPTION A strongly curved oyster (the specimen shown, *L. carinata*, is seen in profile), *Lopha* valves are thickened, with extremely pronounced ribs that form heavy serrations. The thickening is believed to be a defence against carnivorous gastropods, and is still used by living *Lopha* species.
OCCURRENCE Worldwide.
RANGE Triassic–Recent.

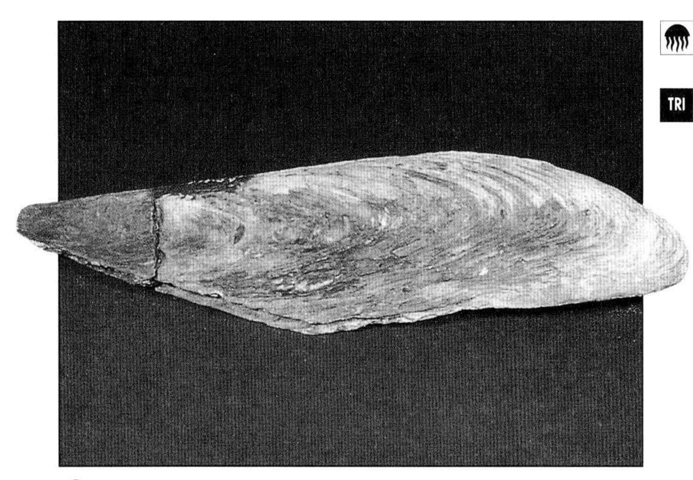

GERVILLELLA SPP.

GENERAL DESCRIPTION Elongated and lanceolate, the valves of *Gervillella* are pointed anteriorly, forming a dagger-like shape, but are unornamented except for concentric growth lines. A medium or large inequivalve, *Gervillella* is found worldwide in appropriate deposits.
OCCURRENCE Worldwide.
RANGE Triassic–Cretaceous.

EXOGYRA SPP.

GENERAL DESCRIPTION *Exogyra* species are inequivalved fossils of the group loosely known as coiled oysters, which includes *Gryphaea*. As in *Gryphaea*, the left valve is enlarged with a curled umbo, while the right valve is reduced and flat. Members of this genus (which includes the illustrated specimen, *E. latissima*) were sedentary, remaining cemented to the ocean floor.

Exogyra belongs to the group of bivalves known as dysodonts, which all but lack hinge teeth. Shell ornamentation varied.
RANGE Cretaceous.

VENUS SPP.

GENERAL DESCRIPTION A large, heavy-shelled clam, *Venus* is oval to circular, with growth lines that form raised, sharp-edged concentric ridges on the circular to oval valves. The species shown is *V. casina* from Pliocene deposits.

The quahog of New England clam chowder fame was once classified with the *Venus* clams, but has since been reassigned to the genus *Mercenaria*.
RANGE Oligocene–Recent.

SPONDYLUS SPP.

GENERAL DESCRIPTION An extremely widespread fossil genus, *Spondylus* is an inequivalve with regular or irregular costae and, depending upon the species, irregular spines or knobs growing from the costae. The right valve is cemented to the substrata.

One of the most dramatic, living members of this genus is the Atlantic thorny oyster (*S. americanus*), which develops long, delicate spines sometimes more than 1in. in length.
OCCURRENCE Worldwide.
RANGE Jurassic–Recent.

Class CEPHALOPODA Cephalopods

Today, the most common cephalopods are octopi and squid, which lack external shells, but during the Paleozoic and Mesozoic the exquisitely built nautiloids and ammonoids reigned, patrolling the seas in their coiled and chambered ram's-horn shells. Nautiloids and ammonoids grow in a coil because the animal's mantle secretes calcium carbonate at varying rates – more quickly on the sides and outer edges, and less quickly on the dorsal surface closest to the inside of the coil. Nautiloids appeared first in the waning years of the Cambrian, with one surviving species, while the ammonoids arose during the Devonian, and were extinct by the end of the Cretaceous.

ORTHOCERAS SPP.

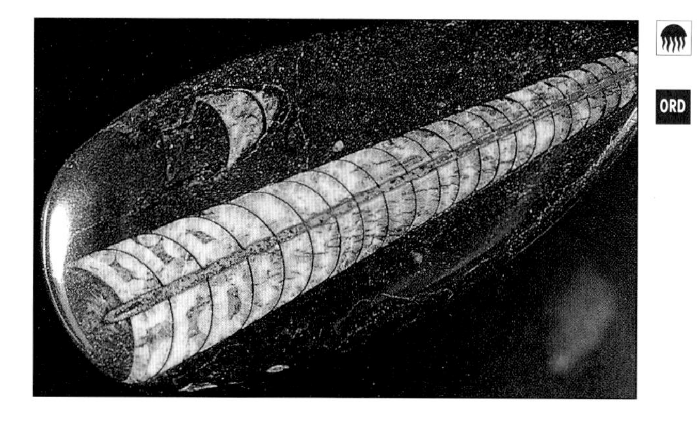

ORD

GENERAL DESCRIPTION The most famous of the fossil cephalopods, the nautilus and ammonites, have curved shells, but the Paleozoic produced many species with straight or only slightly curved shells. One was *Orthoceras*, a large, active predator. This specimen, from Morocco, shows an *Orthoceras* shell in cross-section. The septae dividing the body chambers are visible and the tube-like siphuncle running the length of the shell can be seen clearly.

North American orthocerids that had previously been assigned to this genus have been reclassified as several distinct genera.

OCCURRENCE Europe; North Africa.

RANGE Ordovician–Triassic.

NAUTILUS SPP.

TERT

GENERAL DESCRIPTION More than 180 million years old, this fossil *Nautilus* echoes the sole surviving species of its genus, the chambered nautilus. In *Nautilus*, the shell coils up and behind the body chamber like a ram's horn; the live animal, which was tentacled like a squid, protruded from the aperture, and was able to move by jet propulsion, squirting water through a fold of flesh beneath the head. Buoyancy was controlled through gas-filled chambers inside the shell – spaces that had once formed the body chamber, and had been sealed off as the nautilus grew and secreted new sections.

OCCURRENCE Europe; Australia; East Indies.

RANGE Oligocene–Recent.

DACTYLIOCERAS SPP.

JUR

GENERAL DESCRIPTION A famous, commonly collected ammonoid of Eurasia, Latin America and parts of North America, *Dactylioceras* possesses evolute whorls and simple, relatively straight ribs. There is no keel, and the sutures are strongly lobed. The shell is usually 4in. in diameter or less.

Shown are three specimens of the species *D. commune*, an important index fossil in European strata, in which the ribs divide over the ventral surface of the whorls. In other members of the *Dactylioceras*, the ribs remain undivided over the venter, the portion of the whorl farthest from the central axis of the shell.

OCCURRENCE Worldwide.

RANGE Jurassic.

Hildoceras spp.

General description An evolute ammonoid with somewhat flattened whorls, *Hildoceras* has a shallow groove that runs the length of each side of the whorls as well as along the keel; the ribs are curved. The shell is 5in. or less in diameter. The specimen illustrated is *H. bifrons*.
Occurrence Worldwide.
Range Jurassic.

Amaltheus spp.

General description *Amaltheus* belongs to a worldwide group of ammonoids known as ammonitids, a suborder with rather simplistic sutures, heavily ornamented shells and – in some cases – gigantic sizes, with diameters of nearly 3ft. *Amaltheus* itself, however, is much smaller, with an average size of about 3in. The whorl coiling is involuted, a keel is present, and the ribs form gentle S-shapes. Shown is the species *A. margarinatus*.
Occurrence Worldwide.
Range Jurassic.

Arnioceras spp.

JUR

General description A common Jurassic ammonoid, *Arnioceras* has strong, straight ribs that curve forward on the venter, stopping at the keel. The coiling is evolute, and the saddles and lobes of the sutures are themselves convoluted into smaller subdivisions. The specimen shown is *A. semicostatum* from the Lower Jurassic, the variety most commonly found.
Occurrence North and South America; Europe; Africa; Asia.

Class SCAPHOPODA Scaphopods

Dentalium spp.

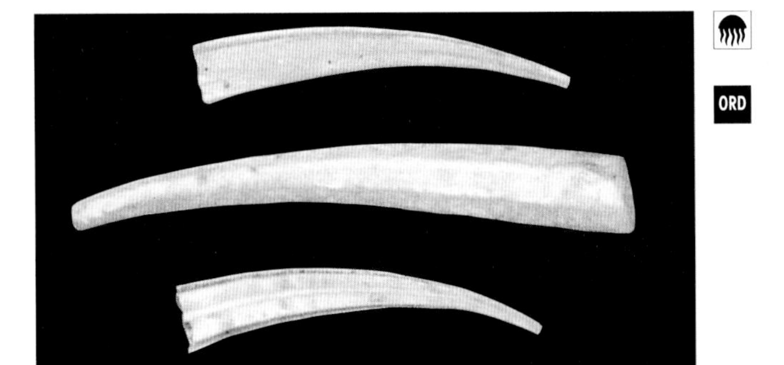

General description Familiar to beachcombers in many parts of the world, the tusk shells of today are largely indistinguishable from fossilized specimens from the Paleozoic. The shell is a long, gentle taper, convex or straight and usually ridged, and as the genus and common names suggest, looks very much like a tooth. Modern species live buried in sediment, both inshore and at the edge of the continental shelf.
Occurrence Worldwide.
Range Ordovician–Recent.

Phylum ARTHROPODA Arthropods

Arthropods have segmented, chitinous exoskeletons that are periodically shed as the animal grows, and jointed legs. This phylum, the largest and most diverse in the world (with more than 80 per cent of all living animal species), includes insects, crustaceans, spiders, scorpions and centipedes. The trilobites, an extraordinarily successful subphylum, became extinct during the Permian.

Class TRILOBITA Trilobites

Extinct for roughly 250 million years, the trilobites were one of the dominant forms of life in their day, which stretched from the Cambrian to the Permian. The name trilobite comes from the body's three-fold shape. In cross-section, it has a central axis and riblike pleurae jutting out to each side, and lengthwise it has the cephalon (head shield), thorax (body) and pygidium (tail section). Even to those generally unfamiliar with fossils, the trilobite is almost instantly recognizable.

Trilobites first appeared in the Lower Cambrian, diversifying incredibly during the so-called "Cambrian explosion" some 550 million years BP, when multicellular life itself underwent radical diversification and almost all basic animal body plans appeared.

Scientists ascribe the great number of trilobite fossils to three causes – trilobites possessed exoskeletons armoured with calcium carbonate, which fossilizes easily; most species lived in shallow oceans, where fossilization is most likely to occur; and not the least importantly, they were simply phenomenally common in their day.

SIL

CALYMENE SPP.

GENERAL DESCRIPTION In trilobites, the cephalon is the most important feature for identification. That of *Calymene*, a widespread genus in North America and Europe, is semicircular, while the glabella is raised, convex and has three lobes that taper to the front. The rest of the body tapers to a small, pointed pygidium. The specimen shown is *C. blumenbachi*, from the Silurian, and is just over 1in. in length.

OCCURRENCE Worldwide.

RANGE Silurian–Devonian.

ORD

FLEXICALYMENE SPP.

GENERAL DESCRIPTION When a trilobite was threatened or injured, it curled into a tight ball, a process known as enrolling that protected its vulnerable, lightly armoured underside. This specimen of *Flexicalymene retorsa* was fossilized enrolled, a common occurrence with this and many other trilobite genera. It may be that the mud slide that encased them triggered this response, just as bumping a modern wood-louse causes it to enroll as well. Shed exoskeletons of some trilobites also enrolled once they were moulted.

Flexicalymene is easily confused with its close relative *Calymene*, but has a more pronounced cephalon border, and the glabella is larger than the pygidium. *Flexicalymene* is found in parts of Europe, and is especially common in eastern North America.

OCCURRENCE Europe; North America.

RANGE Ordovician.

NIOBELLA SPP.

GENERAL DESCRIPTION A mid-sized trilobite, with lengths of up to 4in., *Niobella* fossils show a well-developed cephalon, large pygidium and eyes. There are eight thoracic segments. Like all trilobites, *Niobella* (in this case, *N. homfrayi*) was benthic – that is, it spent virtually all its time on the ocean floor, judging from the shape and position of its appendages, as well as its digestive system. Trilobites appear to have been scavengers or hunters, and were probably a combination of both.
RANGE Ordovician.

OGYGIOCARELLA SPP.

GENERAL DESCRIPTION Trilobites of the genus *Ogygiocarella* are common in European and Latin American deposits from the Ordovician. The genus is macropygous – that is, the pygidium is almost as large as the thorax; in addition, the eye is short and curved, the glabella bulges out anteriorly, and the facial suture cuts the rear border of the cephalon. The species illustrated is *O. debuchi*.
OCCURRENCE Europe and Latin America.
RANGE Ordovician.

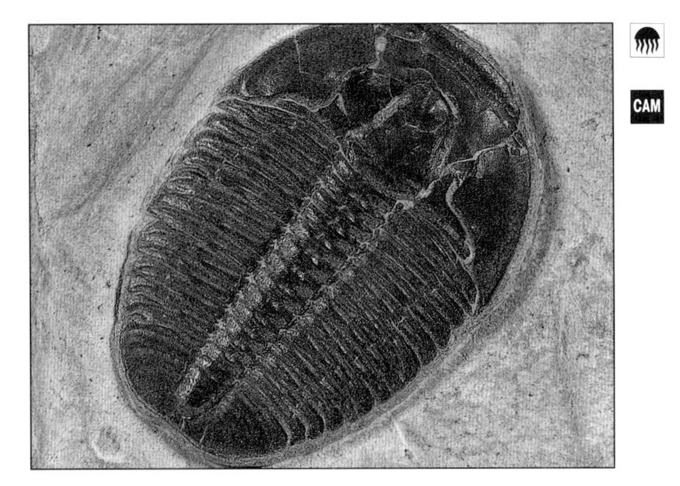

ELRATHIA SPP.

GENERAL DESCRIPTION A North American trilobite, *Elrathia* is a very important member of the Cambrian fauna, with the species *E. kingii* (shown here) being especially abundant and widespread. The glabella is short and tapers to the front, with a broad brim and wide free cheeks; the pygidium is small. *Elrathia* belonged to the large group of trilobites called opisthoparians, named for their distinct head sutures. These uncalcified junctures provided the trilobite with an escape route when it had outgrown its exoskeleton. The opisthoparians were the largest of the trilobites, with some species more than 2ft. long.
OCCURRENCE North America.
RANGE Cambrian.

PHACOPS SPP.

GENERAL DESCRIPTION The phacopids are the dominant genera of trilobites from Middle Paleozoic rocks in North America. *Phacops rana*, shown here, is typical; the glabella is large and bulbous, wider at the front that the rear, with at least two pairs of furrows; the pygidium is the same general shape as the cephalon, with 10–12 segments. Broken and incomplete fossils, usually of molted pieces of exoskeletons, are the most common.

Fossil trilobite eyes retain the faceted surface that in life was a compound lens, a system found in many modern arthropods and providing excellent vision. The eyes of the *Phacops* were so large and high that the animal probably enjoyed a 360-degree field of vision.
OCCURRENCE Worldwide.
RANGE Silurian–Devonian.

ASAPHISCUS SPP.

GENERAL DESCRIPTION A trademark trilobite from the middle Cambrian, *Asaphiscus* is found in deposits in the western United States. The cephalon and pygidium both have wide, flattened borders that are distinctive, with a secondary border in front of the glabella, which has three pairs of furrows. There are between 7 and 11 thoracic segments in this genus, and between five and eight segments on the pygidium. The species shown is the common *A. wheeleri*.
OCCURRENCE North America.
RANGE Silurian–Devonian.

SIL

Class INSECTA Insects

Insects first appeared in the Devonian, the ancient precursors of today's wingless silverfish and springtails. Gaps in the fossil record make sorting out the sequence difficult, but by the Carboniferous, dragonflies – the earliest winged insects – had taken to the air. With no competition from other flying animals, these early dragonflies were massive, with wingspans of nearly 3ft.

LIBELLULA DORIS

GENERAL DESCRIPTION Insects are rare as fossils, partly because of their thin, easily destroyed exoskeletons. This dragonfly larva is one of the unusual exceptions, perhaps because its habitat – probably ponds or slow-moving rivers with mud bottoms, as in living species – is more conducive to fossilization than the terrestrial environments inhabited by most insects. The dragonfly family Libellulidae remains widespread today.
RANGE Miocene.

TERT

TERT

INSECT TRAPPED IN AMBER

GENERAL DESCRIPTION Nearly 40 million years ago, on what is now the island of Dominica, this small insect became trapped in tree resin. Mired and eventually entombed, it quickly died of suffocation, and the complete lack of oxygen that killed it also prevented bacteria from decomposing it. Eventually the resin fossilized into amber, preserving the insect – a member of the Hymenoptera, the large order that includes ants, wasps and bees.

Even though the insect appears to be intact, down to the tiniest details of antennae and wing veins, it is really a hollow mold in the resin, around the edges of which clings a thin, carbonized film. To the observer, however, the amber provides a perfect window to a death many millions of years in the past.

Class CRUSTACEA Crustaceans

Crustaceans evolved at around the same point in the Cambrian as the trilobites, but apparently were held in check by their vastly more successful arthropod relatives. The mass extinctions of the trilobites at the end of the Permian, however, left the niches they once occupied empty, and the crustaceans radiated to fill most of those ecological slots.

CRET

NOTOPOCORYSTES SPP.

GENERAL DESCRIPTION The carapace of crabs and other crustaceans – that is, the shieldlike covering on the thorax and head – is often the only body part to survive fossilization. In the Mesozoic crab *Notopocorystes*, the carapace is oval or shield-shaped, covered with tiny bumps and featuring a series of knobs that form a low dorsal ridge. Illustrated is the species *N. stokesi*, a specimen from England. This genus is sometimes listed as *Palaeocorystes*.
OCCURRENCE Europe; North America; parts of the Middle East and Indo-Pacific.
RANGE Cretaceous.

TERT

XANTHOPSIS SPP.

GENERAL DESCRIPTION Crustaceans usually do not appear as fossils in the abundance that brachiopods, trilobites and molluscs achieve, but *Xanthopsis* is an exception.

Xanthopsis was a stout crab about 2in. across, similar in shape to the rock and mud crabs that live today along the coast of New England. The claws were thick and strong, held close to the body, as can be seen in this specimen of *X. leachi*, which shows the crab's underside. The carapace was oval and convex, with distinct furrows.
OCCURRENCE North America; Europe.
RANGE Eocene.

Phylum ECHINODERMATA Echinoderms

The name echinoderm means "spiny skin", an apt description for many of this phylum's members, which include sea urchins, sea stars, sea cucumbers and crinoids. All are built on a body plan that is based on multiples of five, which covers everything from the number of arms to the branches of the vascular system. They have been entirely marine through their history. Several extinct classes, the blastoids among them, are important fossils.

Class CRINOIDEA Crinoids

Divers know the living crinoids as "sea lilies", since they bear a resemblance to plants, with their sinuous stalks and feathery, petal-like arms. Fossil crinoids are varied and beautiful if found intact, although many are only fragments of the ossicles (stem segments) or the cupped calyx, the body. In some weathered deposits, crinoid ossicles litter the ground like stone buttons.

Fossils can tell a paleontologist only so much, and comparisons with living forms – when possible – can provide valuable insight into extinct genera. Fossil beds provide little on crinoid life history, for instance, but we know from studying modern crinoids that the larvae are mobile before settling down. Interestingly, even crinoids that are stalkless as adults go through a stalked larval phase; such a replaying of ancestral forms in juvenile stages is common, and its study is an important tool for deciphering the past. Even human beings, for example, go through a stage in which the embryos have gill pouches and a fishlike tail.

TRI

PENTACRINITES SPP.

GENERAL DESCRIPTION In this piece of shale, the long arms, or branches, of *Pentacrinites* have been preserved, along with impressions of the pinnules, the smaller, branching armlets, as well as the clasping stem branchlets known as cirri. The pinnules, covered in sticky mucus, served as filtering devices for the crinoid, capturing plankton from the water and transferring it to the animal's calyx.
OCCURRENCE North America; Europe.
RANGE Triassic–Recent.

SIL

CYATHOCRINITES SPP.

GENERAL DESCRIPTION A common Paleozoic crinoid, *Cyathocrinites* had a globular calyx and branching arms composed of a single row of plates, as can be seen in this specimen of *C. arthriticus*, from the Silurian. Stalked crinoids like *Cyathocrinites* were dominant in the ancient seas of the Paleozoic, but in plankton-poor modern oceans they have been largely replaced by stalkless, mobile genera that arose in the Mesozoic. Stalked crinoids are today found only on deep reefs in tropical regions.
OCCURRENCE North America.
RANGE Silurian–Carboniferous.

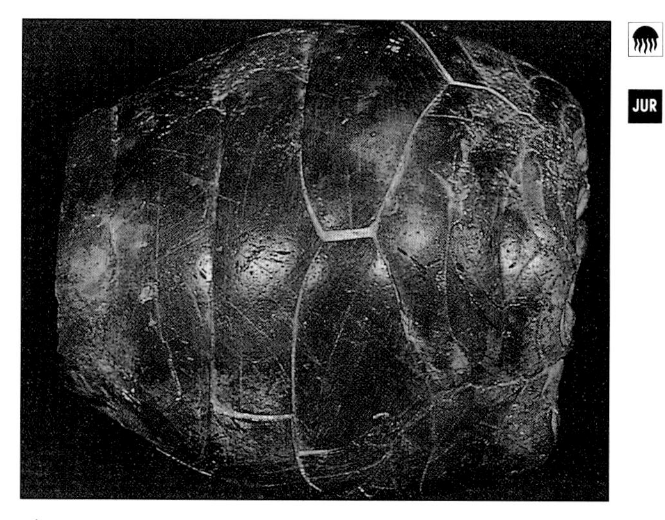

JUR

APIOCRINUS SPP.

GENERAL DESCRIPTION This specimen of *Apiocrinus*, the species *A. parkinsoni*, shows the teardrop-shaped calyx characteristic of the genus. The calyx is composed of the radial, basal and ray plates fused almost seamlessly with the upper ossicles. Fossils of this genus are found only in Europe.
OCCURRENCE Europe.
RANGE Jurassic.

CRET

MARSUPITES SPP.

GENERAL DESCRIPTION All echinoderms show five-fold radial symmetry in their body plans. In *Marsupites*, the calyx is made up of three rows of five plates each, all heavily scored with radial ridging. Found in North American and European deposits, *Marsupites* was a stalkless, free-swimming crinoid. The specimen shown is *M. testudinarius*.
OCCURRENCE North America; Europe.
RANGE Cretaceous.

SIL

BOTRYOCRINUS SPP.

GENERAL DESCRIPTION Crinoids were far more successful than their close relatives, the cystoids and blastoids, outnumbering them nearly five to one in terms of fossil genera, with a total of more than 750. In addition, only the crinoids survived the mass extinctions at the end of the Permian. This specimen of *Botryocrinus* is from the Wenlock limestones.
OCCURRENCE Europe.
RANGE Silurian.

ORD

GLYPTOCRINUS SPP.

GENERAL DESCRIPTION This specimen of a Silurian *Glyptocrinus* shows the long stalk, arms and branching pinnules, but unfortunately not much of the calyx, which in this genus is conical, with radial ridges.
OCCURRENCE North America; Europe.
RANGE Ordovician–Silurian.

Class ECHINOIDEA Sea urchins, sand dollars and allies

This class is marked by the presence of a central, boxlike test composed of hard plates fused together to form 10 bands that radiate from the top. The body is covered with spines, although in most fossils only the test is preserved. The test is usually globular or flattened, although conical species occur.

The large opening on the underside of the test in echinoids is known as the peristome, which contains the mouth. The "jaws" in echinoids are made up of five-pointed, calcareous plates with the non-technical name of Aristotle's lantern, for their fancied resemblance to an old lamp.

HEMICIDARIS SPP.

GENERAL DESCRIPTION The widespread fossil sea urchin is usually preserved as the test alone. The test is knobbed with tubercules like a floating mine, and these become larger as they approach the underside. The test is a flattened sphere, especially so on the venter. The ambulacral grooves – the five zones between the rows of tubercules – are ornamented with regular rows of tiny tubercules. The ambulacral grooves move food to the oral opening underneath the test, while the anus is found at the periproct, the cluster of small, central plates at the top of the test.
OCCURRENCE Worldwide.
RANGE Jurassic–Cretaceous.

JUR

PYGURUS SPP.

GENERAL DESCRIPTION The star-shaped ambulacral grooves make *Pygurus* instantly recognizable as a "sand dollar", the common name for the tests of flattened, short-spined sea urchins. Many similar genera survive in the world's oceans, delighting beachcombers. The edges of the ambulacral grooves are studded with pores, through which tube feet protruded, permitting the animal to breathe and move. In life, *Pygurus* would probably have been buried slightly in sand, allowing wave action to bring food particles to it.
OCCURRENCE Worldwide.
RANGE Cretaceous–Eocene.

CRET

Micraster spp.

CRET

General description Echinoids can be regular (those that are radially symmetrical) or irregular (those in which the test shape is bilaterally symmetrical). *Micraster*, a common European echinoid, is irregular; the test is heart-shaped, with short ambulacral plates. A groove leads from the centre of the test to the oral opening on the side, with a low ridge running the opposite direction, towards the posterior, where the anus is located. This genus (represented here by *M. coranguinum*) is used to identify Cretaceous strata in Europe.
Occurrence Worldwide, especially Europe.
Range Cretaceous–Palaeocene.

Echinocorys spp.

CRET

General description Seen in profile, the test of *Echinocorys* is high, rounded and flat on the venter. The ambulacral grooves are widely separated, with double rows of pores on the slightly granular test. The genus is widespread in North America and Eurasia. The species shown is *E. scutata*.
Occurrence North America; Eurasia.
Range Cretaceous.

Plegiocidaris spp.

JUR

General description Generally speaking, each genus of echinoid has a distinctive spine shape that helps in identification – but the shapes can seem whimsical to the human eye, like that of *Plegiocidaris*, which looks more than a little like an ear of corn. *Plegiocidaris* is usually found with other inhabitants of ancient coral reefs, and it serves as an environmental indicator fossil, especially if found with other echinoids that shared its taste for warm, shallow seawater. The species illustrated is *P. florigemme*.
Range Jurassic.

Class BLASTOIDEA Blastoids

Similar to cystoids, the blastoids possessed a globular or budshaped theca, usually the only part of the animal to be fossilized.

Pentremites spp.

CAR

General description A Western Hemisphere speciality, *Pentremites* is one of the best-known and most common blastoids in North America. The theca is globular to budshaped, with five distinct ambulacral grooves extending from the mouth down the sides towards the base. In life, blastoids probably resembled delicate crinoids, anchored to the sea bed by thin stalks, and seining plankton from the water with the help of waving, mucus-covered arms.
Occurrence North and South America.
Range Carboniferous–Permian.

Phylum HEMICHORDATA Hemichordates

Class GRAPTOLTHINA Graptolites

These extinct colonial animals have left behind delicately beautiful fossils that resemble branches of coral. The colony, or rhabdosome, is made up of stipes, or branches, which are in turn marked by small depressions called thecae, in which the animals lived. Thecae may be small (bithecae) or bigger (autothecae). The rhabdosomes were themselves part of a larger cluster jutting out from a buoyant nematophore. It is believed that graptolite colonies floated near the surface or anchored themselves to floating debris, although some of the earliest forms were apparently bottom-dwellers. The majority of the following graptolites are found worldwide.

Graptolites are most common in black shales, and are, ironically, among the very few fossils ever found in such rocks, which were formed in an almost oxygen-free environment, toxic with hydrogen sulphide, in which nothing could live. If graptolites were bottom-dwellers as first thought, how could they survive without oxygen? Yet, if they were planktonic, why weren't they found in other strata? The answer seems to be that their protein-based exoskeleton was simply too easily decomposed anywhere except in the harsh, poisonous environment that went on to produce the black shales, although some graptolites have been found in limestone.

Graptolites long confused paleontologists, who were not sure if they were plants or animals – and if animals, whether they belonged with the sponges, the bryozoans, the molluscs or the cnidarians. Finally, microscopic examination showed them to be protochordates – the group that later gave rise to vertebrates.

ORD

PHYLLOGRAPTUS SPP.

GENERAL DESCRIPTION The *Phyllograptus* rhabdosome has four joined stipes, creating an X-shape when sectioned. The thecae of this genus are tubular and simplistic. Like most graptolites, the stipes are thinner than a pencil lead.
OCCURRENCE Worldwide.
RANGE Ordovician.

ORD

TETRAGRAPTUS SPP.

GENERAL DESCRIPTION Sadly, fossilization is rarely kind to graptolites, which are usually preserved as squashed, carbonized films with little or no three-dimensional detail, with the stipes often torn and scattered. Most graptolite fossils are similar to the specimen of *Tetragraptus* shown here, but in those in a better state of preservation, the rhabdosomes are made up of four stipes, joined as pairs. The thecae are straight and saw-toothed. In life, the stipes hung from a thread-like support called the nema, arching up and out like the leaves of a ground-hugging flower.
OCCURRENCE Worldwide.
RANGE Ordovician.

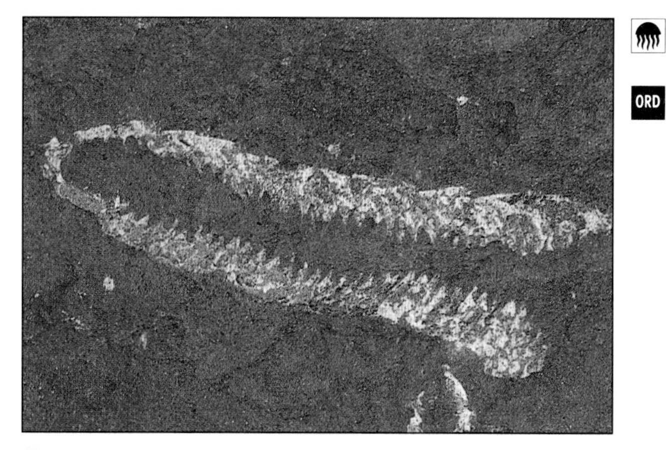

ORD

DIDYMOGRAPTUS SPP.

GENERAL DESCRIPTION This specimen of *D. murchinsoni* displays the characteristic shape of the genus, in which the stipes are folded together like tongs. Occasionally they will have been fossilized in a straight line. The thecae are pronounced and toothlike on the insides of the stipe, like serrations on a pair of pinking shears.
OCCURRENCE Worldwide.
RANGE Ordovician.

ORD

ORTHOGRAPTUS SPP.

GENERAL DESCRIPTION Unlike *Didymograptus, Orthograptus* belongs to the biserial graptolites – those with rows of thecae on both sides of the stipe, instead of just one. The colony consisted of a single stipe, suspended from a thin nema (a short length of which also fossilized in this specimen); the thecae pointed upwards at a 45-degree angle.
OCCURRENCE Worldwide.
RANGE Ordovician–Silurian.

ORD

CLIMACOGRAPTUS SPP.

GENERAL DESCRIPTION Large, squared-off thecae mark *Climacograptus*, another biserial graptolite with a single stipe. Oval body parts found with *Climacograptus* are thought to have been flotation buoys, from which the colony was suspended.
OCCURRENCE Worldwide.
RANGE Ordovician–Silurian.

SIL

RASTRITES SPP.

GENERAL DESCRIPTION With their curved stipes and long thecae, *Rastrites* colonies look a little bit like false eyelashes. The thecae are uniserial and are themselves slightly curved, and are more widely spaced than most graptolite thecae.
OCCURRENCE Worldwide, except South America.
RANGE Silurian.

MONOGRAPTUS SPP.

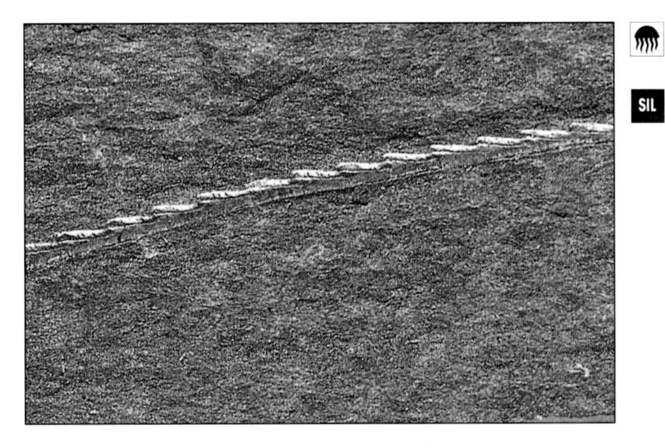

SIL

GENERAL DESCRIPTION A close-up of a *Monograptus* stipe shows the tightly packed, uniserial thecae. This is a highly variable genus, with stipe and thecae shape ranging from straight to gracefully curved. *Monograptus* is one of the most commonly found of the graptolites.

OCCURRENCE Worldwide.

RANGE Silurian–Devonian.

VERTEBRATES

Class CHONDRICHTHYES Cartilaginous fish

The first protofish arose roughly 540 million years BP, around the cusp of the Cambrian and Ordovician, and their jawless descendants reached their zenith during the Devonian before fading away. They were replaced by two groups of fish – the cartilaginous fish, which today includes sharks and rays, and the more advanced bony fish. Cartilaginous fish have skeletons made of tough, flexible cartilage. While this may seem a primitive trait, fish of the class Condrichthyes appear to have evolved from bony ancestors. The most frequently fossilized parts of sharks and rays are their teeth, which can be found in huge numbers in some areas.

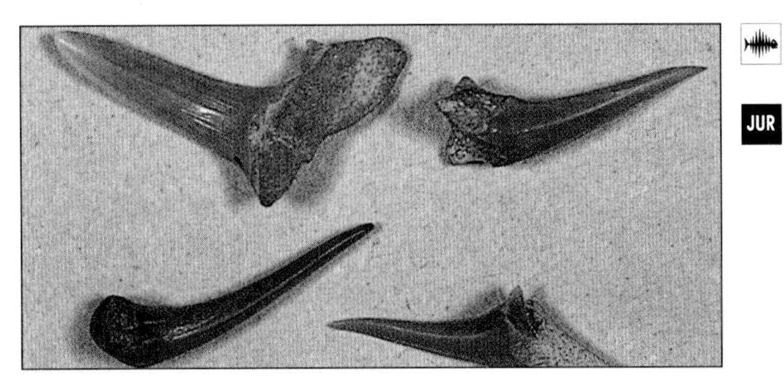

JUR

ODONTASPIS SPP.

GENERAL DESCRIPTION The sand sharks of the genus *Odontaspis* possess long, curved teeth that are often found along ocean beaches; Florida is particularly noted for its aggregations of fossil shark teeth. Because of abrasion in the surf, the bases are frequently worn away, but when intact, there are usually small, auxiliary spines protruding from the top of the base on either side of the tooth.

While *Odontaspis* and its relatives were common in Cenozoic seas, the numbers of fossilized teeth may give a skewed idea of their abundance. Sharks lose their teeth constantly throughout their lives, with replacements constantly migrating forward from rows of backup teeth, so one shark can produce hundreds.

OCCURRENCE Worldwide.

RANGE Jurassic–Recent.

CRET

CARCHARODON SPP.

GENERAL DESCRIPTION The large size, triangular shape and serrated edges of this tooth mark it as belonging to *C. megalodon*, a Cenozoic relative of the modern great white shark. By comparing the size of teeth from *C. megalodon* to those of living great whites, it was once thought the extinct species grew to lengths of more than 90ft., and would have been capable of swallowing a small car. Those estimates are now known to be wrong, but *C. megalodon* was nonetheless at least 50ft. long – certainly one of the most formidable predators ever.

OCCURRENCE Worldwide.

RANGE Cretaceous–Recent.

Class OSTEICHTHYES Bony fish

Far and away the most successful class of fish in modern waters, bony fish first appeared in the Devonian. Not long after, they split into two evolutionary lines; one produced the world's more than 20 000 species of typical bony fish, the other the lungfishes and lobefins, including the famous coelacanths of the genus *Latimeria*. It is thought that this second group gave rise to the amphibians, the first land vertebrates.

TERT

ACANTHONEMUS SPP.

GENERAL DESCRIPTION This fossil fish, a rarity in Tertiary strata, appears to be related to the pompanos and crevalles, and is classified with the Perciformes. The species shown is *A. subaureus*. The genus is found from the Eocene to the Oligocene in European strata.
OCCURRENCE Europe.
RANGE Tertiary.

GOSNITICHTHYS SPP.

GENERAL DESCRIPTION The Green River shales of Wyoming are justly famous for the quantity and quality of the bony fish fossils they produce. In this example, a school of small *G. paruns* have been fossilized as they died, perhaps the victims of depleted dissolved oxygen, which still causes massive fish kills, or a drought. The alignment of many of the fish also indicates a possible water current, or the action of waves, before the fish were buried.
RANGE Eocene.

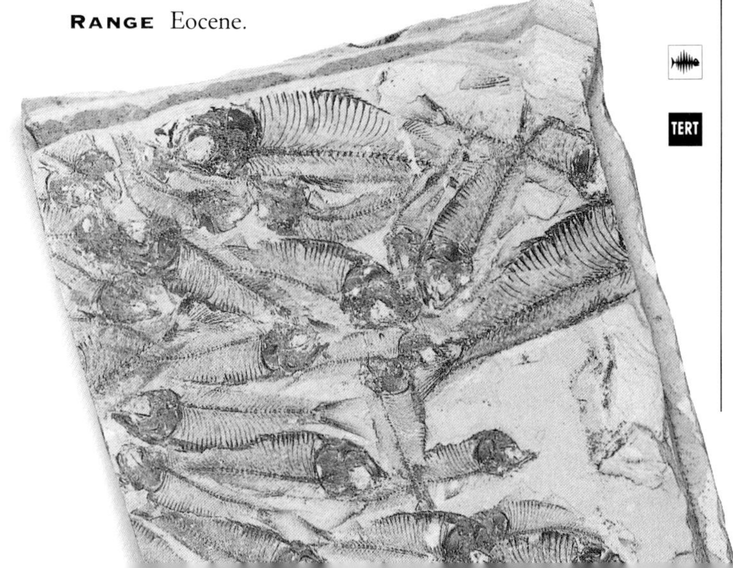

TERT

TERT

PROLATES SPP.

GENERAL DESCRIPTION *Prolates* is one of the earliest examples of the order Perciformes, which is today the largest order of vertebrates in the world. It includes such familiar fish as the sunfish, bass, darters, pike and true perches. The specimen shown is *P. herberti*, found in early Palaeocene strata in France.
RANGE Tertiary.

CRET

LEPIDOTUS SPP.

GENERAL DESCRIPTION *Lepidotus* was a member of the group of bony fishes known as semionotids, heavily built fish with small mouths, simple, peglike teeth and thick scales. The group arose during the Permian and became common in marine deposits during the Jurassic, but none survived the great extinction at the K–T Boundary. These round objects are fossilized vertebrae from *L. marimus*, a species that lived in the Cretaceous, just before the genus died out forever. By examining *Lepidotus* teeth, palaeontologists believe this and other related genera fed on heavily shelled invertebrates.
OCCURRENCE Europe; Africa; North America.
RANGE Cretaceous.

LATIMERIA SPP.

GENERAL DESCRIPTION The coelacanth (as this genus is popularly known) was believed extinct for 30 million years until one was pulled up by a trawler off the coast of South Africa in 1938. Many more have been caught since then, most from the Comoro Islands and all from great depths. This preserved, modern specimen shows the hallmarks of its fossil ancestors – most importantly the lobelike fins, which were supported internally by bones and could act as primitive limbs. The lobefins also had primitive lungs that would have allowed them to breathe on land. It is important to realize that *Latimeria* itself is only an offshoot of this once-diverse group, and while it retains the family's structure, it is not the direct ancestor of the first land vertebrates.
RANGE Devonian–Recent.

DEV

Class AMPHIBIA Amphibians

The first vertebrates to dominate the land were the amphibians, which held sway for nearly 50 million years, beginning in the late Devonian and reaching their peak in the Carboniferous. Amphibians have moist, scaleless skin and lay eggs coated in a gelatinous substance, without a watertight shell. The eggs must be laid in water or in a very damp place, largely restricting this class to humid or semi-aquatic environments.

MICROMELERPETON SPP.

GENERAL DESCRIPTION Not long after the amphibians evolved, they split into two major groups. One, the labyrinthodonts, eventually gave rise to the reptiles, while the other, the temnospondyls, remained an evolutionary dead-end, flourishing from the Permian through the Triassic, then eventually dying out. *Micromelerpeton* was a member of the latter group, in the suborder Rhachitomi. Like many early amphibians it had a wide, flat head, short limbs held splayed out to the side, and a low, waddling carriage. The species shown is *M. amphibia*, a specimen from Lower Permian deposits in Germany.
RANGE Permian.

PER

Class REPTILIA Reptiles

The most famous fossil reptiles – indeed, the best-known fossils of all – are the dinosaurs. While reptiles had evolved as early as the Devonian, dinosaurs themselves did not arrive on the scene until the Triassic, many millions of years later. Today, in fact, there is great debate over whether dinosaurs truly belong to the Reptilia at all. It has always been assumed that dinosaurs shared the typical reptilian trait of ectothermy ("cold-bloodedness"), a sluggish metabolism dependent on external temperature. But recent research indicates that they may instead have been active, warm-blooded creatures with insulating coats of fur or feathers. To some scientists, there is a clear case for reclassifying dinosaurs with their warm-blooded descendants, the birds, in a new class called Dinosauria.

JUR

STENOPTERYGIUS QUADRISCISSUS

GENERAL DESCRIPTION Judging from their relative abundance in Jurassic marine deposits, the group of fishlike dinosaurs known as ichthyosaurs (which included *Stenopterygius*) must have been the pre-eminent vertebrates of the middle Mesozoic seas. They were superbly streamlined, as can be easily seen in this extremely well-preserved specimen, which shows the outline of the soft parts surrounding the skeleton – the high dorsal fin, stabilizing flippers and forked tail flukes. Ichthyosaur teeth are commonly found, and can be distinguished by their deep lateral grooves; the teeth have barrel-shaped roots and are set into grooves in the jawbones. The skull tapers drastically beyond the cranial cavity, as does a modern dolphin's skull. In fact, the similarities in appearance between this extinct dinosaur and the living, mammalian dolphins are an excellent example of evolutionary convergence, in which two unrelated animals adapt in similar ways to similar environments.
OCCURRENCE Western and Central Europe; North America.
RANGE Jurassic.

LUFENGOSAURUS

TRI

GENERAL DESCRIPTION The earliest and most primitive of the large dinosaurs, the prosauropods (or anchisaurids) were ancestors, indirectly, of the massive sauropods. Five to forty feet long, they had long tails and moderately long necks, although neither end of the animal was tapered to the extreme that sauropods would exhibit. Although probably four-footed most of the time, anchisaurids were able to rear up on their hind legs for feeding, using the tail as a brace. Another clue to their posture is found on the front legs, which are armed with curved claws. Such weapons would have been effective against attackers, especially if the anchisaurid stood upright. The variety shown is *Lufengosaurus*, a prosauropod of about 20ft. in length.
RANGE Triassic–Jurassic.

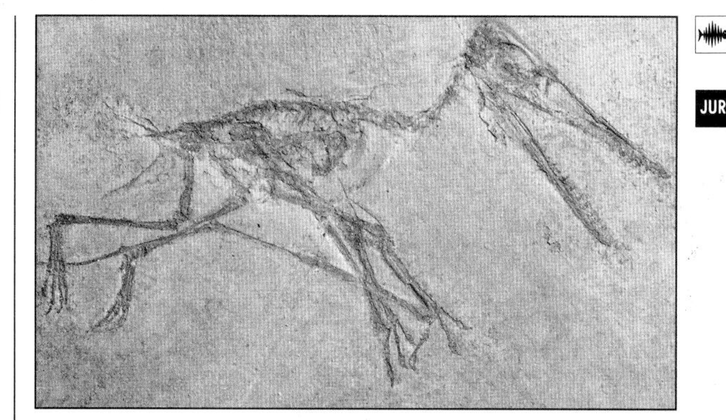

JUR

PTERODACTYLUS SPP.

GENERAL DESCRIPTION The first of the flying reptiles to come to light, this small species was discovered in a German quarry and described by Baron Georges Cuvier, the great, pioneering paleontologist of the early nineteenth century. Noting its elongated front digit, he named it *Pterodactylus*, meaning "wing-finger". Even though this species was the first pterodactyl discovered, it was a late-comer to the history of this varied group, which included long- and short-tailed species, and head shapes that ranged from the tapered jaws of the *Pterodactylus*, to blunt triangles and even an upcurved beak fitted with filter plates, which may have functioned much as a flamingo's beak. Most were small, but one, named *Quetzalcoatlus* after the Aztec feathered snake god, may have had a wingspan of more than 50ft.
RANGE Jurassic–Cretaceous.

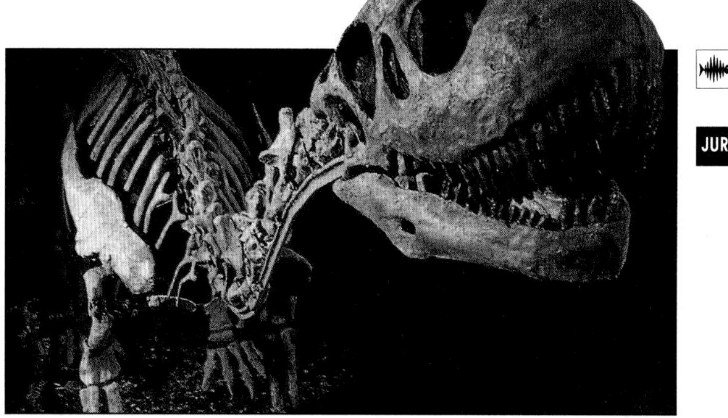

JUR

SHUOSAURUS

GENERAL DESCRIPTION The sauropods, the famous clan that included *Diplodocus* and *Apatosaurus*, were big dinosaurs, with one species that may have been more than 100ft. long. But not every sauropod was a giant; *Shuosaurus*, discovered in Asia, was only about 30ft. long, and was one of the earliest sauropods to evolve.

Shuosaurus had an impressive set of teeth. Although they may appear long and predatory, they are actually designed for cropping and chewing vegetation. In many species, the teeth show the kind of abrasion usually associated with tough land plants like conifer needles, lending strength to the argument that sauropods were terrestrial browsers with a lifestyle more like giraffes than hippos.
RANGE Jurassic.

JUR

Mamenchisaurus

General description With 19 neck vertebrae, *Mamenchisaurus* holds the record for the longest neck among the dinosaurs, and perhaps in the whole animal kingdom. This Asian dinosaur belonged to the group known as diplodocids, the long-tailed, long-necked browsers, of which *Apatosaurus* (formerly *Brontosaurus*) is the most famous.

Despite its prize-winning neck, *Mamenchisaurus* was not the longest diplodocid; at about 70ft., it was exceeded by several other species with total lengths of more than 90ft. As part of the recent revision in thinking, the diplodocids and their relatives are now thought to have been land animals, capable of rearing back on their hind legs (braced by their tails) to feed in the highest branches of the coniferous forests that covered the landscape.
Range Jurassic.

JUR

Tuojiangosaurus

General description The stegosaurs were a varied group of herbivorous dinosaurs in the Jurassic and Cretaceous, best known for *Stegosaurus*, with its double row of bony plates running down the back. There were many other genera, however, whose fossils have been found across the Northern Hemisphere, India and Africa. *Tuojiangosaurus* is another recent find from the fertile deposits in China, source of so many new dinosaur discoveries. Somewhat smaller than the 30ft. *Stegosaurus*, it bore twin rows of spiky plates and a double pair of tail spines.

There is a great deal of disagreement over the correct placement (and function) of the stegosaurs' back plates. Some paleontologists see them as a strictly defensive adaptation, while others argue for their role in a heat-regulation system.
Occurrence China.
Range Jurassic.

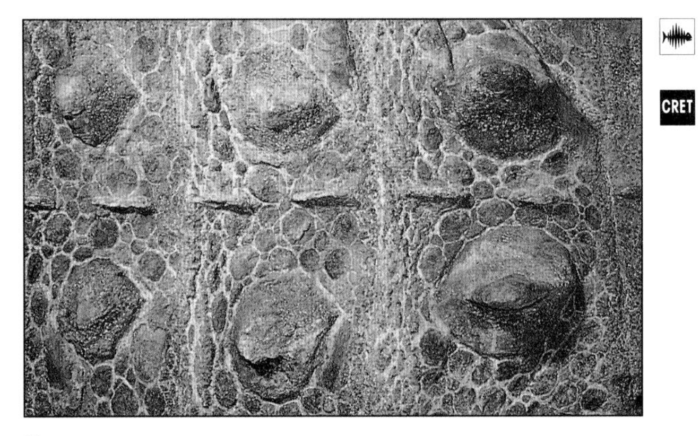

CRET

Scolosaurus

General description Fossilized dinosaur skin is rare, and provides an invaluable glimpse of their appearance and lifestyle. This fossil skin impression is from one of the ankylosaurs known as nodosaurids – squat, barrel-bodied dinosaurs with short legs, broad backs and long tails. They were among the most heavily armoured of living things, sheathed in strong plates, and many species grew thick spines around the body and down the tail.
Occurrence North America.
Range Cretaceous.

CRET

Protoceratops spp.

General description The discovery of the first dinosaur eggs, in 1923 by the Andrews expedition to central Asia, captured world attention. Further field work has since shown the eggs of *Protoceratops* to be surprisingly common in the Gobi Desert, suggesting that this predecessor of the horned dinosaurs (like *Triceratops*) was an abundant dinosaur in the Asian Cretaceous.

The eggs are usually found in circular groupings inside the remains of the hollow scrape that served as a nest. The adult *Protoceratops* was less massively built than its later relatives, without the exaggerated horns (just a knob on the end of the snout), and only a small head shield.
Occurrence Central Asia.
Range Cretaceous.

CRET

TRICERATOPS SPP.

GENERAL DESCRIPTION It was one of the great confrontations of pre-history: the towering, predatory dinosaur *Tyrannosaurus* against the tanklike, heavily armoured herbivore *Triceratops*. *Triceratops'* weaponry was formidable, to say the least: two curved, sharp horns angling forward from just above the eyes, with a third, shorter horn on the snout. The vulnerable neck was protected by a wide head shield that flared back several feet, and was rimmed with short spikes.
OCCURRENCE North America.
RANGE Cretaceous.

JUR

GASOSAURUS

GENERAL DESCRIPTION The theropods began as small, meat-eating dinosaurs in the Triassic, and eventually produced the reigning carnivores of the "Age of Dinosaurs": *Allosaurus* in the Jurassic and *Tyrannosaurus* in the Cretaceous. *Gasosaurus* was a much smaller theropod, but was built along the same lines as its more notorious relatives – large, powerful hind legs, comparatively tiny forelegs adapted for grasping, a long tail to counterbalance the body while running, and a mouth armed with curving, knifelike teeth.
RANGE Jurassic.

Class AVES Birds

Birds first appear in the fossil record during the Jurassic with *Archaeopteryx*, an obvious intermediary between small, fast-moving dinosaurs like *Deinorhynchus* and true birds; in fact, *Archaeopteryx* fits just as well among the dinosaurs as it does among birds, and one specimen was misidentified for years as a pterodactyl.

In order to fly, birds have hollow, thinly walled bones that rarely fossilize, so that their history is spotty. From the fossils that have been found, however, we know that by the Cretaceous, toothed birds with fully functional wings had evolved, followed by wholly modern birds at the Cretaceous–Palaeocene border.

ARCHAEOPTERYX

GENERAL DESCRIPTION First there was a feather – a startling imprint found in Germany in 1860, from Jurassic rock where dinosaurs, not birds, were expected. Less than a year later, the same limestone of the fabled Solnhofen quarries in Bavaria had given up a nearly complete *Archaeopteryx* fossil, riveting world attention. This exceedingly fine-grained limestone, perfect for lithographic plates, is also nearly perfect for fossilization, preserving details that would be lost in a coarser matrix. So it was with *Archaeopteryx*, which could be seen to have a dinosaur-like skeleton, a long, bony tail and reptile-like teeth. And as the limestone clearly showed, *Archaeopteryx* also had feathers.

The fossil illustrated is the famous "Berlin Specimen", unearthed in 1877. The head, with its toothed mouth, is flung backwards, while impressions of the wing and tail feathers are easily seen. The three long "finger" bones in *Archaeopteryx* eventually degenerated into the three small, partially fused digits found in modern birds.
OCCURRENCE Germany.
RANGE Jurassic.

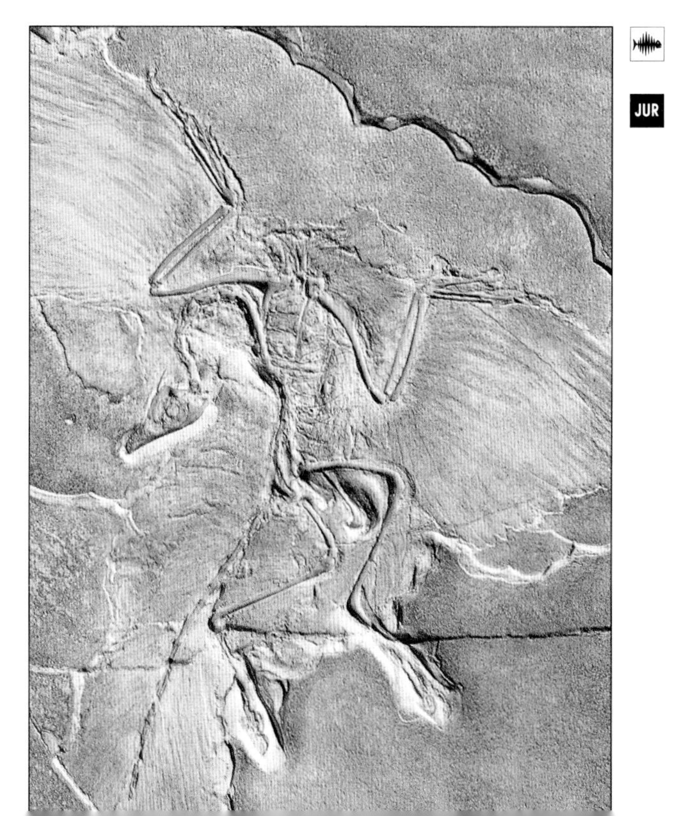

JUR

Class MAMMALIA Mammals

Our own class, the Mammalia is wonderfully diverse, encompassing everything from whales to bats to gorillas – all united by warm-bloodedness, body hair and the production of milk for the young. Mammals first evolved about 215 million years BP, apparently arising from a group of mammal-like reptiles known as theraspids during the Triassic. Initially, mammals laid eggs (a reproductive process still used by echidnas and the platypus), while a later group, the marsupials, gave birth to scarcely developed young called neonates, retained in a nursing pouch for months thereafter. The marsupials' spot at the top was eventually usurped by modern, placental mammals everywhere but in Australia and, until the Middle Cenozoic, South America.

TERT

MAMMUTHUS SPP.

GENERAL DESCRIPTION By the Pleistocene, mammoths and mastodons were found all over the Northern Hemisphere, Africa and South America. The smaller mastodons survived in North America until after the last glaciers retreated, and were hunted by Paleolithic Indians less than 10 000 years ago.

The proboscidians, including the elephants, arose in the late Eocene or early Oligocene, first in the form of piglike creatures known as *Moeritherium*. Over time, the snout elongated into the famous trunk, while the jaw shortened and the teeth were reduced to only eight active molars in modern elephants, with two upper incisors (not canines, as often supposed) transformed into tusks. The gigantic steppe mammoth *(M. trogontherii)* was the largest European elephant, with a shoulder height of more than 14ft., and tusks more than 16ft. long. The photo, showing a jaw of North America's *M. columbi* from South Dakota, demonstrates the size of these extinct mammals.

Woolly mammoths *(M. primigenius)* from Siberia and Alaska have provided some of the most unique fossils in paleontological history – almost perfectly frozen specimens from the Pleistocene, many still with mouthfuls of grass and wildflowers.

OCCURRENCE Africa; South America.

RANGE Oligocene–Pleistocene.

QUA

SMILODON SPP.

GENERAL DESCRIPTION Popularly known as "sabre-toothed tigers", these large, unusual cats were apparently common carnivores in North and South America during the Pleistocene. The most startling feature of the skull is the upper canine teeth, which have evolved into sweeping fangs.

The fangs certainly look deadly, and it has long been assumed that *Smilodon* used them to great effect against such thick-skinned prey as mammoths and mastodons; the discovery of sabre-toothed cat skeletons and those of primitive elephants, together in California tar pits, would seem to seal the argument. But others have argued that *Smilodon*'s fangs were too big to be efficient biting tools, and are awkwardly placed for stabbing. They theorize that the cat may have been a scavenger, and the huge teeth might have played a social, rather than predatory, role.

Whatever the function of the sabre-teeth, they must have been effective, for the same style of dentition had evolved earlier, independently, in a South American marsupial known as *Thylacosmilus*, which lived during the Pliocene but died out when the Central American land bridge joined North and South America, permitting a flood of placental mammals to move south. The unique marsupial fauna of South America were overwhelmed by the placentals, and the marsupials largely vanished.

OCCURRENCE North and South America.

RANGE Pleistocene.

TRACE FOSSILS

Not true fossils in the strictest sence, trace fossils record biological activity without preserving the animal itself. In this category are found fossil worm tubes, mollusc borings and insect tracks, as well as such non-biological pseudo-fossils as "fossil lightning".

BIOLOGICAL TRACE FOSSILS

Many trace fossils must remain anonymous, but sometimes the palaeontologist can determine what species made the trace by comparing it to markings found in association with animal fossils or living species; very often, particular genera leave recognizable trails or burrows. These mollusc holes in chalk, for instance, were made by *Pholas* razor clams or *Ensis* angel-wings. Both bivalves are common in the fossil record from the Cretaceous, and remain abundant in today's oceans. Trace fossils are especially important in deciphering the lives of extinct animals. By measuring the stride lengths of dinosaur footprints, paleontologists have surmised everything from herd social structure to posture and speed.

CRET

WORM TUBES AND MOLLUSC BORINGS

GENERAL DESCRIPTION Many species of aquatic worms secrete cement-like substances to bond the substrata into a hard tube; since the tubes were buried in mud to start with, they are frequently found in fossilized form. The worms themselves, on the other hand, are rarely found – the usual fate of soft-bodied animals, which are fossilized only under the most remarkable of conditions.
OCCURRENCE Worldwide.
RANGE Pleistocene.

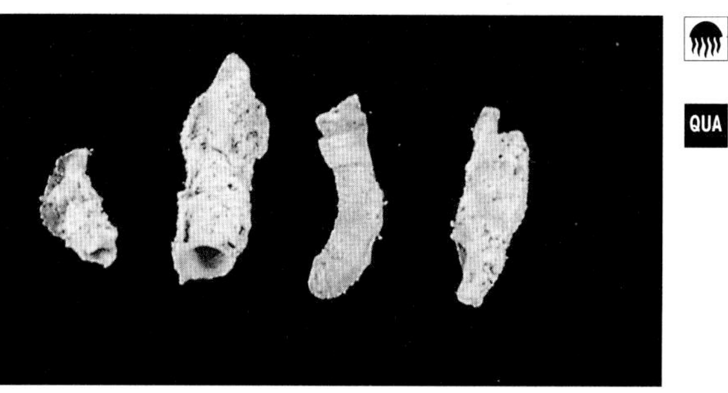

QUA

NON-BIOLOGICAL TRACE FOSSILS

Sometimes, the same forces that create a fossil from a dead organism do the same for non-biological phenomena. While not truly fossils, they are often found by fossil hunters, and are fascinating in their own right. The illustration here shows volcanic fulgurites, formed when lightning struck a field of volcanic pumice, melting and solidifying the mineral into thin, glassy tubes covered with rough pumice.

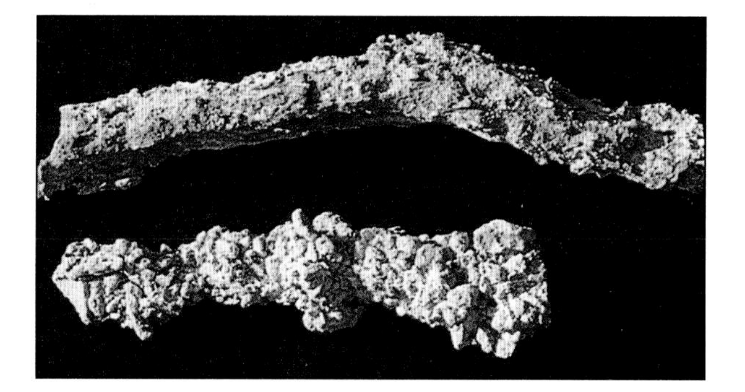

GLOSSARY

MINERALS AND GEMS

ABSORPTION SPECTRUM The pattern of dark lines seen when white light is examined by a spectroscope after the light has passed through a gemstone.
ADAMANTINE Very bright mineral luster.
AMORPHOUS "Without shape". Amorphous substances have no regular internal structure, i.e. they are not crystalline.
ASTERISM The star effect seen in a gemstone when cut and polished *en cabochon*.
BASAL CLEAVAGE Cleavage parallel to the basal plane of a mineral.
BIREFRINGENCE The difference between the maximum and minimum *refractive indices* of a *doubly refractive* stone.
CABOCHON Style of cutting used for opaque gemstones or to show *asterism* or *chatoyancy*.
CHATOYANT Cat's eye effect in gemstones.
CLEAVAGE Tendency of a stone to break along a definite direction giving a smooth surface.
CONCHOIDAL FRACTURE Uneven breaking of a stone which gives a shell-like appearance to the surface.
CRYPTOCRYSTALLINE Crystals are so small that they can only be seen with the aid of a microscope.
CRYSTAL Form bounded by flat *faces*. The external shape of the crystal is directly related to its internal atomic structure.
DENDRITIC Moss- or branch-like shapes or markings.
DICHROISM See *pleochroism*.
DIFFRACTION Splitting of white light into the colors of the rainbow (spectral colours) as light passes through narrow slits, for example in a spectroscope.
DISPERSION Splitting of white light into the spectral colors when it passes through a gemstone; also known as "fire".
DOUBLY REFRACTIVE A gemstone which refracts rays of light by different amounts to give a range of *refractive indices*.
EARTHY Non-reflective mineral luster.
FACES Flat external surfaces which make up a crystal.
FACETS Flat surfaces of a cut and polished gemstone.
FLUORESCENCE Emission of visible light when a stone is exposed to invisible light such as ultraviolet light or X-rays.
FORM Describes a number of identical flat *faces* that make up a crystal. More than one form may be needed to describe a crystal.
FRACTURE Uneven breaking of a stone. The direction of breaking is not related to the atomic structure of the stone (see *cleavage*).
HABIT Form in which a gemstone is usually found.
HACKLY Fracture with a rough surface.
ICOSITETRAHEDRON Solid figure with 24-sided faces.
INCLUSIONS Cavities, fragments of crystal or other substances found with the crystal structure of a gemstone.
IRIDESCENCE Due to interference of light in the internal structure of a stone, which causes white light to split into the spectral colors.
ISOTROPIC Substances in which the properties, for example refraction, are the same in all directions.
LUSTER Effect produced by light reflecting off the surface of a stone. Luster may be *vitreous* (glass-like), *adamantine* (like a diamond), waxy, resinous, silky and so on.
MASSIVE Mineral habit of no definite shape.
METALLIC Luster like fresh metal.
MINERALS Naturally occurring inorganic substances that have a constant chemical composition and internal atomic structure.
PASTE Artificial silica glass. It may be colored and used to imitate a number of gemstones. It is easily scratched and worn.
PEGMATITES Igneous intrusions caused when residual liquids cool from magmas; gives an ideal growing region for crystals.
PLEOCHROISM Occurs when a stone appears to be two (dichroic) or three (trichroic) different colors or shades of body color when viewed from different directions.
REFRACTION Occurs as a ray of light passes from one medium to another of different density and is slowed and bent.
REFRACTIVE INDEX (RI) Constant relationship between the angle at which light enters a gemstone and the angle of refraction.
SCHILLER (SHEEN) In a gemstone is caused by reflection of light off the internal features of a stone.
TRICHROISM See *pleochroism*.
TWINNING Occurs when a crystal grows in two different directions from one face.
VITREOUS Luster of broken glass.

ROCKS

ARENACEOUS Sedimentary rocks derived from or composed of sand.
BOTRYOIDAL Resembling a cluster of grapes.
CONCRETION Nodular rock masses found in shale or clay.
DRUSY CAVITY Hollow space within a rock that is filled with a collection of secondary minerals.
IGNEOUS ROCKS Formed from volcanic magma or lava which has cooled and solidified.
MAGMA Molten rock.
METAMORPHIC ROCKS Formed from *igneous* or *sedimentary* rocks that have been changed by high temperature and/or pressure.
PEGMATITE Igneous rock with large, individual crystals.
PORPHYRITIC Igneous rock texture with relatively large crystals set in the matrix.
SECONDARY MINERAL Mineral that has formed in a rock due to secondary processes.
SEDIMENTARY ROCKS Formed from the breakdown and deposition of *igneous* or *metamorphic* rocks.

SHELLS

ADDUCTOR SCARS Impressions on the inner walls of bivalve shells left by the muscles used by bivalves to close the shells.
APEX The point from which a shell begins to grow; the top of the spire of a gastropod shell.
AXIAL A term usually applied to gastropods to describe markings or whorls that follow, or are parallel to, the axis of the shell.
BIVALVE A mollusc, such as an oyster, that has a hinged double shell.
BODY WHORL The largest and last formed section of a gastropod shell; it encloses the soft parts of the creature.
BYSSUS Tuft of silky filaments by which some molluscs adhere to rocks.
CALCAREOUS Made of, or containing, calcium carbonate.
CANCELLATE Shell marked with crossing lines that form a lattice-like pattern.
CANCELLATION An area of a shell sculptured by lines crossing each other at right angles; also referred to as reticulation.
CARDINAL Projection below the umbo on the hinge plate of a bivalve.
CARINA Structure or part of a structure of a shell that resembles a keel or ridge.
CHITIN Substance that forms the horny constituent in the exoskeleton of arthropods.
CHITON Mollusc with a shell formed of eight overlapping plates.
COLUMELLA Spirally twisting pillar surrounding the axis of a gastropod shell, which is visible in the aperture.
CORD Rope-like, usually spiral ornamentation on a gastropod shell.
CORNEOUS In shells, horn-like or horny; made of chitin.
CORONATED In shells, crown-like; bearing nodules on the shoulder or spire.
DENTATE or **DENTICULATE** In shells, toothed or bearing tooth-like notches.
DORSUM Back of a shell, opposite to the aperture.
FUSIFORM In shells, shaped like a spindle; rounded and broadest in the middle and tapering towards each end.
GLOBOSE In shells, rounded or spherical; like a ball.
KEEL In shells, a raised, often sharp edge or carina.
LAMELLA Thin plate or scale.
LIP Inside or outside edge of the aperture of a gastropod shell.
MACULATE In shells, marked with irregular spots or blotches.
MANTLE Glandular flap or fold of the body wall of a mollusc that secretes the shell-forming material.
NACREOUS Of or like mother-of-pearl.
NODULAR Bearing or decorated with nodules.
NODULE Sharp or rounded knob; a lumpy protuberance.
OPERCULUM Oval or round structure, which may be calcareous or corneous, on the foot of many species of gastropods, which is used to close the aperture when the creature withdraws into its shell.
OVATE Egg-shaped or oval.
PALLIAL SINUS Curved scar line visible on the interior walls of bivalve shells at the point where the edges of the mantle were attached.
PARIETAL Area or wall, sometimes referred to as the inner lip, in a gastropod shell that lies opposite the outer lip and above the columella.
PERIOSTRACUM Fibrous, skin-like membrane that covers many live shells.
PLICATE Having parallel folds, like a fan; usually used to describe the plaited or folded portion of the columella of a shell.
PORCELLANEOUS In shells, having a porcelain- or china-like appearance.
PROTOCONCH Tip or apex of a gastropod shell, formed during the creature's larval stage.
RADIAL Ray-like ornamentation or sculpturing diverting from the umbo of a bivalve shell.
RADULA Ribbon-like structure with rows of teeth, used by molluscs to tear up food and take it to the mouth.
RETICULATE Net-like pattern of intersecting ridges or striations.
SIPHONAL CANAL Tube-like structure used to protect the fleshy tube of gastropods and bivalves that is used for drawing in or ejecting liquid; it is situated at the front (base) of the aperture.
SPINOSE or **SPINOUS** In shells, bearing or covered in spines.
TROCHOIDAL In shells, shaped like a spinning top.
TUBERCLE Small rounded projection.
UMBILICUS Open point at the base of a gastropod shell around which the body whorl is coiled.
UMBO (plural **UMBONES**) Part of a bivalve shell that was formed first; it is also known as a beak.
VARIX (plural **VARICES**) In shells, rib-like thickening, representing a growth resting stage, which appears as a raised ridge.
WHORL One complete coil about the axis of a gastropod shell.

FOSSILS

ALLOCHTHONOUS Fossil displaced from or deposited outside its habitat.
ANCESTRULA Early stage in bryozoan life cycle.
ANGIOSPERMS Flowering plants.
ANTERIOR Having to do with the front; in bivalves, the beak points towards the anterior side.
APERTURE Opening in shell, especially in gastropods and cephalopods.
APICAL WHORLS In gastropods, the whorls comprising the apex or spire.
ARISTOTLE'S LANTERN Five plates that comprise echinoid "jaw".
AUTOCHTHONOUS A fossil deposited within its habitat.
BISERIAL In graptolites, when thecae are found on both sides of the stipe.
BRACHIAL VALVE Upper valve in brachiopods.
CALYX Bud-like body segment of crinoid and similar echinoderms.
CARAPACE Shield-like exoskeleton that covers the head and thorax of crustaceans.

CEPHALON Trilobite head shield.
CIRRI Prehensile armlets on crinoid stems.
CLASTIC Sedimentary rock composed of rock, mineral or fossil fragments.
CORALLITE Calcereous exoskeleton of an individual coral animal.
CORALLUM A coral colony, made up of many corallites.
COSTAE Radial ribbing on mollusc shells.
COUNTERPART Imprint or impression left in rock by a fossil.
EQUIVALVE In bivalves, when both valves are the same size and general shape.
EVOLUTE In cephalopods, a type of coiling in which the loose outer coils do not greatly overlap the inner coils.
GROWTH LINES Radial marks on mollusc and other shells that record shell growth.
GONDWANALAND Southern supercontinent comprising South America, Antarctica, Africa and Australia.
GYMNOSPERMS Non-flowering plants, including conifers, cycads and seed-ferns.
IGNEOUS Rock formed from crystallized magma or lava.
INEQUIVALVE In bivalves, when the valves are of differing size and shape.
INTERNAL MOULD Fossil created when a mineral fills the internal gaps in an organism, which later dissolves.
INVOLUTE In cephalopods, a type of coiling in which the tight outer coils overlap the inner coils.
K–T BOUNDARY Division between Cretaceous and Tertiary, marked by mass extinction.
LANCEOLATE Shaped like a lance, narrowly tapered at both ends.
LAURASIA Northern supercontinent composed of Europe and North America.
MATRIX Rock surrounding a fossil or crystal.
MEDUSA Free-swimming, saucer-shaped body form rimmed with tentacles, especially jellyfish.
METAMORPHIC Rock that has undergone change due to heat or pressure.
MOLD Gap in matrix left when a fossilized organism completely dissolves.
NATURAL CAST A *pseudomorph*; the resulting fossil formed when a substance fills an empty mold.
NON-CLASTIC Sedimentary rock formed by the deposition of animal or plant matter or minerals.
OSSICLE Crinoid stem segment.
PALAEONTOLOGY The study of fossils and the extinct life forms that they represent.
PANGEA Supercontinent formed by juncture of *Gondwanaland* and *Laurasia*.
PART The fossil itself; opposite of *counterpart*.
PEDICLE FORAMEN Opening for stalk in pedicle valve of brachiopods.
PEDICLE VALVE Lower valve in brachiopods.
PERISTOME Oral opening in echinoids.
PERMINERALIZATION Partial mineralization of a fossil.
PINNULES Armlets on crinoid branches used for food gathering.
PLEURAE Trilobite "ribs".
POLYP Sedentary, columnar body form topped with tentacles, especially of cnidarians.
POSTERIOR Having to do with the rear.
PSEUDOMORPH Process by which a fossilized organism completely dissolves, leaving a gap in the matrix which is filled by another substance, creating an external mold of the specimen.
PTERIDOPHYTE A true fern.
PTERIDOSPERM A seed-fern.
PYGIDIUM Trilobite tail section.
REPLACEMENT Complete mineralization of a fossil in which the original substance is replaced by an invading mineral like silica.
RHABDOSOME Graptolite colony.
SEDIMENTARY Type of rock formed from layers of deposited sediment.
SEPTA Dividing wall between chambers in a cephalopod shell.
SEPTAE Lateral dividers inside a corallite.
SESSILE Stationary or attached.
SIPHUNCLE Thin tube that joins the flotation chambers in cephalopod shells.
SHOULDER In gastropods, the flattened portion of the whorl just below the suture.
SILICEOUS Containing or consisting of silica.
SIPHONAL CANAL In gastropods, a tubelike extension of the aperture.
SPATULATE Having a broad end and a narrow, tapered base.
SPICULES Mineralized structures found in sponge tissue.
SPIRE All whorls in a gastropod shell except for the body whorl.
STEINKERN Internal mold.
SUTURE Line of juncture between two body parts. In gastropods, the seam between two whorls; in cephalopods, the intricate divisions between the shell wall and septa.
TABULAE Horizontal dividers inside a corallite.
TEST The hardened outer shell; especially of Foraminifera and some echinoderms.
THECA Calyx, or cup, of crinoid and similar echinoderms.
THECAE Tube on graptolite stipe that encased the living animal.
THORAX Middle of three body sections among arthropods.
UNISERIAL In graptolites, when thecae are found on one side of the stipe only.
VALVE Half of a bivalve mollusc or brachiopod shell.
VENTER Having to do with the lower, or ventral, side. In ammonoids, it refers to the portion of the whorl farthest from the central axis of the shell.
ZOOECIA Individual bryozoan animal.

INDEX